# Life of Evel

W/D

*For Ally Cubbon*
*and Shannon Chloe Greenwood*

*Best buddies*

# Contents

# Acknowledgements

Thanks to the following (in alphabetical order) for their assistance and/or support in compiling this book: Roger Atyeo, Jim Barker, Josie Barker, Karen Boyle, Steve 'Biggsy' Bygraves, Ally Cubbon, Mary Cubbon, Stewart Cubbon, Paul Downey, Clark Gibson, Paul 'Green Dog' Greenhead, Shannon Chloe Greenwood, Angela Hewitson, Emily Hewitson, Neil Hewitson, Paul 'Jonah' Jones, Jim Loughran, Donnie McCleod, Leigh McQueen, Nick Mullen, Ben Purvis, Bertie Simmonds, Heather Temple, Pete 'Scouse' Whittington, Tracy Wisbee and to all at The Briars for keeping me sane.

A special thanks to Michael Doggart, Tom Whiting, Tarda Davison-Aitkins, Rachel Nicholson, Juliette Davis, Sara Walsh and all at HarperCollins*Publishers* for making this book possible.

# Introduction

Evel Knievel's incredible career reached its literal and metaphorical apex on 8 September 1974 when he attempted to jump the Snake River Canyon in Idaho in a custom-built, rocket-powered Sky Cycle.

The world held its breath as the 35-year-old daredevil from Montana blasted into the sky at 350mph in a bid to span the three-quarter-mile chasm. It had taken seven years to plan and execute the attempt and Knievel had invested $1 million of his own money to make it happen. Audiences packed cinemas across America to watch the event live on closed-circuit television (also known as pay-per-view), and newspapers around the world held their front-page headlines. It was the most-hyped stunt in history – and it didn't work. Knievel's drogue parachute blew out on take-off and, after soaring a thousand feet into the Idaho sky, his X-2 Sky Cycle started drifting down towards the murky green depths of the Snake River. Once he was hidden from view of the thousands of spectators on the canyon rim, many feared Knievel had finally gone too far and had ended his remarkable life in a watery grave.

When he was rescued by boat and helicopter and returned to the canyon rim, Knievel was dazed and bloodied, and, having just bombed out of the biggest stunt event of all time, he considered retiring to enjoy the reputed $6 million he had earned from the event. But having already tried to blow a million dollars on a 'last supper' drinking party before the jump, Knievel needed more money to fund his extravagant lifestyle and within nine months he was back with a sellout performance at Wembley Stadium in London in what was to be the only UK appearance of his career.

Even by today's Extreme-sports standards, Knievel's Snake River jump remains a monumental act of daring, bravado, showmanship, courage and, for some, sheer stupidity. But whatever anyone's personal take on the Snake River attempt, there is no denying that it represented the zenith of Evel Knievel's career. His fame continued into the late Seventies and he carried on performing for a further six years after his most famous stunt, but never again did he capture the collective imagination of the world in such a way, nor attempt anything quite so spectacular and original, or on such a magnificent scale.

It mattered not. Knievel had already secured his title as the 'King of the Daredevils', the self-styled 'last of the gladiators', and he is currently being embraced by a whole new generation of skaters, snowboarders, freestyle motorcycle riders and base jumpers, among others, as the Godfather of daring – the original Extreme athlete. Here was a man who transformed what was nothing more than a county-fair sideshow act into a global spectacular; a man who had reportedly broken every bone in his body and, while that was some way from the truth, had certainly suffered more pain and injury during his 15-year career than most people could ever imagine in a lifetime.

A natural-born hustler, Knievel's career would never have progressed from state fairs and local car-race meetings had he not possessed a Herculean aptitude for self-promotion. Right up until the Snake River Canyon attempt, Knievel handled all of his own

PR, bookings and promotions; not because he couldn't afford hired help, but simply because he knew he was the best man in the world for the job. He frequently referred to himself as a P. T. Barnum for the modern age.

Evel's first promotional masterpiece was the jump which made him famous all over the world – his attempt to leap over the majestic fountains outside the newly opened Caesar's Palace casino in Las Vegas in 1967. The film footage of the crash, which resulted in Evel spending 29 days in a coma, was said to have been screened over the following years more than any other roll of film since the Zapruder footage of President Kennedy's assassination. It is certainly one of the most watched pieces of sports footage in history. Children and adults alike around the world were captivated by the gory, slow-motion images of Knievel's body being battered, torn and crunched over the Tarmac surface of his landing area. No one had ever seen anything quite like it before, and few thought they would see anything like it ever again. Surely Knievel would never be able to ride again after such a horrendous crash, even if he wanted to?

He did ride again and he did crash again, but he always came back for more. If there's anything that Evel Knievel stands for it's the will to carry on against all the odds; to never say die and to never, *ever* give in. In that arena he had few peers. Jumping motorcycles from ramp to ramp may not be the most noble of careers, and neither is it a pursuit likely to affect the world in any significant way, but that does not detract from Knievel's achievements over huge adversity and pain. His unique brand of spirit and determination could have been showcased in many arenas, the most natural alternative being motorsport, but that would have been following a trend, and that was never Knievel's style. The very fact that he single-handedly created the arena in which he became famous highlighted the other outstanding attribute of the man from Montana: his originality.

When combined, Knievel's courage and originality gave out the message to an entire generation that they should pursue their dreams, whatever they may be, and never give up in their pursuit no matter how tough things got and no matter how much hardship had to be endured. His own favourite and often-quoted phrase – 'A man can fall down many, many times in life but he is never a failure until he refuses to get up' – captured Evel's attitude superbly, even if he never openly credited it as being an adaptation of Confucius's proverb, 'Our greatest glory is not in never falling, but in rising every time we fall.'

Evel's timing in promoting such a message could not have been better, at least as far as American audiences were concerned. The country had lost its innocence with the assassination of JFK in 1963, just two years before Knievel's first public stunt performance, and as Knievel's career progressed, so did the conflict in Vietnam and so too did the nationwide protests against it. At the peak of his career in the run-up to the Snake River jump, the Watergate scandal piled further shame on both the US government and the nation as a whole. The American people badly needed a hero and an escape from the depressing events of the time. They needed someone who could not only provide distracting entertainment but who could give them faith in their nation's virtues once again. For a never-say-die daredevil to come along dressed in assorted variations of the American national flag, facing danger with all the front of a real-life superhero and refusing to be beaten by pain or injury, must have seemed too good to be true. The Knievel phenomenon happened in exactly the right place at exactly the right time and the man himself had both the courage and the promotional know-how to milk the situation for all it was worth –

and he's still milking it now, almost a quarter of a century after his retirement.

Along the way there were excesses that would put most hell-raising rock stars to shame. Knievel was fond of boasting that he made $60 million and spent $63 million. At one time he owned 14 aeroplanes, 16 boats, five Rolls-Royces and more sports cars and motorcycles than he could remember. He lost and won millions of pounds in the casinos of Las Vegas and had his own private walk-in bank vault in Butte, into which he literally shovelled his cash.

Evel counted Elvis Presley, Frank Sinatra and Muhammad Ali among his friends, and his appetite for beautiful women was unrivalled. He claims to have slept with over 2,000 women during his lifetime, despite the fact that he was married for 38 years.

But there were dark times too. Knievel was sentenced to six months in prison, a small proportion of which was served in a cell next to Charles Manson, for breaking a former colleague's arms with a baseball bat. The colleague's crime? He wrote a book about Evel which the daredevil took exception to. A $13 million lawsuit followed, but it was the shame of Knievel's prison sentence that destroyed his reputation and ultimately his fortune, as every company he was associated with withdrew their endorsements. At the same time, the Internal Revenue Service were hunting down Knievel for anything up to $21 million in outstanding taxes. Knievel all but disappeared as the IRS stepped up the hunt.

For the best part of 15 years, from the late 1970s to the early 1990s, Knievel was neither seen, heard of nor talked about as he toured the US in a converted bus and trailer that he called home. He hustled for whatever money he could get by betting on games of golf just to buy his next bottle of bourbon. It seemed he had lived his somewhat extended 15 minutes of fame and was destined to fade into complete obscurity, with only hazy, booze-tinged memories as souvenirs of his time as one of the most famous people on the planet.

Then a remarkable thing happened. By the mid-Nineties, all those thirty-somethings who had grown up with the name Evel Knievel discovered a nostalgia for their lost Seventies youth, and suddenly the forgotten decade became fashionable again. Boot-cut denims were the new flares, satellite TV showed re-runs of all the cult, classic programmes from the Seventies; programmes like *The Incredible Hulk, Starsky and Hutch, The Dukes of Hazzard* and *The Bionic Woman* (in which Knievel himself once starred). Classic disco anthems like the Bee Gees' *Staying Alive* were being sampled by contemporary artists, and the star of the film of the same name, John Travolta, was shot dramatically back into the limelight in Quentin Tarantino's huge box-office hit *Pulp Fiction.* It seemed there was no escaping the retro phenomenon and more and more forgotten stars of the Seventies were hunted down and brought out of mothballs to be lionised once again. Inevitably, their twenty-years-after appearances shocked many who could only remember them as the fresh-faced stars they had once been, but they were welcomed back into the limelight all the same.

At some undefined moment, the retro-mongers realised there was one very significant name missing from the Seventies cele-bration: Evel Knievel. What had happened to him? Was he dead? It seemed likely, given his chosen occupation and the fact that no one could really remember him officially retiring, since his career had simply fizzled out rather than ended in a blaze of glory. Knievel suddenly found himself making after-dinner speeches and being sought out by the media again. But it was the appearance of the once handsome and well-built man that shocked more than the revelation that he was still alive. Time had taken a heavy toll on Knievel, and the frail, grey-headed and bespectacled man who hobbled back blinking into the bright limelight which had for so long neglected him seemed as far removed from the King of the Daredevils as it was possible to be. Apart from the 16 major open-reduction surgeries he had gone through, Knievel's appearance had also been ravaged by hepatitis C and Type II diabetes and he was suffering from liver failure as well as the to-be-expected arthritis. He was in poor shape for a man in his late fifties, but the fact that he was alive at all still seemed a miracle to most.

In 1999, Knievel needed another miracle. Hepatitis C had ravaged his liver to such an extent that he was given just 48 hours to live. Signing himself out of hospital in order to die quietly at home with his partner Krystal, his 12-mile journey home was interrupted by a phone call that told him a suitable liver donor had been found. He was rushed back to the hospital and underwent a successful transplant operation.

With a new lease of life, Knievel was more determined than ever to enjoy his second shot at fame. The revival of his name took many forms: his famous wind-up toys which had grossed over $300 million in the 1970s were re-released; documentaries on his incredible life were screened both in America and the UK; DVDs of his famous jumps were compiled; tribute bicycles, motorcycles and even cars were manufactured. Rights for an Evel Knievel rock opera were signed over, computer games were churned out and various artists even penned songs about their childhood hero. The new marketing weapon of the late twentieth century, the Internet, provided a perfect platform for the sale of staggering amounts of Evel Knievel paraphernalia – some old, much new. Fans could now buy Evel replica jackets, T-shirts, lingerie, cigars, commemor-ative coins, aftershave, and almost any other saleable commodity imaginable. If something could be branded, someone stamped 'EK' on it and added instant commercial appeal.

But one of the greatest compliments for Knievel during his second, and surely now eternal, period in the limelight must have been the founding of an annual Evel Knievel week in his home-town of Butte, Montana. The inaugural event, held in the July and August of 2002, featured a ride-out led by the man himself, as well as freestyle motocross events, car and bike stunt shows, performances from big-name live bands, an Evel Knievel exhibit and a grand fireworks finale. Few living celebrities can lay claim to such an honour.

Knievel's remarkable comeback had brought him full circle, back to his beloved hometown of Butte where he once held court as its most famous son before disappearing from the public eye. It had been in Butte that a young Bobby Knievel learned his trade as a bank robber before becoming famous, and it was in the town jail that he was given the nickname 'Evil', which would eventually become a byword for anything daring or dangerous.

Throughout his career Knievel never missed the chance to tell the press and the people where he came from. He was proud of his roots in the tough, former mining town and probably realised more than most just how much that upbringing had shaped the man he became. There is no widely acknowledged birthplace for daredevils, but if they're going to come from somewhere it may as well be Butte, Montana. It certainly provided Robert Craig Knievel with all the right stuff to become the most famous daredevil the world has ever known.

# 1
# The Richest Hill on Earth

*'In Butte, if you weren't a pimp or a thief you were nothing.
And I needed a few bucks to get out.'*

Situated in southwest Montana, approximately halfway between
the Yellowstone and Glacier National Parks, Butte is the largest
city in the state, even though its population only numbered 33,892
citizens during the census of the year 2000. The figure speaks
volumes about the decline in the town following the closure of the
copper mining pits it was once famous for; one hundred years
ago there would easily have been 100,000 entries on the census.

Butte was founded on a collection of small mining claims and
eventually became a massively prosperous mining centre in the
early part of the twentieth century. Described as 'the richest hill
on earth' for more than 100 years due to the wealth of ore lying
beneath its surface, the town was once the most important source
of copper anywhere in the world, with 2,590 miles of tunnels
connected by 41 miles of vertical shafts – some of which reached
6,000 feet down – allowing access to the valuable commodity. It
is also home to the famous Berkeley Pit, once the biggest truck-
operated open-pit copper mine in the United States.

Where there's copper there are usually miners, and where there are miners there's always a lively, noisy, hard-living community. Butte was no exception. If there was any exception, it was that the city was even livelier, noisier and harder-living than most of its peers, operating largely as it did by its own rules and code of conduct, much like the pioneer towns of the old Wild West.

To live in Butte was to work hard and play hard. At one time the city was reputed to have more bars per capita than any other city in the US – and for almost every bar there was a brothel. Such was the importance of brothels in Butte until very recent times that one of the more famous examples, the Dumas Brothel, has now been turned into a museum to celebrate the city's sinful past. With miners working shifts round the clock, many bars in Butte were open twenty-four hours a day and there were always prostitutes on hand to accommodate the miners. At one time there were no fewer than 500 women working the red-light-district area of Butte.

As far back as 1863 the area surrounding Butte had been famed for its gold deposits, and when they ran out of this the prospectors found an abundance of silver in the same Tobacco Root Mountains. When the silver too was mined to exhaustion it could have spelled the end of mining in the area, and the city of Butte might never have developed as it did. But the discovery of vast resources of copper kept the prospectors coming, and this would prove to last much longer than the sources of silver and gold. Copper was the making of Evel Knievel's hometown, just as his hometown was the making of Evel Knievel.

With large companies like the Anaconda Copper Mining Company (which Knievel would later work for) establishing big-time operations, mining work became plentiful and by 1917 the population of Butte had soared to upwards of 100,000 people. It would never again reach this peak but while it did the city was an absolute haven of all the major vices: gambling, drinking and prostitution were practised on a scale not seen since the days of Dodge City and Tombstone in the previous century, and the rough, tough copper miners were just as ready with their guns as the outlaws of the Wild West had been. Butte was one tough town.

But it was not only populated with hard-drinking, hard-gambling and prostitute-friendly miners, it was also home to a new breed of millionaires who had made their money from the mines without actually having had to work in them. It was this nouveau-riche clientele who made possible the construction of the resplendent parlours, brothels, bars and hotels which set Butte aside, at least aesthetically, from the other rough-and-tumble mining towns. The presence of great wealth was evident even as drunks lay in the streets and men shot each other over card games. It was a town of contrasts and a town where a fast buck could always be made by anyone who was prepared to operate on the wrong side of the law.

The Wild West mentality hadn't entirely subsided by 1938 when an unremarkable couple named Robert Edward Knievel and Ann Knievel (née Keaugh) had their first child on 17 October who they called Robert Craig Knievel. As the Knievels would soon discover, it was not the ideal time or environment to raise a child. The town was already a rough place and the great depression of the 1930s wasn't making things any easier. Jobs were hard to come by, money was scarce and a world war was just around the corner; a war which would eventually damage the economy even further.

Robert senior was a handsome man of German ancestry, while his young wife could trace her own family roots back to Ireland. The uncommon surname of Knievel can be traced to Germany as far back as 1265 with a family coat of arms that places great emphasis on 'military fortitude and magnanimity'. While the name is unusual, the hard pronunciation of the 'K' in Knievel is genuine and not an American corruption, nor is it a gimmick dreamed up by its famous bearer to enhance the rhythmic qualities of his stage name.

For reasons he has never openly discussed, presumably because the subject-matter remains a source of some anguish, Bobby Knievel's parents separated in 1940 when he was just under 18 months old and not long after Ann Knievel had given birth to another child, Bobby's younger brother Nick. It was not an uncommon scenario under the circumstances. Living conditions were extremely tough for any young family in America during the great depression and having two young children to clothe and feed stretched many families to breaking point. The Knievels were no exception. Knowing they would struggle to provide a stable and secure upbringing for their children, the decision was taken to hand the boys over to their paternal grandparents, Emma and Ignatious Knievel. While Robert Senior believed a brighter future might lie in California, Ann moved to Nevada, and the young Knievel brothers were left with their grandparents in a small house on Parrot Street in Butte, unaware at such a young age of exactly what was happening to them and why.

Ignatious J. Knievel owned a tyre shop in Butte and worked long hours trying to make it more profitable than it actually was. While it was no gold mine it did put food on the table and clothes on Bobby and Nick, a burden the ageing couple could well have done without but a duty they fulfilled to the best of their ability. With Ignatious devoting so much time to the shop it fell mostly to Emma to raise the boys and instil in them the rights and wrongs, the do's and don'ts, that would prepare them for life in a difficult world.

Having been taken in by their grandparents at such an early age,

Bobby and Nick quite comfortably and naturally called them 'Mum' and 'Dad' and, apart from the greater age gap, life in the small Knievel house probably felt much like that of any other working-class family in Butte. There wasn't much to go around and survival was a daily struggle, as Evel explained many years later: 'Everything that my grandparents got they worked morning, noon and night for. Nothing was ever given to them and nothing was given to me; I either worked for it or stole it.'

As soon as Bobby and Nick were old enough to play outside in the streets they found out what it really meant to be a resident of Butte. Pimps, prostitutes and drunks were everywhere, and one of the boys' earliest childhood pastimes was throwing stones at prostitutes in order to bait their pimps into chasing them down the street. And it wasn't as if Bobby had to go out of his way to locate the city's prostitutes; a good many of them were working quite literally on his doorstep. 'There were 500 prostitutes working in one square block on Mercury and Gallina Street and my grandfather's tyre shop was right on Gallina Street. I was raised right in it. Blonde Edna's whorehouse was right across the street from it [his grandparents' house] and Dirty Mouth Mary's was on the other side.'

When he came of age, Knievel stopped throwing rocks at prostitutes and began throwing money at them instead. 'In ten years in these whorehouses,' he admitted, 'I must have spent at least five or six thousand dollars, at three dollars a time. Every whore in this town knew me. There just wasn't anything else to do there but go into a bar or a whorehouse. When you got tired of going to the whorehouse, you went to the bar.'

But as a kid there were often more conventional games to be played than pimp-baiting, and Big Sky Country was a better place than most in which to play them. Like any young American boy,

Bobby loved playing cowboys and Indians, and since Montana had been as much a part of the Wild West as anywhere else in the States it formed the perfect backdrop for escapist cowboy games. Television cowboy Roy Rogers was Bobby's greatest childhood hero and he would spend hours pretending to be him, dressing up in a makeshift cowboy outfit complete with sheriff's badge and his grandfather's hat. By the time he reached his mid-teens, Bobby even had a real horse, Alamo, gifted to him by his step-grandfather, Roy Buis, to add a touch more realism to his escapades. It would have dumbfounded the young Knievel to imagine that he would not only meet but befriend his hero Roy Rogers in later life, but for the time being he was content just to imitate him.

Another of Bobby's childhood idols was boxer Joe Louis, better known at the time as the 'Brown Bomber'. Bobby was a huge boxing fan and always tuned the radio in to listen to Louis fight the likes of Billy Conn, Max Baer and 'Jersey' Joe Walcott. As a kid, Bobby owned a pair of boxing gloves but had no punchbag. Being as inventive as any other child without the resources to actually buy what he wanted, Bobby soon found a solution to this, albeit an unlikely one. 'My dad was in the Second World War and he sent me his canteen from Japan, so I hung it up in my grandmother's [house] upstairs and I used to use it for a punching bag.' When Knievel's father managed to get Joe Louis's autograph for his son, Bobby was so thrilled he carried it in his wallet for 12 years.

Despite having being abandoned by his parents, a scenario that can often result in children becoming rebellious and delinquent, Bobby Knievel wasn't an inherently bad child – he simply had a mass of energy and an inclination to mischief like most young boys. In other words, he was perfectly normal, but he did seem to have an inherent fondness for danger and so sought out thrills whenever and wherever he could. Apart from the adrenalin rush he enjoyed when being chased by pimps, Bobby also loved to build his own ramshackle soapboxes and race them down the hill at the end of Montana Street. Naturally there were crashes – the first of many in Knievel's life – but they rarely amounted to more than a blood-ied knee or scuffed elbow and injuries were always something to boast about in a town like Butte. Bobby was also extremely fond of football and would don his leather safety helmet and play with his brother Nick every night after school as their grandmother cooked dinner.

There was nothing about Bobby's early childhood to suggest he would be anything other than a regular working Butte man when he grew up; nothing which marked him out as being particularly different to the other kids he played with on the block. It was not until he was eight years old that he witnessed the event which would ultimately inspire him to carve his own way in life and become famous the world over for doing so.

In 1946, Butte's Clark Park played host to Joey Chitwood and his Auto Daredevil Show, and when Emma Knievel took her grand-sons to watch the performance she could never have imagined the far-reaching consequences their day out would have; in fact, if she had known, it is most probable that the family would have stayed at home. Bobby was completely mesmerised by the performances of the daredevils and thrilled to see their Ford V-8s crash through fire walls, jump from ramp to ramp and perform choreographed rollovers. 'I had never seen anything like it,' he later recalled. 'Using a take-off ramp, Chitwood had leapfrogged his car over an automobile while stuntman Cliff Major jumped a motorcycle through a hoop of fire. This set the course for the rest of my life.'

Although he didn't decide there and then that he was going to become a professional stuntman, Knievel did set about imitating the stunts he had seen on his bicycle. 'I went home and took the mudguards off my bicycle and put cards in the spokes so it would sound like a motorcycle and I built little ramps and jumped off of them. I'd put on little shows for the kids in the neighbourhood.'

Even those early shows combined the three key elements to Knievel's later career: his love of performing in front of an audience, his willingness to be hurt while doing so, and his entrepreneurial skills for making a fast buck – Bobby charged his friends two cents apiece to watch. Using his grandfather's garage doors as ramps, Bobby's brother Nick would chalk a mark where Bobby landed before moving the doors further apart to allow him to try and better the distance. When this became too mundane, the brothers set flame to piles of scrub and Bobby would amaze his young audience by leaping over the flames. Leaping fire proved to be a real showstopper until both doors caught fire and left the budding stuntman with no ramps. Needless to say, Bobby's grandfather was none too impressed upon discovering that his garage no longer had doors, but after reprimanding Bobby he merely chalked the experience down to 'boys being boys'.

Witnessing the Chitwood show was certainly the defining moment of Bobby Knievel's childhood. At the time it may have simply been a fantastic spectacle and an exciting escape from the realities of growing up in Butte, as well as being the inspiration for his own little stunt show, but at a deeper level the experience had a more profound and lasting effect on Knievel. He had learned that people would pay to watch men risking their lives – and would love them for doing so.

But while Knievel's marketing and PR skills would become legendary, they certainly weren't learned in Butte High School where he showed little aptitude for the discipline of scholastic pursuits. He was more interested in the opportunity school gave him for meeting girls. 'I didn't like school very much – I never did. The only time I liked it was when I had a girlfriend and I wanted to go to school to see her.' Knievel later rued the fact that he had not persevered in school, admitting that 'Education is so important. I didn't have much schooling and regret it now.'

While he was still in formal education, Bobby relied on sports rather than academic pursuits to provide the inspiration for getting out of bed each morning. He enthusiastically played hockey and football and tried his hand at pole-vaulting and most other track and field events, usually with a considerable degree of success. In fact he became so competent at skiing that he went on to win the Class A division of the Northern Rocky Mountain Ski Association men's ski-jumping championship in 1957 – his first real, high-profile jumps of any kind and another crucial piece in the jigsaw that was to make up his unique and bizarre career. Years later, Knievel would utilise ski-jump-style ramps for several of his motorcycle jumps when there was insufficient space to reach the required take-off speed.

Further refining the necessary skills for the career path he would eventually choose, Knievel also tried his hand at rodeo riding all over Montana. Again, the physical involvement and danger appealed to Bobby just as it did on the football pitch or hockey rink; he was a natural-born thrill-seeker and those thrills simply could not be found sitting behind a desk listening to a lecture on the American Civil War, much as he enjoyed tales of the Old West. Rodeo riding also happened to be another discipline that would stand Bobby in good stead when it came to muscling a bucking and weaving Harley-Davidson down a landing ramp.

But the sport that most of his childhood friends and sports coaches remember him as being particularly good at was ice hockey, even though he was never noted as being much of a team player as his high-school hockey coach Leo Maney recalls: 'He was an individualist and he did not learn, at any time we were associated with him, this matter of team play; passing the puck to the other players. He'd get the puck at one end of the ring and away he'd go all by himself.'

That streak of individuality, that preference to rely on himself instead of others and that desire to attract the glory of the limelight for his own achievements were all crucial elements in the making of Evel Knievel. While his grandparents did all they could for him, Bobby was continuously aware that he had been abandoned early in life and that the only person that was going to be able to help him make something of himself *was* himself.

But, much as he would have liked to, Bobby couldn't spend his entire time at high school playing sports and, when the pressure and boredom of class work finally became too much, he decided to leave school at 16, before graduating, much to the disappointment of his grandmother. Emma Knievel had tried everything she could to make sure Bobby had a solid education which would earn him a respectable job, but in the end his own will was too strong. If he didn't want to do something, Bobby Knievel simply wouldn't do it – for anyone or anything. But his lack of education meant there were few options of employment in Butte and it was almost inevitable that he would find himself working down the mines.

Mining for any substance is hard, gruelling and dangerous work but it was even tougher before today's high standards of safety and occupational health came into being. Apart from the multitude of physical mining accidents, which were all too common, there was also silicosis – or miner's consumption as it was known locally – to worry about. Caused by breathing in tiny particles of silica, quartz or slate, over time silicosis affects the lung tissue and can ultimately prove fatal. Regardless of the dangers (or more probably because he just didn't have any other viable options) Bobby Knievel landed a job with the Anaconda Copper Mining Company after leaving school, and worked in the Stewart and Emma mine shafts a mile below the surface of the richest hill on earth as a contract miner, skip tender and diamond driller. 'I did every job in the mine from the top to the bottom and I remember my first cheque – $57 for a week's work.'

Apart from silicosis there were other potentially lethal hazards, including the constant threat of cave-ins, fires, floods and the escape of poisonous gases, not to mention the additional and usual hazards of working with heavy equipment in a poorly lit environment where temperatures often soared above 100 degrees. Conditions were so bad that more than 2,100 miners lost their lives in Butte's deadly labyrinth of mine shafts over the years, 168 of which perished in a single fire in 1917. Knievel soon discovered it wasn't for him. 'I could hardly wait to get out. I had many friends killed in the mines [from] accidents; ore dumped on them in the shafts and killed falling to the bottom, and being crushed to death in the slopes. I just wanted to get out.'

Knievel did have one other option open to him apart from working down the mines and that was to work in his father's Volkswagen dealership, which he had opened upon his return to Butte in 1956. But Bobby, perhaps needing to find his own way in the world or maybe because he still harboured a grudge against his father for abandoning him, declined the offer and stuck with his mining job, however desperate he was to get out of it.

Salvation from the pits eventually came in the form of a driving job for the same Anaconda company. Bobby could escape the perils of the mines by driving his less fortunate colleagues to and from work. It was a safer and more comfortable job but Bobby found it mundane work and often spiced it up by trying to scare his passengers witless, to the point where he claims they refused to ride with him any longer. The final straw in his career at Anaconda came when he reputedly told a colleague to drop a giant boulder into the back of a truck he was driving so that he could perform a 'wheelie'. According to Knievel, the truck reared up so high that it brought down overhead power cables and led to his dismissal.

Glad to be out of the mining business, an experience he would 'never forget', Knievel was nonetheless still short of career options and decided that his physical prowess would be put to better use in the US Army. He joined the 47th Infantry in the late 1950s (most probably 1958, though Knievel himself offers varied dates) for one year's full service to test the water. As a non-team-player and a young man who did not respond well to authority, the armed forces may have seemed a strange choice, but for Knievel it represented one of the few opportunities to escape the grimness and hopelessness of Butte. He had to give it a try.

Knievel was stationed at Fort Lewis in Washington, and although he initially claimed he hated his time in the Army his opinion appeared to have mellowed in later years when he was asked if it was a particularly grim period in his life. 'Not really. I served two years in the infantry full-time then seven years in the Reserves when I was in my twenties, but it was okay. I even managed to do a bit of pole-vaulting, sky-diving and parachuting.'

Despite becoming proficient in the use of Browning automatic rifles, it would seem that Bobby's premier contribution to Uncle Sam was in his role as a member of the Army's pole-vaulting team where he could stand by his own merits – just the way he preferred it. Having already become a proficient ski-jumper, his pole-vaulting prowess (he claims to have been able to clear a bar at 14 feet) seemed to prove that jumping really was in Knievel's blood, one way or another.

Whatever his true feelings about the Army, he didn't enjoy the experience enough to sign up for any longer than the minimum term, and after a short period of service he opted out, even though he didn't have any other immediate prospects.

Once again it was his love of sport that provided the prospect of a possible alternative career. Having attended a summer hockey school at the University of North Dakota in Grand Forks in 1959, Bobby saw a glimmer of hope in carving out a career as a professional ice-hockey player.

Perhaps disliking the formal approach adopted by an official hockey school, Bobby claimed to have declined the offer of a full-time scholarship, opting instead to throw his lot in with the semi-professional Charlotte Clippers who were members of the Eastern Hockey League. Yet again he appeared to be restless and easily bored and he quit the team after completing just one exhibition season. By then Knievel felt he had no chance of making it into the professional National Hockey League and, after failing a try-out with the semi-professional Seattle Totems of the Western Hockey League, he headed back home to Butte, a little more worldly but still lacking any real direction in his life.

While he may not have been good enough to cut it on the national scene, Knievel was now armed with the experience he'd gained on his travels and he viewed himself as a big hockey fish in a pretty small pond. He saw a new opportunity of making a living from the sport, and decided to form his own team, the Butte Bombers, which he would not only own but also play for, manage and coach. If he couldn't cut it solely as a player, maybe a jack-of-all-trades approach would reap rewards. The Bombers established themselves as a semi-professional team and Knievel claims they only lost one game in the two seasons they existed. That game was against the Czechoslovakian Olympic team, whom Bobby had shrewdly coerced into playing his Bombers as a warm-up game for the 1960 Winter Olympics that were being held at Squaw Valley in California.

This may have appeared to be a shrewd move at the time but it soon turned into a farce and threatened to ruin Bobby financially. He had hired the Civic Center in Butte and promoted the entire event himself, as well as still being one of the team players. He stood to make some decent money on the gate and a few bucks more from selling beer and snacks, but when forty Czech players, officials and hangers-on turned up in Butte, all expecting their expenses to be paid, Bobby knew he was in trouble. He had only anticipated an entourage of 20 and immediately realised he was going to lose money, and what was more, it was money he didn't have to lose. After the game he told the Czechs he couldn't pay their expenses without receipts (which Knievel later admitted to stealing) and an international incident was only avoided when the US Olympic Committee stepped in to pick up the bill.

The whole event must have left a sour taste in Knievel's mouth as he finally turned his back on ice hockey and set about looking for other ways to make a quick buck. 'There's no money in hockey,' he later lamented. 'It was my dream to be a pro-hockey player but there's just no money in it.' He certainly needed to make some money somehow because Knievel had by now married his childhood sweetheart, Linda Joan Bork.

Knievel had known Bork from his days at Butte High, and even after he dropped out he still hung around outside the school looking for any opportunity to talk with Linda. Three years younger than Knievel, Bork was caught between her youthful love for the handsome but unpromising 20-year-old and the disapproval of her parents, who saw Bobby as little more than a hoodlum who couldn't hold a steady job. And if Knievel's often-repeated tale about kidnapping his future wife is true, then he certainly justified the Borks' assessment of him. According to Knievel, he became so frustrated by the Borks' ban on their daughter speaking to him that he kidnapped Linda from the local ice rink. He reportedly dragged her off the ice by her hair and headed for Idaho where he proposed to marry her. Knievel's grandmother recalled the incident many years later, adding a ring of truth to the story. 'He did kidnap her of course and they were hunting for them all night long. The police were hunting for them and we were hunting for them but he was not put in jail or anything.'

Driving conditions on the night of the 'kidnap' were terrible and the young couple were forced to pull over and sleep the night in Bobby's grandparents' car, hoping the blizzard would abate by morning. But, by the following day, word of Knievel's escapade had got out and the couple were intercepted by a police road-block before they could reach Idaho. Knievel was charged not with kidnapping but with contributing to the delinquency of a minor, but since Linda did not want to press charges he was merely reprimanded by the authorities.

However, now feeling fully justified in his assessment of Knievel, Linda's father subsequently succeeded in obtaining a restraining order against Bobby, forcing him to stay away from Linda for a period of two years. Knievel had little choice but to obey – at least in public – but he still never gave up hope of one day marrying Linda Bork. His patience paid dividends and that day finally came on 5 September 1959 when the pair tied the knot having eloped with the help of a $50 loan from Knievel's grandmother and the use of the family car. Linda had only managed to elope because her father was away on a fishing trip at the time of the marriage and by the time he discovered the truth there was nothing he could do to change matters, no matter how furious he was.

A married man he may have been, but Bobby Knievel was still without gainful employment and the only money he was bringing in to the caravan he and his young wife were staying in was from a number of petty criminal activities. Knievel had long since realised that most of the people he saw in Butte with money had gained it on the wrong side of the law and he wanted a piece of the action, having seen the benefits of a life of crime. 'All that you can desire in life or want to be is what you can see immediately around you,' he explained, 'and what I saw immediately around me was a pimp with a shiny pair of shoes and a '49 Mercury. In Butte, if you weren't a pimp or a thief you were nothing. And I needed a few bucks to get out.' It was all the incentive Bobby needed; if he couldn't earn an honest buck, he'd earn some dishonest ones.

Knievel had long been used to the wrong side of the law, having been involved in several fights and charged with petty theft, but that was not exactly out of the ordinary for young men in post-war Butte. He was no stranger to dreaming up scams to make money either. One particular favourite was stealing hubcaps from cars to sell on as replacements or as scrap metal, a technique he perfected while still at school but one which escalated over time to almost industrial proportions. 'One time the police caught me and another boy with about three hundred hubcaps. I sold them for about a buck apiece. Christ, I needed a few bucks to go out. I could steal a guy's hubcaps when he was sitting in the car. You know, those ore trains go by, make a lot of noise. A guy's sitting in his car, I didn't care whether he had the radio on or not, I'd just steal the hubcaps right off his car. Every kid in town knew I could do it. But I moved on to bigger and better things.'

Those bigger and better things included running a 'protection agency', which was, by Knievel's own cryptic admission, really an extortion racket. While his well-meaning police-officer friend Mo

Mulchahy politely referred to Bobby's 'job' as being that of a merchant policeman, there were others in Butte who recognised it as something rather more corrupt. Knievel visited various businesses around Butte and asked if they would like him to keep an eye on their properties when they were closed. If they paid up, Bobby would check locks, make sure there were no open windows or doors and generally scare off any prowlers. Job done. If, however, any particular business refused his offer, they were very likely to find their premises had been broken into shortly afterwards.

The differing accounts of Knievel's 'job' among those who knew him show just how undefined his role was. Officer Mulchahy believed it to be legitimate, saying, 'He went around on the south side of town and he'd rattle doors and shake windows; he was one of us. He went to different merchants down on the south side and asked them for a job. Course, a lot of people who knew Knievel, they said "we'd rather not do that". They didn't have break-ins, they had breaks; they had breaks in their windows or breaks in their doors but he'd be back the next day and tell the businessmen "If I was watching your place, this wouldn't have happened", and they'd hire him.'

Knievel's own take on the situation was rather more telling, even if it did stop short of an absolute confession. 'When I was a merchant policeman I had a deal – you don't want to give a little kid that's trying to make a dollar a five-dollar bill every 30 days to watch your place then you might get robbed. That's what it amounted to. You pay me ten dollars a month, five dollars a month, to watch your place of business, you don't get robbed. They found out that my protection was well worth the five or ten dollars a month after not subscribing to it for a while.'

Knievel's friend Bob Pavolich, who ran the Met Tavern in Butte at the time – one of Knievel's favourite watering holes – showed no such ambivalence when asked for his interpretation of Bobby's scam. 'When he was a doorknocker here he used to come around my place at two o'clock in the morning – he was a merchant cop is what they called him. Well I would have to say that he probably knocked over mine and about a dozen others on the route. He always had money and he didn't make that kind of money knocking doors. Really, he told me he'd knocked over my place.'

Knievel eventually owned up – and apologised for – committing a string of burglaries around Butte, and he confessed that he tried for a whole weekend to break into the Prudential Federal Savings building but couldn't manage it. Addressing a meeting of Butte townspeople in the late 1990s, he blamed his misdemeanours on his youth and insisted he had eventually made amends for those acts over the years and was now a model Butte citizen.

But the money Bobby was spending in Butte bars was coming from increasingly more dangerous criminal activities. He had by now become so desperate for more money that he'd started robbing grocery stores, pharmacies and even banks all over the western United States. Knievel teamed up with a gang of six other men in order to be able to carry out more and more ambitious crimes. He claimed most of them were drug users, hence their penchant for turning over pharmacies to steal drugs as well as whatever was in the cash registers.

The techniques employed by his crew usually followed a similar pattern: they would stake out whichever building they planned to rob to gain the usual information about workers' shifts, opening and closing times, and where the entry points and exits were, then Bobby would drill a hole through the roof to allow the gang to drop down into the premises, by which point the adrenalin would really start to flow. Knievel, for one, found he liked the rush. 'That feeling I got inside a bank was the same feeling I got later when I started to jump [a motorcycle]. I could crack a safe with one hand tied behind my back faster than you could eat a hamburger with two.'

But Knievel soon realised that the prize of adrenalin alone wasn't enough to justify the risks he was taking. 'When we dropped through a hole in the roof there was so much pressure we'd sweat our shoes off. And it wasn't really worth it. We'd have to split the money between four or five people (depending on how many were in on any particular job) and averaged only a few grand apiece.'

If the FBI really were on the gang's trail, as Knievel claims, then the risks could not have been worth the slight rewards. After all, Bobby may have had a few dollars to throw around on beer but he and his young wife weren't exactly living in the lap of luxury as a result of his endeavours – and things would only be worse for Linda if Bobby was thrown in the county jail.

One long-standing mystery from this period relates to whether or not Knievel used dynamite stolen from his former employers, the Anaconda Mining Company, to blow up and rob the local courthouse in Butte. While Evel has sometimes boasted of carrying off the job, he has at other times backtracked and claimed, 'The courthouse was not blown up, the courthouse was burglarised. As to whether I did it or not, that's nobody's business but mine and that's the way it'll always remain.'

Either way, it was only when one of his accomplices was shot while trying to flee from a crime scene that Knievel was shocked into abandoning his evil ways. It brought him to the verge of a nervous breakdown, which in turn made him feel so low that he actually contemplated suicide. His accomplice, Jimmy Eng, had been shot dead in the street by police while on a job in Reno, Nevada, and while Knievel escaped with his life, he broke down on the way home and vowed to change his ways and turn his back on crime. 'I was crossing a bridge when I stopped and took out all my burglar tools – ropes, crowbars, nitroglycerine, drill bits, all of it – and dumped it into the Sacramento River in California. I just vowed right then that I would never steal another dime or rob another place and I never did.'

Knievel may have decided to go straight but he would continue to have run-ins with the law throughout his life, even after he had given up trying to make a living from crime. His skills as a bank robber appeared questionable anyhow and are perhaps best summarised by his childhood friend Paddy Boyle who once said of Evel, 'Actually he wasn't a bank robber cos he never got nothing. I think that's why he started jumping motorcycles – cos he couldn't make it as a burglar.'

Further pressure for Knievel to find a legitimate job came with the birth of his and Linda's first child, a son, Kelly Michael Knievel, on 21 August 1960. Now with a wife and child to feed, Bobby needed not only to find a source of regular income, he also needed to ensure he wouldn't be facing a lengthy jail sentence and leaving his family helpless.

In 1961, Knievel formed the Sur-Kill hunting service, another scheme which was not quite above board. Bobby would assure his clients that he knew the countryside of Montana so well that he could lead them to whatever game they chose to shoot, thereby guaranteeing them a good day's hunting. The problem was, much of that game was to be found only in protected national parks and was therefore off limits to hunters. Bobby being Bobby, however, wasn't about to let a small matter like that stand in the way of business.

It was during this period of being involved in hunting that one of the stranger episodes of Knievel's life occurred. Hearing that the US Department of the Interior had decided to cull half of

Yellowstone Park's 10,000-strong elk population to maintain nature's balance, Bobby decided to intervene in what would prove to be his first ever publicity stunt. He (illegally) shot an elk in the park then cut off its antlers and slung them across his shoulders and set out to hitchhike all the way to Washington DC in protest at the cull. After all, how could a hunting guide like Knievel expect to make any money if there were no more elk to shoot? Bobby, backed by the Montana Fish and Game Commission, wanted to initiate a relocation programme so the elk could be re-homed all over the state for hunters to legitimately shoot. Bobby could then run his business legally.

Knievel claimed he gave the antlers to President Kennedy himself and told him, 'If you don't do something about this immediately your son John-John will look at the head of an elk on a nickel like my kids do the head of a buffalo.'

Whether or not he actually gained an audience with the president (he was pictured in local newspapers with the antlers but JFK was conspicuously absent) it is nonetheless doubtful that a 22-year-old hitchhiker from Butte would have single-handedly persuaded the government to complete a U-turn on its culling policy. Even so, Knievel had played his part in stirring up publicity for the campaign and the idea was abandoned and a programme instigated whereby the elk were transported to sites across Montana as fair game for hunters. For the elk it was a stay of execution; for Knievel the trip represented a double victory. The first bonus was that Bobby now had some elk he could legally lead his clients to as part of the Sur-Kill experience, but the other plus point was to be far more important in the long-run. Bobby's picture had appeared in the *Washington Post* along with details of his plight, proving to Knievel for the first time that publicity wasn't that hard to come by if you just used a little imagination.

Hitchhiking may have been his only means of getting to Washington but it had added a novelty factor to the trip, as did the elk antlers. Knievel had discovered he was a natural at promoting himself and his ideas, and the lesson would not be lost on him.

Somewhat surprisingly, Bobby tired of the hunting game before he could take advantage of the new elk policy and decided to try his hand at a 'proper' nine-to-five job as a car insurance salesman with the Combined Insurance Company of America. He was hired by a certain Alex Smith, whom Knievel later acknowledged as being the man who finally helped steer him away from a life of crime and who 'probably saved my life' in doing so.

Knievel has never been short of boasts when talking about his skills as a salesman, but given the phenomenal manner in which he managed to promote and sell himself to the world some years later, they perhaps aren't completely idle. He claimed he broke all company records for selling 110 policies in one day to staff at the Warm Springs mental hospital in Montana and quipped that he 'might have even sold some policies to the patients'. There have been comments from more than one party over the years that Knievel in fact sold *all* those policies to mental patients. Whatever the case, he also claims to have gone on to sell an incredible total of 271 policies in that same week. But, if the stories are to be believed, then Bobby became a victim of his own success. Feeling he should have been rewarded with very swift promotion after his success in the field, Knievel determined he was going to ask the president of the company, Mr W. Clement Stone, for just that; he demanded, rather arrogantly in a face-to-face meeting, to be promoted to the position of vice president. Not surprisingly, Stone declined and Knievel immediately resigned. 'He refused me and I quit. He said he was sorry to see me go and wished me the best of luck. I thought

I'd regret it but in every adversity there is a seed of benefit. Mr Stone taught me a lot about the value of a positive mental attitude and he taught me to do the right thing by others simply because it's right.'

Significantly, as well as being president of Combined Insurance, Stone was also a self-made millionaire and author, and his book, *The Success System that Never Fails,* became one of Bobby's favourites. Preaching the benefits of a positive mental attitude, Stone's book would be a constant source of support and guidance in the making of the star that was Evel Knievel. Also present at the meeting between Knievel and Stone was Napoleon Hill, another author who promoted the benefits of positive thinking. Hill had written a book called *Think and Grow Rich,* and while Knievel had been trying to do just that over the last few years with varying degrees of failure, he would have the art mastered within the next ten years and would be rewarded with riches beyond his wildest dreams. All he had to do was think of a field in which he could grow rich.

# 2
# Happy Landings

*'I could do a wheelie either sitting on the motorcycle or standing on it better than anyone else in the world.'*

Having flunked out of school, tried his hand at so many occupations and moved from one sport to the next, it seemed that Bobby Knievel would never be able to maintain enough interest or enthusiasm in any particular field to make a decent living. He was too restless, too ambitious to make something of himself and too opposed to knuckling down and accepting a regular nine-to-five job. The only real constant in his life, the only thing he hadn't tired of since his schooldays, was riding motorcycles. Bobby simply loved to fool around on bikes.

Motorcycles had first entered Knievel's life when he was 15 years old, although he had fantasised that his bicycle was motorised long before that. He was given his first motorcycle by his father while visiting him in El Sobrante, California, where Robert senior had eventually settled with his second wife Jeanie Buis and had three daughters: Christy, Renee and Robin. After working as a bus driver for a time, Knievel's father had managed to save and borrow enough money to open a Volkswagen dealership in Berkeley (he would later return to Butte and open another dealership there), and while young Bobby was visiting his father presented him with a little British-built 125cc two-stroke BSA Bantam – a massively popular machine at the time and one which was responsible for launching countless racing careers as well as the less-travelled route Knievel would eventually follow on two wheels.

It might have seemed an extravagant gift, given the relative poverty Bobby was accustomed to living in, but it may have been his father's way of assuaging his own guilt at deserting his son at such a young age. And, as the bike was part of a trade-in on a car sale, it probably didn't cost him too much.

As well as running a garage, Robert Knievel also raced cars on occasion in local events. He was never serious enough about the sport to attempt to make a career out of it but he was a competent driver and was responsible for generating Bobby's interest in cars and bikes.

Perhaps surprisingly, Bobby never displayed any real anger or bitterness at having been abandoned by his father (and mother) as a child. On the contrary, he usually spoke well of his dad. 'Jeez, I thought my dad was a helluva guy,' he would later say. 'I used to go down there [San Francisco] when he raced midgets and sports cars. Helluva good driver.' Whatever his true feelings were about being given up as a child, Bobby certainly had his dad to thank for kick-starting his two-wheeled career.

The pattern for Bobby's wild-riding style was set right from the first time he ever rode his little bike. Without any formal tuition, Knievel threw a leg over the Bantam, pulled in the clutch lever, engaged first gear, popped out the clutch, roared off down the street and smashed straight into a mailbox. 'I couldn't control it. I really got in trouble on that motorcycle that day. I almost got killed.'

Undeterred, Bobby brought the Bantam back to Butte and set about learning the skills of his future trade as well as annoying and amusing the good citizens of the town in equal measure. 'I used to ride through bars here and ride down the sidewalk, and my dad said, "What is the matter with you? You're going to get killed."'

Tales of his cop-baiting (in which he would spark off chases from Butte's finest) have become legendary and are, at least in part, due to the depiction of such events in the 1971 George Hamilton movie *Evel Knievel.* Officer Mo Mulchahy lends some credence to the legend, however, with his testimony that 'It got to be kinda fun. Most times you chased him you'd go have a coffee. If he didn't wanna be caught, you didn't catch him. But it was never nothing serious.'

While Mulchahy's version of events is certainly within the realms of possibility, other versions show how the legend of Evel Knievel has been added to over the years to the point of absurdity. In his book *Evel Knievel: An American Hero,* author Ace Collins relates one particular incident involving Knievel and the local police. Without crediting anyone as a source or witness, Collins tells of Knievel being trapped in a dead-end alley by police, who had barricaded the entrance with their patrol vehicle. Undeterred, Knievel rides straight towards the police car, but bears to the right at the last minute, hits a convenient earthen ramp and sails straight over the police car! At best it's a highly unlikely scenario, and had there been any element of truth in the tale it's certain that Knievel would have told and retold it over the years. The fact that he hasn't done so would seem to prove that it is just another myth.

However much truth there is in the cop-baiting tales, there is no doubt that Bobby Knievel loved his motorcycle and spent countless hours riding round Butte on it, his thrill-seeking character making him a natural when it came to trying wheelies and rear-wheel slides and gunning the little Bantam flat out for all it was worth. 'I learned to do wheelies on my little BSA and when I later had bigger bikes I could do a wheelie either sitting on the motorcycle or standing on it better than anyone else in the world. And I mean that – better than anybody in the world. I was the first guy to do one standing on the seat. I could wheelie until the oil ran out of the pan and the engine seized up.'

Knievel's two-wheeled antics became something of an institution in Butte, and locals were particularly fond of turning out to watch Bobby race up impossibly steep mine hills on his bike. 'I was goin' up and down mine hills here in Butte. Everybody thought I was a nut. Fifty or sixty cars used to come out every night to this mine-hill dump. I used to climb it; I'd fall off ten times and make it once. They'd all sit there and blow their horns.'

Bobby also started to discover that people would actually pay to see his motorcycle pranks, and he found he could make a buck here and there by amusing his drinking buddies. On one occasion outside Bobby's favourite watering hole, the Met Tavern, a friend bet Knievel $10 he couldn't ride over a Volkswagen car which was parked outside. With friend and Met owner Bob Pavolich riding pillion, Knievel hoisted the front wheel of his Bantam onto the boot of the car, rode up over the rear window, smashing it in as he went, then revved the bike up and over the roof and finally back down over the bonnet and onto the street. He scared the life out of Pavolich, amused the hell out of the gathered drinkers and won his $10. The owner of the Volkswagen was presumably less than pleased.

Knievel may have been good at performing stunts on his BSA, but back in the 1960s there was no obvious means of pursuing motorcycle stunt-riding as a career. Therefore it was to becoming a motorcycle racer, rather than a stunt rider, that Knievel aspired, and in America in the early 1960s there really was only one kind of motorcycle sport and that was dirt-bike racing. Had Knievel been born 20 years later there is every chance he would have taken to road racing on purpose-built Tarmac circuits but back then this was almost exclusively a European pursuit. The Americans preferred to race 'flat-trackers' round dirt or shingle-based ovals ranging from a quarter-mile to a mile in length. It's a fearsome spectacle, with riders racing their bikes flat out down the straights at around 140mph before slewing their machines sideways to scrub off speed into the corners. The nearest European equivalent is speedway, but speedway bikes are far less powerful than the big 750cc American flat-trackers, personified by Harley-Davidson's legendary and enduring XR-750 V-twin machine – the same bike Evel would later use in his jumping career.

Having gained his national racing licence from the AMA (American Motorcycle Association), Bobby headed out to California to try his hand at dirt-track racing. Borrowing all he could from his ever-supportive grandparents, Knievel was still extremely poor and his accommodation at race meetings, as often as not, was the back seat of his car, usually with Linda and Kelly along for the ride. On many nights the young family would camp out under the stars and wash themselves in rivers or creeks, all so Knievel could pursue his dream of becoming a professional motorcycle racer.

Knievel did meet with some success in the racing world, but the prize money was poor and barely enough to keep him going to the next meeting. He also found his six-foot frame put him at a disadvantage next to the smaller riders. 'When the AMA put us on 250s, the little guys who didn't weigh anything would go past you like a rubber band,' he complained. It was during one of these races in May 1962 that Knievel achieved something of a landmark in his life: he broke his first bone. It was his collarbone and it was to be the first of many bones he would shatter; enough, in fact, to earn him a place in the *Guinness Book of Records* as the man who had broken more bones than any other. The 1972 entry for this, however, is laughably inaccurate. It states that in that year alone, Knievel fractured 431 bones. As Steve Mandich correctly points out in *Evel Incarnate: The Life and Legend of Evel Knievel*, that would average out at 1.2 bones being broken every single day of the year, a feat which even Knievel would find hard to admit to with a straight face.

But back in May 1962, apart from being a month memorable for breaking his first bone, Knievel had good reason to celebrate as his second son, Robert Edward Knievel, was born on the seventh day of the month. He would become known to the world as Robbie Knievel, the world-class motorcycle jumper, but his relationship with his father would be stormy in the extreme. But right now, Robbie was just another mouth to feed and his father was still not earning any money worth talking about. Bobby knew he would have to try harder to support his family.

His interest in racing and bikes in general had become such that by late 1962 Knievel made his first attempt to earn a proper living from motorcycles. Having been disillusioned with the car-insurance business, Bobby borrowed as much money as he could from his grandmother and his friend Joe Dosen, put it together with his own meagre savings and opened a motorcycle dealership in Butte called 'Imported Motors'. He stocked a range of bikes including Hondas, Triumphs, BMWs, Indians, Ducatis and Matchless machines. With his innate gift for promotions and sales techniques Knievel should have been a natural as a bike dealer, but money was scarce in Butte and there simply weren't enough people in the position to buy a motorcycle. The shop did a poor trade and in 1963 Bobby was forced to close the business, whereupon he fled to Spokane, Washington with his young family, which grew again to include a daughter, Tracey Lynn, born on 22 October of that year. In Spokane, Knievel tried, yet again, for a new start in life.

The experience of having raced and of owning a bike store, albeit an unsuccessful one, stood Knievel in good stead when he arrived in Spokane. He'd made lots of contacts and friends within the bike industry and one of those, a man named Darrell Triber, readily offered Bobby a job in one of his Honda dealerships. This time Knievel flourished in the trade and was soon made a partner of the Spokane branch. Later, when Triber decided to add another franchise in Moses Lake, also in Washington State, he trusted Knievel enough to allow him to run the business. When Triber eventually wanted out of the motorcycle business entirely he sold the Moses Lake branch to Knievel, who was obviously determined to have another stab at being a successful businessman.

Bobby knew from his previous experience that the challenge of running a successful bike dealership was in learning how to attract potential customers to his particular store rather than anyone else's, and, once he'd got them there, how to persuade them to part with their money to buy a motorcycle. At first, Knievel thought small: he offered a $100 discount off the price of any Honda to anyone who could beat him at arm wrestling. (According to Knievel, no one ever did qualify for the discount.)

But such wacky fairground gimmicks were never going to be enough to attract serious business, and as sales continued to be sluggish Knievel started thinking bigger. Having become more and more adept at the art of riding a motorcycle and, more importantly, at performing stunts and tricks on a bike through his racing, Knievel got round to thinking back to his childhood and the Joey Chitwood Auto Daredevil Show. It might now have been nineteen years ago, but childhood memories, especially such exciting ones, are forged strongly within the psyche and Knievel had never forgotten the experience. But only now, in 1965, did he see a way to turn what was just a happy memory into a potential money-spinner, or at the very least, a way to attract more customers through his shop doors. Robert Craig Knievel, at the age of 26, decided he was going to jump a motorcycle off a ramp over some obstacles in front of a live audience. A star, and a whole new medium of entertainment, was about to be born.

Not content with an 'ordinary' ramp-to-ramp jump (which was anything *but* ordinary at the time), Knievel decided upon adding more danger and more novelty to the event. His elk protest from 1961 had taught him the value of original thinking when it came to drumming up publicity and this time around he excelled himself. In future years the world would know Knievel as the man who soared over cars, trucks and buses on a motorcycle, but his first ever jump was one of the most unusual of his entire career: Bobby had made up his mind to leap over two mountain lions and a crate containing 100 live rattlesnakes.

Once more displaying a keen eye for promotional opportunities, Knievel chose a 350cc Honda from his dealership to make the jump on. Honda, now the world's largest manufacturer of motorcycles, was a relative newcomer in 1965, and many people still mocked the little bikes from the land of the rising sun, associating them with cheaper, unreliable produce manufactured in the Far East. American riders in particular referred to Hondas as 'rice burners' and preferred their machines to be of wholesome American or British stock. But if Knievel could prove that a little Honda was good enough to jump 40 feet over a cage of rattlers then just maybe he could convince them to buy one from his store.

The obvious choice for the jump site was at the Moses Lake Raceway, not far from Knievel's bike shop, and it was arranged that he would perform his madcap stunt during the halftime break in race proceedings. Knievel says he never formally practised the 40-foot leap but it seems safe to assume he had attempted some sort of jumps prior to his public debut, even if they were on a much smaller scale. On the other hand, given that he never made a habit of practising for any of his later bigger jumps ('No use practising – if you kill yourself in practice you'll never make the jump for real'), it is possible that he was prepared to just twist the throttle and see what happened. He was, after all, well versed in the merits of positive thinking and was more than happy to take a risk if he thought there was money to be made.

Obtaining the lions and snakes was in itself quite an achievement, and it would be hard to imagine such a performance being permitted today in our animal-friendly society. However, Bobby used his connections well and arranged to 'borrow' the hapless creatures from the zoo in Cooley City. The zoo's manager was dating a girl Knievel knew well and he used all his charm in persuading her to fight his case. 'She used to come into the store and sit around all the time and go to lunch with me and this and that and the other thing, so she talked him into doing it.'

Even so, the owner of the mountain lions was still understandably nervous about subjecting his animals to the potential harm that could be caused them by a lunatic on a motorcycle. 'The guy that owned the mountain lions was afraid I was going to kill them so he put both of them close to the take-off ramp,' Knievel explained. No one seemed to care much for the well-being of the rattlesnakes, however, the general consensus probably being that if there were to be a hundred less poisonous critters slithering around Washington State then so much the better.

With the snakes and lions in place and blissfully unaware of what was about to happen next, Knievel rode out in front of the crowd on his little Honda to prepare for his first ever professional appearance as a motorcycle jumper. There was little of the glitz and glamour which was associated with his later appearances; no sparkling red, white and blue jumpsuit, no spectacularly custom-painted Harley-Davidson and no entourage of helpers and hangers-on. But the showmanship was there from the very beginning as Knievel revved his bike and made several runs past the take-off ramp, an action which both excited the crowd and allowed Knievel to assess the speed he would need to be travelling at to safely make the jump. This was a technique Knievel would use throughout his career to great effect.

When he felt he had whipped his audience into a suitable frenzy, Knievel rode slowly back to his starting position and prepared to face the unknown. What he was about to attempt was no illusion, nor was there any trickery involved. If he didn't carry enough speed he was going to be seriously hurt right there in front of a live audience, and if he couldn't hold on to the bike as it smashed back down to earth he could even be killed. Like taking an aeroplane on its first test flight, there was no safe way to practise what Knievel was about to attempt, and that is precisely what drew the crowd's attention.

Racing cars or motorcycles is a matter of progressively gaining speed through experience. Jumping a motorcycle is do or die, Russian roulette on two wheels. Knievel would twist his throttle, launch himself off a flimsy wooden ramp and put his fate in the hands of the gods. He was little more than a human cannonball and the crowd knew it.

But by his own admission, the young Knievel had 'balls like a rhinoceros' and a whole heap of faith in himself. He wasn't about to back out, even if his nerves were on edge; on the contrary, the feeling of raw fear and excitement was just like the feeling he got when robbing a bank, but this time the source of his excitement was legal and it felt good. Better than the gloomy prospect of being lowered into a mineshaft, better than the drudgery of doing the rounds as an insurance salesman and better than being told what to do in the Army. Knievel was finally alone and calling the shots; he would quite literally stand or fall by his own decisions and his own skills. He felt more alive than at any other time in his life. It was time to go.

Knievel twisted the throttle on his Honda and kicked his way up through the gearbox, gaining crucial speed before shooting up the ramp that would launch him into the void. As he left the end of the ramp, the Honda's revs dropped away as the rear wheel continued to spin, seeking a purchase on anything solid. Knievel tried to hold the handlebars up high, sensing he must bring the motorcycle down rear wheel first for a stable landing. He was now little more than a passenger; while he could control the angle the bike would descend at, he could no longer increase or decrease his speed, and it looked, even to his inexperienced eyes, that he was not going to clear the gap. He needed just a few more miles per hour to bridge the last few feet clearly. With a resounding 'thud' the Honda smashed back down to earth amid the noise of splintering wood. Knievel had in fact come down short and smashed open the far end of the wooden box containing the rattlesnakes. But he had made it. He had landed his bike safely and was still in one piece.

The crowd, having never seen anything like it in their lives, yelled and cheered their approval. They had looked at the 40-foot gap and thought Knievel would never make it, but he had. And as he hauled on the brakes and scrubbed off speed, the crowd started to notice that the rattlesnakes were making a break for freedom – right in the crowd's direction. 'This guy started running around trying to catch them,' laughed Knievel, 'and I rode back by those mountain lions because I was so excited I didn't know what I was doing. There wasn't any grandstands and these snakes started crawling up there in the crowd. It was funnier than hell. I just buzzed on out and watched it from up on a hill somewhere. People were runnin' every which way. It was a real crowd-pleaser you might say.'

Despite the success and novelty of his first ever motorcycle jump, Knievel's business did not benefit enough from after-show publicity to make it worthwhile persevering. He sold the store and relocated to Orange County in Southern California where he continued racing bikes as the only means of getting a thrill in an otherwise bleak existence. But it wasn't long before he started thinking about trying to make a career out of motorcycle stunt-shows. His first attempt had been a fantastic success and he had totally loved the adrenalin rush that jumping had provided. He was beginning to think that people all over the US might just pay to see him jump on a regular basis. 'I thought that if the auto industry could support an auto-daredevil show like Joey Chitwood or Daredevil Lynch, maybe the time had come that the motorcycle industry could also support a stunt thing.' It wasn't a sure-fire bet by any means but, optimistic as ever, Knievel decided to give it a go. After all, what did he have to lose? If he didn't make any money he'd still get a rush.

But rather than perform alone again, Knievel decided he needed to model his new act on Joey Chitwood's well-established set-up. To put on a whole show he would have to keep a crowd entertained for more than a few minutes and that would require a whole troupe of stunt riders. Bobby found no shortage of talented riders among his racing buddies, who were prepared to try their hand at stunt riding even if it wasn't going to pay much money; there were still bound to be a few laughs in it. By late 1965, Knievel had convinced five other riders that it was worth a shot: Eddie Mulder, Swede Savage, Rod Pack, Skip VanLuwenn and Butch Wilhelm, the midget who stood only four-feet four-inches high and was billed as the 'midget daredevil'. Many of the gang would remain friends with Knievel after he shot to fame and they dropped by the wayside. Mulder would act as Knievel's stunt double in his future movies, Savage would become a golfing partner, and Van-Luwenn remained close to Knievel as well as managing to set up one of the largest motorcycle and helmet distribution companies in the world.

Having secured a fleet of British-built Norton scramblers from the Berliner Motor Corporation (the official distributors of Norton motorcycles in the US), the self-styled daredevils planned and rehearsed their act until they felt they were ready to make their debut in front of a live audience. The only thing the team lacked was a name. It was made clear from the start that Knievel was to be the main attraction; after all, it was his show and he was the only member who had any experience of jumping in front of an audience. But 'Bobby Knievel and his Motorcycle Daredevils' just didn't have any ring of glamour to it, and since the group was billing itself as being 'from Hollywood', a touch of showbiz glitz was essential. In solving the problem, Bobby created one of the best stage names of the twentieth century and one that would eventually become known throughout the world. With only a slight alteration to the spelling, he decided to use his old nickname: from now on he would be Evel Knievel.

# 3
# What's in a Name?

*'Evel Knievel was a character I created. He was even hard for me to live with sometimes. He wouldn't do anything I told him, the dumb son-of-a-bitch.'*

Very few people become so famous that they are identifiable to the mainstream public by a single name. The vast majority of people in the Western world would know exactly who Sinatra, Ali or Hitler were, but these are all surnames and the Recognisable-by-a-single-name Club becomes much more exclusive when only first names are permitted. Elvis can certainly claim membership, but so can another white-jumpsuited icon: Evel.

Perhaps it is because both names are unusual, although Elvis is genuine while Evel is merely a nickname-cum-stage name; or it may be that both men were the single-handed creators of the phenomenon they respectively gave rise to. Whatever the case, Evel can rightly lay claim to being one of the few celebrities of the late twentieth century who is recognisable by his first name without any need for further expansion or explanation. Yet how he came to have one of the most recognised stage names in showbiz is not quite so simple, and it is quite possible that the origins of it are hazy even to the man himself, given, as he is, to repeating tales with such frequency that, true or false, he certainly seems to believe in them himself.

The most commonly repeated anecdote of how Bobby Knievel became Evel Knievel is the jail-cell theory, which holds that Bobby was being held in a Butte police cell overnight along with a man called William Knoffel. According to the legend, a police officer quipped that he had better double the guard because he was housing both 'Awful' Knoffel and 'Evil' Knievel on the same night. Contemporary newspaper reports prove that a William Knoffel did exist, and Butte police officer Morris Mulchahy has actually testified to this version of events in the documentary *Evel Knievel: The Last of the Gladiators*.

The problem with this theory is that Evel himself later claimed he was nicknamed 'Evel' at a much younger age. In *Evel Ways: The Attitude of Evel Knievel*, he is quoted as saying, 'The first one to call me Evel Knievel was Nig McGrath, a friend of the family. My brother Nick and I stole his hubcaps and he hollered "You're just a little evil Knievel." It sort of stuck . . . even though I was somewhat ashamed of the name.' (Although later in the very same book there are claims that the nickname was started by a neighbour and/or the local police due to Knievel's bike-riding antics.) The name McGrath turns up again in *Penthouse* magazine but under different circumstances when Evel explains, 'The guy that actually named me "Evil" was *Nick* McGrath, a baseball umpire. Every time I'd come up, even in Little League, he'd call me "Evil Knievel".' Whether this Nig McGrath and Nick McGrath are one and the same person (their names are repeated here as they were spelled in the respective publications) is open to debate, but the salient point is that Knievel is claiming to have been nicknamed 'Evel' from a young age.

One aspect of the famous name which Knievel does not contradict in his explanations is the changing of the spelling from 'Evil' to the less demonic 'Evel'. He has always claimed that he didn't want any young fans to think he was a truly bad man or an evil man, or, as he once wittily suggested, 'I didn't like it [the spelling] the other way. It was an unnecessary evil.' Although the change in spelling does not affect the sound of the word, it does neatly mimic the spelling of his surname, adding to the sense of alliteration, and there's never been any harm in a self-publicist having his very own unique name to market – and eventually copyright.

However long he may have had the nickname of 'Evil', Bobby was never actually officially billed as 'Evel' in any of his shows until 1966, the year after he started performing motorcycle stunts and several years after he'd started dirt-track racing, where the name, one presumes, would have been equally beneficial in attracting attention. Indeed, another version of how he got his name relates to his time as a bike racer, as Knievel explained in the BBC documentary *Touch of Evel*: 'I put together a stunt group called Bob Knievel and his Motorcycle Daredevils, Hollywood, California. My sponsor [Bob Blair of the Berliner Motor Co. who supplied Knievel's team with bikes] said, "The nickname you have at the racetracks is Evil Knievel, why don't you use it? It's a better name." So anyway, I did. I wasn't too sure about it because I was ashamed of being called Evil.'

So it was that on 23 January 1966 the newly christened Evel Knievel and his Motorcycle Daredevils made their public debut in the grounds of Indio's National Date Festival, where the team performed a selection of stunts, some original and some borrowed and adapted from car stunt-shows. It would presumably not have been known to Knievel that there had been a troupe of riders performing similar stunts in Britain for years. The Royal Signals Display Team – The White Helmets – was formed in 1927 as a means of demonstrating the skills of its Army dispatch riders, and their repertoire included jumping through hoops of fire, fast crossovers (where two riders race towards each other narrowly avoiding a collision) and six-bike pyramids. But while Knievel's daredevils were not an entirely new conception, they were new to American audiences and their presentation was certainly a far cry from the officious military performances of The White Helmets.

Knievel often claims to have used 750cc Norton Commandos in these early jumps, but this must be the result of an inaccurate memory. The first Commando was not released until 1967, and since Knievel started jumping a Norton in 1966 he obviously could not have been mounted on a Commando. Early pictures of Evel's stunt-shows clearly demonstrate him riding a Norton Scrambler with 'knobbly' off-road tyres, but it is difficult to ascertain exactly which model due to the grainy nature of the photographs. The most accurate description he could offer in later years when asked which model it was, was 'It was similar to the Triumph [Triumph Bonneville, which he would later ride]. It had two cylinders; I think it was a 750.' He may have been a great stunt rider but Knievel's knowledge and memory for makes and models of motorcycles is questionable.

The team's first stunt show lasted for approximately two hours during which Knievel and his motley crew smashed through burning wooden boards, performed wheelies and even jumped over small ramps which were being held up by other members of the team as they lay underneath them. At one point Knievel even parasailed behind a racing car at speed, though claims that he reached speeds of 200mph are clearly ridiculous. The show's grand finale was to feature Evel leaping over two pick-up trucks parked tail-to-tail, a distance of about 45 feet. It was a short distance compared to what he would later achieve, but since few had seen this sort of stunt attempted before it proved a genuine crowd-pleaser.

Knievel was paid $500 for putting on his show, which didn't go far between his team members. But even in those early days he must have realised what would become one of the biggest downfalls of his newfound career: once he'd cleared any given distance he would be forced to better it next time. No one wanted to see Knievel churning out the same old stunts in the knowledge that he was operating well within his limits. Over the next ten years Evel would have to continue pushing the envelope by jumping further and further until those two small pick-up trucks would be replaced by 14 full-size Mack trucks – and even a canyon.

Entertaining it may have been, but at this stage Knievel's show was exactly where it belonged: in a small-town festival. It was a county-fair attraction, much as Elvis Presley's music had been at the outset, and both men vied with coconut stalls and other fairground novelties to gain the attention of the gathered crowds. There was certainly nothing to suggest that the rough-and-ready motorcycle stuntman jumping battered old pick-up trucks would eventually capture the world's imagination to such an extent that he would be able to single-handedly sell out the 90,000-capacity Wembley Stadium.

Significantly, Knievel had still not yet hit upon one of the most memorable aspects of his shows: his famous white jumpsuit. For his early performances he wore a much duller black leather suit with golden stars down the legs, a suit much more typical of motorcycle racers at the time. Like any entertainment act, Knievel's would need time to become fully polished and presentable, but for the first time in his life he had finally found something he enjoyed enough to persevere with, and with each performance he would introduce new levels of showmanship and professionalism.

Television cameras were present to record what was only the Daredevils' second-ever performance on 10 February in Barstow, California. It's a date Knievel is unlikely to forget, it being the first time he was injured in his stunt career. It was also the one and only time he attempted the insane stunt which led to his injury.

Knievel stood facing an oncoming motorcycle being ridden at speed by one of his colleagues. With timing being the critical factor, Evel would leap up into a star-jump position, allowing the bike and rider (who was tucked down flat on the tank) to pass through safely. At least, that was the theory, and it had worked in practice every time, but on show day it all went wrong. Knievel got his timing wrong by a split second as the speeding motorcycle approached and the bike smashed into his groin, flipping him over 360 degrees and leaving him writhing on the ground. 'The motorcycle hit me right in the balls,' he cringed. 'I was thrown 15 feet into the air and my body turned a couple of flips. I landed on my back on the ground. I was in no pain, but felt paralysed. Most of my ribs were cracked or broken. Someone covered me with a blanket. That was the last time I ever tried that particular stunt.'

He perhaps didn't realise it at the time but Knievel had just added another very attractive, however morbid, addition to his show – the very real possibility that he could get a stunt wrong and suffer a spectacular injury. Getting it wrong would ensure crowds kept flocking back for more in numbers, which surely would not have been possible had Knievel always successfully pulled off his stunts. If there was no danger there would be no sustained interest. Knievel may have suffered serious injuries after being smashed in the groin, but if he was going to get paid for it he wasn't complaining. And when pictures of his ugly mishap made it into several

West Coast newspapers the following day, Evel knew he was on to something.

But the money he earned in those early outings was pitiful, and if Knievel imagined he would one day make millions from his carnival act he was more of a visionary than he has been given credit for. The $500 the team was typically paid for a show had to be split up to six ways on occasion, and each man's share was reduced further by the expenses incurred by travelling to and setting up each show. As Evel had already proved, the risks were extremely high for such scant rewards, but since he had no other obvious means of making cash he got straight back to stunting after being released from hospital. Knievel simply couldn't allow the momentum to be halted; if he was going to make anything of this bizarre business he couldn't let an inconvenience like pain stand in his way.

In his fourth appearance with the Daredevils, Knievel suffered even more serious injuries. At Missoula in Montana he attempted to leap over 13 cars, having already realised that two pick-up trucks was old news. He came up short and ploughed into a van parked at the end of the line of cars. Apart from being knocked unconscious, Knievel broke his left arm and several ribs – again. He was in bad shape and wouldn't be up to working again for at least five months. And when Evel wasn't working his show had lost its main attraction; gigs had to be cancelled and all of a sudden the other riders weren't getting paid. While some performances went ahead, such as the one at Montana's Great Falls Speedway on 21 August where Evel acted as host but could not perform, others were cancelled and Knievel's co-riders began seeking out more consistent forms of employment. They simply couldn't afford to hang around for months waiting for Evel to recover from injury. During those months of recuperation it must have appeared to Evel that his new career was over before it had really got started. It seemed that everything he turned his hand to would be doomed to failure.

With the benefit of hindsight, however, the disbanding of the Daredevils proved to be the best thing that could have happened as far as Evel was concerned. He had never been a team player and, since he was the main attraction anyway, he began to realise he could now perform on his own and keep all the money to himself. The shows would have to be shorter and more spectacular, even more risky, in order to keep audiences' attention, but Evel Knievel the solo artist had finally arrived.

Wasting no time, Knievel started calling up racetrack promoters touting for gigs. He'd ask them what size crowd they usually drew then boldly promise he'd double it for them. The promoter would profit from sales of popcorn, peanuts, beer and car-parking, as well as half the gate money, while Knievel would settle for the other half of the gate money. He invariably instructed the promoters to 'jack up your tickets by a buck or two', and so, with minimal outlay and a percentage of the gates guaranteed, Evel Knievel hit the road.

Being a solo artist may have entailed a lot more work for Knievel but he didn't seem to mind: it was, after all, in his own interest. So as well as performing he built all his own ramps, promoted and emceed his shows, and drove all over the western United States to whichever venue would have him.

Evel Knievel's first-ever solo performance took place at the Naranche Memorial Drag Strip near his hometown of Butte on 30 October 1966. Undeterred by his failure to clear 13 cars in Missoula, Knievel attempted, and cleared, 14 cars on his solo debut. To the crowd present it seemed an impossible number and, given his previous failure, many were expecting blood. Knievel may have denied the more ghoulish members of the audience their kicks but he thrilled the rest of his home crowd with a feat they thought impossible. Montana had a new home-grown hero.

While his fame began spreading all over the west coast of America, Knievel was still desperately short of money, and while out on the road he and his young family were still sleeping rough under the stars, still bathing in rivers, and constantly aware that another big crash would sideline the only breadwinner in the family and make things even worse. Knievel's existence truly was hand-to-mouth in the late 1960s.

But despite the hardships of a life on the road, the jumps continued and Evel reached another landmark in the spring of 1967 when his performances in between motorcycle races at the Ascot Park Speedway near Los Angeles were filmed for ABC's *Wide World of Sports*. This was his first real chance at the big time. So long as he only performed live at small-time race meetings in front of a few thousand people then he could only ever hope to be a local hero. But with the promise of television coverage came the chance to make it as a national star, and, if he could achieve that, the riches he so desperately craved would surely follow.

The relationship between Knievel and ABC would prove extremely beneficial to both parties in the coming years, and the timing on Knievel's part couldn't have been better. ABC's policy was to offer coverage of lesser-known sports, more often than not with an oddball quality, which is why Knievel's antics slotted right into place. He was perfect fodder for the network and the link-up would ultimately inspire thousands of American kids to emulate Knievel. In one article describing the relationship between ABC and Knievel, writer Christopher Ross went as far as to say 'it can be argued that today's increased popularity of extreme sports can be directly traced to Knievel and *Wide World of Sports*.'

ABC certainly helped spread the Evel word to a national

audience, and he, in turn, rewarded them with five of their 20 most successful broadcasts ever. His 1975 jump over 14 Greyhound buses at King's Island still ranks as the highest rating the channel has ever had, with an incredible 52 per cent audience share – better than Muhammad Ali and George Foreman's rumble in the jungle and every Super Bowl ever held.

But that was all still in the future; for now, Knievel kicked off his first national television performance by successfully clearing 15 cars, breaking his own record by one. The television coverage did not go out live, however, and American audiences had to wait for another two weeks before getting their first taste of Evel Knievel on 25 March 1967.

Encouraged by his success, Knievel continued gathering momentum and moved on to clear 16 cars at the Ascot Raceway near Los Angeles before attempting the same number again at the Graham Speedway near Tacoma, Washington. This time things didn't go quite so smoothly and Knievel lost his balance on landing and parted company with his bike, sustaining a slight concussion in the process. Just under three weeks later he returned to the same venue to see the job through successfully, proving to his audience that he was no quitter and that he would see anything through if he had given his word to do so.

This was another crucial part of the Evel Knievel phenomenon: to Knievel his word was his bond, and he could offer nothing more to anyone than that. It stemmed from his Butte upbringing where a man could only be seen as a man if he kept his word. If you say you're going to do something in Butte, you had better do it, and it was a code that Evel lived by. Throughout his career he attempted jumps he felt he couldn't make, even at the risk of serious injury or death, because he'd given his word he'd try. It was this strongly held belief that led Knievel to try the biggest and most outrageous stunt of his entire career some years later, and, ultimately, to his undoing.

Evel had by now abandoned his Norton in favour of another British bike, a 650cc Triumph T120 Bonneville, now one of the most revered of all classic British motorcycles. Despite his later association with Harley-Davidson, Knievel never hesitated in naming the Bonneville as his favourite bike of all time for jumping. 'The Triumph was a much better handling motorcycle than the Harley. The XR-750 Harley had way too much torque. When it got up in the air it wanted to twist because it had so much torque. The Triumph 650 went as straight as a bullet.' His praise for the 650cc model, however, did not extend to the 750cc version, which he rather amusingly berated as '. . . a piece of crap. It couldn't pull a sick whore off a piss-pot with Vaseline on her.'

But, as Evel was finding out, there was more to jumping a motorcycle than simply twisting the throttle and hoping the bike went as straight as a bullet. 'The big thing about jumping over cars on a motorcycle is to hit the take-off ramp just right. I don't want the bike's front wheel to hit the ramp too hard. That might throw me over the handlebars. I have to hang on tight. And then I fly through the air and hope for a safe landing. When I jump I stand or lean forward on the balls of my feet. The motorcycle has a tendency to buck and come over backwards on me so I try and lean forward to hold it down. I want to go off the take-off ramp right at the top of the power curve. If I do, the bike'll go straight through the air. If I don't, the motorcycle has a tendency to drift sideways and cross up. It's just like crouching in a crouch; if you crouch too much you can't jump very high, if you don't crouch at all you don't jump very high. You gotta be on the power curve.'

It is, as Evel often explained, only when the rider has left the take-off ramp that the real skill of motorcycle jumping comes into play. 'Anyone can jump a motorcycle, the trouble comes when you try to land it. I never missed a take-off in my life. It's like I put you in a Learjet and help you take off but then I give you the controls and say "all right, big boy, now you go ahead and land it". That's where you'll have your ass knee deep in crap, boy.'

The most incredible thing about Knievel's jumping technique was that it was all based on feel and instinct rather than being scientifically calculated in the way that modern jumpers prepare their jumps. As he openly admitted, 'I did everything by the seat of my pants. That's why I got hurt so much.' One of Knievel's former friends and helpers, Joe Delaney, recalls being amazed at Knievel's haphazard approach to jumping. Turning up for the first time to help Knievel set up his ramps he was expecting a much more high-tech approach than what he actually witnessed. 'He told me, "Step off 40 steps." I said, "What for?" He said, "That's how far I'm gonna jump. Just draw a line in the dirt." So we did and he set his ramps up.'

Knievel's Triumph Bonneville was slightly customised to meet his unique demands, but it was still far from being an ideal tool for the job; unlike the modern motocross bikes, which are light-weight, have massive suspension travel and heaps of power. Like the motorcycle racers who have no need for road-going gear, Evel ditched the lights, mudguards and numberplates and fitted a racing engine and racing exhaust to help increase the bike's standard top speed of around 110mph. Less necessary and more for show was the drogue parachute, which was fitted in the rear-seat unit; it was designed to slow him down after big jumps but, as he proved when he had no parachute, this was not a major problem anyway unless his landing area was extremely confined. However, the flurry of the chute as it opened added to the drama and further created the impression that Knievel was pushing motorcycle technology to the limit.

Throughout 1967 Knievel toured and performed wherever he could secure a booking, and by the year's end he had pulled off more than eight major jumps. Notable performances included a leap on 24 September over 16 Chevrolets in front of 4,000 demolition-derby race-goers at the Evergreen Speedway in Monroe, Washington. Knievel actually approached the jump too fast and overshot his landing ramp, though he somehow managed to keep the bike upright despite a heavy landing and steered it to safety. He did, however, suffer a compression fracture to his lower spine on landing and had to be administered with painkilling injections.

As successful as Knievel's assorted dates were becoming, he was realising by now that it was going to take something extra special to drum up the level of public interest he dreamed of. Jumping rows of cars could only look impressive for so long – there had to be something else, something bigger, better and more spectacular. Knievel had been aware since his first jump when he leaped over snakes and mountain lions that what lay between his ramps was just as important as how far apart they were. 'Right then,' he told the press after his 1965 debut, 'I knew I could pull a big crowd by jumping over weird stuff.' It was a lesson well learned and one which would stand him in good stead throughout his career. The problem lay in dreaming up novelty obstacles that would be just possible to jump while retaining precisely the right amount of risk and danger, while convincing an audience that they could *not* be jumped. This balance between the possible and the impossible was another key element in Knievel's unique brand of entertainment.

It's easy to imagine Knievel, wherever he went from 1965 onwards, keeping one business eye on anything of note which could possibly be jumped on a motorcycle, just as an artist never stops searching for scenes to paint and a songwriter always has one ear open for potential melodies, lyrics and song titles. It's even easier to imagine him dreaming up more and more crazy ideas during his regular drinking binges, and this was, in fact, how his most famous stunt of all originated in 1966.

Somewhat the worse for wear, Knievel had been boozing it up in a bar called Moose's Place in Kalispell, Montana with his friend Chuck Shelton. Shelton spotted a calendar on the wall of the bar with a picture of the Grand Canyon on it and told Knievel he should try jumping that. Anyone other than Knievel would have laughed off the idea for the joke it was intended as, and, at least initially, that's what Evel did. But gradually, through a haze of alcohol, the laughing stopped and Knievel began to realise he might just be on to something big. Very big. 'The more I studied on it, and the more Montana Marys I put back, the narrower that durned [sic] hole in the ground seemed to get. People talk about the Generation Gap and the Missile Gap, but I suddenly saw that the real gap was right there in the heart of the Golden West. And I knew I could bridge the bastard.' As an afterthought he added, 'Ah well, what the hell? I always liked drinking and jumping.'

The Montana Marys Knievel was consuming on that particular evening have become as much part of his legend as his jumps, but the actual contents of Evel's favourite drink have long been a source of speculation. Some claimed it was a near lethal combination of beer, tomato juice, Wild Turkey and vodka, while others suggested a touch of engine oil added to his beer was the magic ingredient. Like most things surrounding Knievel, the facts have been misinterpreted, distorted and exaggerated, and Evel has, more often than not, been prepared to play along – or at least not deny any of his legend. However, he did finally put an end to the speculation surrounding the contents of a Montana Mary in 1998 when he disappointed many by confessing it was '. . . just beer and tomato juice [a drink favoured by Butte miners]. The stuff about Wild Turkey and vodka in it is just crap.'

Of course, even a daredevil wildly drunk on Montana Marys would realise that the massive, gaping chasm that was the Grand Canyon could never be jumped by any standard motorcycle. It was, after all, two miles wide at the spot Knievel was considering jumping and was as much as 5,700 feet deep in places. But that in itself was not enough to put Knievel off and he started making preliminary plans which would one day allow him to tackle the ultimate stunt. He initially conceptualised the building of a giant take-off ramp, 200 feet high and 740 feet long, which would allow him to tackle the canyon in the same way he tackled any other jump but on a much, much grander scale. He would have a custom bike built specially for the stunt, featuring a jet engine, wings and a parachute. Knievel even went as far as to claim he had made scientific calculations (for once) that would allow the bike to bridge the chasm. The bike was to be 13 feet long and weigh in at almost 1,000 kilos and, according to his calculations, it would reach a top speed of 250mph and would accelerate to 158mph in just 3.7 seconds. The total cost of building the ramp and bike he estimated at $1 million.

The whole idea seemed nothing short of ridiculous but, if nothing else, it gave Knievel something more to talk about and he announced these plans on national US television in late 1967, saying, 'I'm going to try and jump across the Grand Canyon but I may have to parachute off the bike before reaching the other side. I know how to parachute and I can "track" with my body. If I bail off the bike, I'll just aim my body toward the opposite rim of the canyon, open my parachute and land there.' To those who scoffed at the idea and claimed Evel was just a publicity seeker, he added, 'Before I even make the jump I may show these sceptics I mean business by riding a motorcycle across the Grand Canyon on a cable. I'll be just like a tightrope walker in a circus, but I won't have a safety net to catch me. That'd show those sceptics.'

In actual fact, the sceptics did have the last laugh as Knievel never did manage to jump the Grand Canyon, nor did he ride over it on a cable. Despite gaining preliminary permission from the Department of the Interior (who owned the land where Knievel proposed to take off from) to make the jump, this was later withdrawn when it was realised that Knievel was actually serious about the attempt. He had already announced a tentative jump date of 4 July 1968 but permission was withdrawn just a few months beforehand. For the time being, Knievel was grounded, at least as far as flying over the Grand Canyon went. But the seeds for jumping a canyon had been sewn; Knievel had promised his public he would see it through and the idea refused to go away. It would change shape and, eventually, location but it did not go away. One day, Knievel vowed, he would jump a canyon, some darned canyon, if only to prove the doubters wrong.

Unable to realise his ultimate dream for the time being, Knievel looked elsewhere for a means of breaking out of the rut that was jumping over cars. He finally found his location at the newly opened Caesar's Palace casino and hotel resort, which was situated, somewhat appropriately, in the gambling capital of the world – Las Vegas. It was here, he decided, that he would take the gamble that would ultimately lead to worldwide fame and fortune or, equally likely, his own death.

Knievel was in Vegas for a middleweight title fight when he first clapped eyes on the spectacular fountains in front of Caesar's grand entranceway. They gushed intermittently high up into the dry Vegas air and Evel realised straight away that they were perfectly suited to his needs: he vowed there and then to jump them. But even though he had built up a big-enough reputation to command national media coverage when he announced his jump, it wasn't so easy gaining permission from the casino's owners.

It is worth pointing out that Evel Knievel is a notorious yarn teller and it's often difficult to separate whole truths from half-truths, and half-truths from complete fantasy, when listening to his animated and entertaining speech. Over the course of almost 40 years he has repeated and exaggerated the same tales to the point where he appears to believe even the furthest-fetched stories himself. Knievel didn't become the legend he is by telling modest, mundane anecdotes about himself; his larger-than-life character is very much part of the reason why he attained such fame, and his enthusiastic and often over-the-top story-telling has gone a long way to creating that character. Knievel himself may well be having the last laugh by telling tongue-in-cheek stories and fooling many into believing them. Indeed, it was once a running joke that in 20 minutes Knievel could tell enough yarns about his early life to keep a reporter busy for 20 years just checking them out. His famed rhetoric is exemplified in his explanation of how he gained permission to jump the Caesar's fountains.

The day after the aforementioned Vegas title fight, Knievel called Caesar's founder and executive director Jay Sarno, claiming to be a certain Frank Quinn from *Life* magazine. Knievel takes up the story from both men's points of view:

Knievel:  *Do you know Eval Neval?*
Sarno:    *Eval Neval? Who the hell's he?*

Knievel: *He's the guy who's gonna jump the Grand Canyon, says*
*he's gonna jump over your hotel.*

Sarno: *I heard about that nut, he ain't gonna jump nothin'*
*around here. I gotta go, goodbye.*

The following day, Knievel called Sarno again, this time posing as
a reporter:

Knievel: *Hi, this is Larson with* Sports Illustrated. *You ever heard of*
*Evel Neevle?*

Sarno: *Evel Neevle? Who the hell's this Evel Neevle?*

Knievel: *He's the guy that's going to jump the Grand . . .*

Sarno: *Oh yes, some guy called me yesterday about that guy. I*
*don't know, something around here . . . something's going*
*on. I don't know. Call back.*

Two days later, Knievel called again, this time impersonating a
friend who worked for the ABC television network.

Knievel: *This is Dennis Lewen from ABC's* Wide World of Sports.
*Do you know Evel Knievel?*

Sarno: *Eval Neval, Evel Neevle, Evel Knievel? Who is this crazy*
*guy? Everybody's calling me up about him. I think we've*
*got a deal with him, I don't know, call back.*

With the ball rolling, Knievel then sent his fictitious business
partners to work. Because he admired the Jewish community
for their financial skills, Knievel had created three fictitious Jewish
businessmen to head up his company, 'Evel Knievel Enterprises',
the idea being that the list of names on his headed stationery would
look impressive and persuade people to take him more seriously.

The president was named as H. Carl Forbes, the vice president was Mike Rosenstein and the secretary and treasurer listed as Carl Goldberg. Knievel himself does a very fine, if stereotyped, Jewish/American accent and claimed he often called people up, on his own behalf, in this accent pretending to be any one of the three fictitious businessmen. With Sarno at least now aware of who Evel Knievel was, it was time for the killer punch and this time Knievel called impersonating Rosenstein:

Knievel:  *Hello, this is Rosenstein.*
Sarno:   *Who?*
Knievel:  *Rosenstein.*
Sarno:   *Who the hell do you represent?*
Knievel:  *Evel Knievel. He's going to be in your office this afternoon about two o'clock to see you about this big jump. He's gonna make you famous. Nobody ever heard of this Caesar's Palace.*

With the meeting set up, Knievel finishes the story. 'So I go to this Sarno, knock on his door, the secretary lets me into these big executive offices; she ran to the back [office] door and says, "It's him, it's him." He comes running out of his office and says, "Kid, where you been? I been looking all over for you!"'

It's an unlikely scenario and would depend on an extremely switched-on businessman like Sarno being fooled no less than four times, but it is indicative of the way Knievel worked, which was very much along the same lines as ex-carnival huckster Colonel Tom Parker who became a multi-millionaire representing Elvis Presley by promoting him in a similarly unorthodox but effective fashion. Knievel never took the obvious approach when it came to promoting himself, and in an era before PR executives and massive marketing agencies became all too commonplace his imagination and flair for self-promotion served him well.

However, Knievel actually gained permission to jump the fountains at Caesar's, and he bartered a deal with Sarno which would see him performing three leaps there: on New Year's Eve 1967 and on 3 and 6 January 1968. Promotional posters were placed all over Las Vegas inviting the public to see Knievel, who was already billing himself as 'The King of Stuntmen'. By leaping over what the promotional posters billed as the 'highest fountains in the world', Knievel was claiming a world-record attempt and the posters even boasted that 'a two-hundred-yard elevated takeoff runway ramp' was 'now under construction'.

The pre-jump publicity campaign was enough to rouse interest among Vegas regulars who would never dream of showing up at a small-time county fair, and crowd estimates on the evening of 31 December reached 25,000 – a figure which would later prompt Evel to boast that 'Frank Sinatra couldn't draw that crowd if he jumped naked off the hotel roof.'

With the ramp in place, the rear suspension on his Triumph Bonneville stiffened and special cams, pistons and valve springs fitted to give faster acceleration and a higher top speed, Knievel readied himself for his 2 p.m. matinée performance with what had, by now, become his standard preparatory routine: a few shots of Wild Turkey bourbon and a quick prayer. He was confident to the point that even a bad omen en route to his waiting motor- cycle didn't dampen his spirits. 'The one thing I remember was coming downstairs [from his hotel room] for the jump. I'd had my good-luck shot of Wild Turkey, like always, and was walking past the tables and stopped at the roulette and bet $100 on red. It was black. I thought nothing of it, just put my helmet under my arm and kept walking.'

As he appeared outside the entrance to the hotel to the cheers of the crowd, Knievel waved and soaked up the applause before donning his helmet and mounting his motorcycle. Under normal circumstances, Evel would perform a few practice runs by heading straight for the take-off ramp before veering off left or right at the last second. At Caesar's, however, there simply wasn't the space to allow for such a luxury and Knievel would effectively be flying blind. All he could do was dump the clutch on the Triumph, hope his rear wheel would hook up and grip the wooden runway, then kick his way up through the gears to gain whatever speed he felt he needed. If he dropped the clutch too harshly when setting off his back wheel could easily lose traction and spin up, and if he fluffed just one gear change he could easily fail to gain the required momentum. There could be no stopping at speed halfway up a ramp to have another run. Apart from possible rider error, there was also the danger of component failure – and that risk was much more pronounced in Knievel's era than it is now. British bikes in particular, like Knievel's Triumph, were renowned for spouting oil leaks back in the 1960s, and that was only one potentially lethal hazard. Another very real danger was the possibility of a chain snapping under the strain of the launch, leaving Evel with no drive and the threat of the chain becoming entangled in his rear wheel, which would almost inevitably cause a crash. Or the engine could develop a misfire for any number of reasons, again leaving Knievel down on power and unable to clear the distance. His throttle could stick open as he sped down the runway, meaning he would be travelling way too fast and would overshoot his landing ramp, again putting him in great personal danger. And those were just the problems he faced on the take-off. Other problems, like a rear wheel collapsing on landing (which would actually happen during a 1970 jump in Seattle), or the rear suspension bottoming out and spitting him off (which happened many times), or even brake failure, were all to be considered. Motorcycle jumping, especially in Knievel's pioneering days, was extremely dangerous.

But it was danger which had drawn 25,000 people out onto the streets of Las Vegas and Knievel wasn't about to have any second thoughts and disappoint the biggest audience he had ever attracted. It was make-or-break time and Evel knew it. His reputation and career would stand or fall on this one jump alone. There could be no backing out, even if his nerves were screaming, his palms sweating and his heart racing.

With Knievel and his mechanics satisfied that the bike was set up as well as it could be and sounding as it should as he revved it in neutral, Knievel finally decided the crowd had waited long enough and kicked the Triumph into gear. He gunned the bike down the runway, revving it out to maximum revs in each gear until he reached 90mph. It was the highest speed he could achieve in the distance he had to work with but he still had no more idea than anyone watching if it would be enough to carry him to safety. Still, Evel's run was looking good. He seemed to have the speed and his launch looked perfect; he even had the measure of the bike in mid-air, purposefully dropping its tail in search of a smooth rear-wheel landing. He sailed through the spray of the ornate fountains, travelling what seemed an impossible distance for anything without wings, and the Las Vegas revellers gawped in disbelief at what they were seeing. He had done it. This crazy kid had actually gone through with what he'd promised, and hell, did it look impressive. As man and machine descended back down towards the landing ramp things still looked good; it still looked like Knievel was going to pull off the apparently impossible. Then his worst nightmare happened.

Just one foot further and Evel may well have got away with it.

He'd travelled a distance of 141 feet – way further than he'd ever managed before – but he landed just inches short and his rear wheel smashed into the safety deck which guarded the lethal edge of his landing ramp to prevent him from being decapitated in the event of him falling short.

The term 'rag doll' is over-used when describing a rider being thrown from a motorcycle either in racing or stunt riding, but there is no other way to describe how Knievel's body was slammed and battered down the Tarmac when the impact of the landing threw him off the bike, tearing its handlebars from his grasp. He was thrown over the front of the motorcycle and landed first on his back before tumbling at great speed end over end, limbs flailing helplessly as his head took an equally brutal battering from the Las Vegas asphalt. The crowd, who split seconds earlier were expecting victory, looked on in horror.

Some reports said that Evel actually slid further than he had jumped, and the only thing which eventually stopped him from tumbling even further was a decorative brick wall which he slammed into while still carrying speed. What happened next was nothing short of chaos. The crowd went hysterical, screaming and wailing, convinced they had just witnessed a man killing himself right in front of their eyes. Smoke poured from the twisted metal of the once-immaculate Triumph as medical crews, hangers-on and rubberneckers surged round Knievel's battered and apparently lifeless body. General panic reigned until Knievel was removed by ambulance to the nearby Sunrise Hospital. It would be 29 days before he woke up again, but when he did, he would be a star.

# 4
# Theatre of Pain

## 'I'm Evel Knievel. I'm not supposed to be afraid.'

The Caesar's Palace crash resulted in the worst injuries of Evel Knievel's career. He landed so hard that his left hip was forced up into the pelvis, leaving both structures comprehensively smashed. He also broke his nose, sustained several broken ribs, smashed out several teeth and fractured his jaw. But the immediate and most serious concern was for the head injuries which left Knievel in a coma. His head had taken repeated blows as he was thrown viciously along the Tarmac, and even though crash-helmet technology in 1967 was extremely basic by today's standards, Knievel's Bell Magnum helmet had at least saved his life. In acknowledgement of the fact, he has kept it to this day.

Evel lay unconscious for day after day and week after week with his devoted wife Linda at his bedside, wondering if her husband would ever wake up and, if he did, would he be brain-damaged? Would he be able to walk again? She knew better than anyone that a man as active and daring as her husband would never tolerate being confined to a wheelchair and would never be able to accept being dependent on others.

As the weeks crept by, feeling like years, it became increasingly unlikely that Evel would regain consciousness, but after an agonising 29 days for Linda, Kelly, Robbie and Tracey Lynn, the man they all loved and admired showed his true mettle: he woke up. The family, not to mention the nurses who had tended him night and day, were understandably beside themselves when Knievel not only opened his eyes but proved that he'd lost none of his abilities of speech and understanding. It was a moment of unadulterated joy that few experience. Evel Knievel had, to all intents and purposes, prised himself from the very jaws of death and returned to life.

When he was stable enough and when his doctors were confident that he was in a fit state of mind to be told, Knievel learned the true extent of his horrific injuries, which, while they were gruesome and painful, were at least not life-threatening. A successful operation was carried out to insert an 18-inch steel rod between his left femur and pelvis, but, as a result of his hip being pushed up into his pelvis, his left leg was now almost an inch shorter than his right. Knievel would be left with a permanent limp, but that seemed almost irrelevant; the only thing that mattered was that he was alive when he really shouldn't have been.

Surprisingly, Knievel remembered every bone-crushing moment of the crash (at least up to the point of being knocked out), but to this day he still doesn't know quite what went wrong. When asked at what point he knew he wasn't going to make the landing he replied, 'I never knew it. I thought I'd made it. It was a surprise and a shock – a big shock.' He added, 'I was hurt real bad – landed on my head. That was the most serious of all. I remember the whole thing; every tiny bit of it. There was a little six-foot safety ramp and I landed right on top of it. It was just a piece of steel sitting on a van.'

When asked if he had any idea what actually went wrong,

Knievel replied 'I just wasn't going fast enough', while also explaining that he simply *couldn't* go fast enough because the run-up ramp wasn't long enough. But what was done was done, and, besides learning from the experience, there was nothing more that could be done about it. All he could do now was focus on getting better.

Knievel remained in hospital for a total of 37 days. It wasn't his first hospital stay and it wouldn't be his last, but it was certainly his longest. As he lay in bed recuperating, the world outside was going Knievel crazy, and it was largely down to the fact that Evel's horrific crash had been captured in all its bone-crunching detail, not by ABC or any of the other mainstream networks but by future *Dynasty* actress Linda Evans. Evans was at the time married to movie director John Derek, who later married and made a huge star out of Bo Derek. Many years later, Knievel actually claimed that he was responsible for introducing John Derek to Bo, despite their insistence to the contrary. 'John was filming a project at a Harley store where Bo worked for her father. I didn't know her but I introduced her to John anyway. She has a sister that looks almost exactly like her. Anyway, to hear John and Bo say it they met on the Mediterranean. They met at a Harley store in Long Beach.'

Whatever the case, Knievel had struck a deal with John and Linda Derek allowing them to exclusively shoot his Caesar's jump on 16mm IMO cameras. It proved to be a wise move, as Knievel explained: 'The film that was shot of the Caesar's Palace jump has been said by a lot of people who are in the film business to be one of the greatest pieces of film footage ever filmed. This was filmed by one of the most beautiful blondes; her name was Linda Evans. John Derek shot the jump at the take-off and Linda shot the landing and the accident.'

The footage shot by the couple was aired over and over again, both in real time and in slow motion, and it was unquestionably responsible for transforming Evel Knievel from a fairground attraction into a national star. So frequently was the footage shown that it was widely believed to have been played more times than any piece of film since the infamous Zapruder footage of John F. Kennedy's assassination in Dallas back in 1963. Knievel always believed that 'In any adversity there is the seed of benefit', and that never proved to be more true for Knievel than now. He may have come close to losing his life, and, having survived, had to endure enormous pain as physiotherapists forced his limbs back to life, but the upside of the Palace crash was that it had captured the attention of the great American public: Evel was famous at last.

Someone crashing a motorcycle is, in itself, not usually an act which guarantees widespread mainstream celebrity. If it was there would be no end of motorcycle racers and stuntmen who would qualify as household names. While the American public had thrilled, cringed and been utterly amazed upon seeing footage of Knievel's accident, it was the unsaid, almost intangible reasons behind why he had crashed – why he had been prepared to crash – which appealed to the collective subconscious.

For the first time in modern history, Americans had become disillusioned with their government, their society, and their country as a whole by the late 1960s. The massively unpopular war in Vietnam, which America had been involved in since 1961, had polarised the nation, and mass protests and riots were literally tearing the country apart. Being an American suddenly wasn't so simple any more. Millions believed the government was wrong to commit so many young soldiers to lay down their lives in a war on the other side of the world for a cause most did not understand.

The American people were, quite simply, confused. It was no

longer clear-cut as to who were the heroes and who were the villains. Thousands performed the previously unthinkable act of burning the Old Glory, the starred and striped American flag. For one brief moment in time, Evel Knievel offered an escape. He offered Americans the kind of hero they could believe in, one who gave hope and inspiration to anyone facing problems, challenges, danger – or all three combined. Here was a man who gave his word that he would attempt to fulfil his dream right there in front of anyone who cared to watch and he would not back out of the challenge, even in the face of hideous injury or possible death. If it is true that God loves a tryer then so does the public, and Evel's was a simple one-act stage play which preached the message that if you want to achieve something then don't let fear get in your way. In a modern-day version of Robert the Bruce and his spider, he encouraged the nation to believe that if at first you don't succeed then try and try again. 'I always said you can fall many times in life but you're never a failure as long as you try to get back up. Use your body or use your head, or use anything you got left to be a worthwhile human being. And I think America needed that kind of figure when it was on its knees with Vietnam. You have dreams in your life which require taking risks, and if you see someone else taking risks to get what they want you are inspired to try yourself.'

Knievel was more than a performer; he offered a service to his audience. Too many worked in dull nine-to-five jobs and would never have the chance – or courage – to attempt anything as dangerous and outrageous as Evel did. He symbolised all their struggles and condensed them into a lightning strike, death or glory leap, which he would either triumph over or suffer in spilled blood and crushed bones. Those without his courage – and there were many – could watch from afar as he took all the risks.

The phenomenal success of the James Bond movies has often

been attributed to the fact that all men want to be like Bond while all women want to be *with* Bond, and Knievel struck a very similar chord in the psyches of his male and female audiences. While the men were content to admire his guts, the women were attracted to him not only for his movie-star looks but also because of his courage. And Knievel's appeal to kids as some kind of real-life superhero who flies through air is easy to understand. Evel Knievel had all angles covered.

When asked to reflect on what he thought made him so famous and universally appealing after Caesar's, Knievel answered, 'America was down on its ass when I came along and needed somebody who was truthful and honest; someone who would spill blood and break bones and suffer brain concussions. Somebody who wasn't a phoney. People pulled for me because they pulled for the underdog. I got hurt bad but I kept trying – I refused to lay down and die. I always tried to get up.'

As he recovered in hospital, Knievel slowly became aware of his growing celebrity. He was inundated with requests for interviews for radio and television and would proudly pore over the printed newspaper and magazine stories in his bed. But something else was beginning to take shape, something that was harder to put a finger on than just fame: he was slowly becoming an 'attitude'. Comedians and chat-show hosts began referring to anyone doing something daring or dangerous as being worthy of Evel Knievel. The name began to enter the American language on an everyday basis: 'Not even Evel Knievel would try that', 'Who do you think you are, Evel Knievel?', or, 'He's broken more bones than Evel Knievel.'

In the ensuing years, even major Hollywood movies would pass reference to the daredevil whenever a scene gave rise to a mention. In the 1998 Bruce Willis movie *Armageddon*, Ben Affleck is about to leap a space buggy over a canyon on an asteroid but not before he turns to his passenger and asks, 'You ever heard of Evel Knievel?' In the 2003 remake of *The Italian Job*, when one of the lead characters falls off his motorcycle another quips, 'Help Knievel get up for his next jump.' Even the James Bond movies paid homage in 1974's *The Man with the Golden Gun*. When Roger Moore as Bond prepares to make a leap over a river in a car, which will include a 360-degree barrel roll, he too asks his passenger, 'Ever heard of Evel Knievel?' There were countless more examples on television.

To become a byword for anything crazy, daring, risky or down-right mad; to become the name that most people the world over associate with motorcycle riding was probably Evel Knievel's single most enduring achievement, and it all started with his Caesar's Palace wipe-out.

Ironically, the fact that he had failed in his attempt to clear the fountains had made him way more famous than he would have been if he had completed the challenge successfully. It was a valuable lesson to Knievel, which taught him to always seek advantage in an apparently disadvantageous situation. He even managed to turn the fact that he had a limp to his advantage by obtaining one of the most instantly recognisable Knievel props – his famous jewelled cane.

While he did have a genuine physical need for such a device, it was typical of Evel to seek out something different, something which would uniquely identify him as well as adding a touch of glitz, and for that the cane was perfect. But just like his name, the origins of the cane are shrouded in the contradictions and myths of Knievel folklore. He often claimed the cane dated back to 1883 when it had belonged to the mayor of Philadelphia, but he would then contradict this by admitting it was custom-made for him by his jeweller friend, G. Darrell Olson. It certainly seems odd that the mayor of Philadelphia would have owned a cane featuring a motorcycle engraved into its gold top, since motorcycles hadn't even been invented then! In another version of the story, Evel said he picked the cane up from a pawnshop in Spokane, Washington for $35 and was later offered $35,000 for it by legendary pianist and entertainer Liberace. Knievel refused the offer.

What was never in doubt, however, was that his cane (or at least one of them, for there appears to have been several incarnations) opened up to reveal six shots of Wild Turkey. Knievel even demonstrated this novelty on national television, explaining how the top of the cane screwed off to allow access to six test-tube-style vials of booze. The true origins of the prop are ultimately irrelevant; what matters is that instead of appearing like a crippled old man after his operation, Knievel emerged with even more swagger and lordliness, his cane becoming as much a recognisable part of him as a Stetson was to John Wayne.

After leaving the Sunrise Hospital in Las Vegas, Knievel was lauded as a celebrity and he milked it for all it was worth. After all, this was what he had been striving to achieve for so many years. Having attempted numerous scams and successive oddball professions, each seeming doomed to failure, he had finally hit upon a formula that the public seemed to love and he was going to make the most of it. He could hardly fail to be aware that such a novelty act carried with it the risk of being a mere flash in the pan; a sideshow with a sell-by date. If this was to be Knievel's 15 minutes of Warholian fame, he sure as hell wasn't going to waste it.

In today's climate of manufactured fame, Knievel would have been sucked in by stylists, PR people, marketing companies and spin doctors, but in 1968 he had the intuition to do it all by himself and quickly set about growing into the role of a celebrity. He started hanging out in the glitziest bars, clubs and casinos in Vegas, began to wear increasingly loud and ostentatious clothes (even by 1970s standards), rode around in flash cars and dated beautiful women, ignoring the fact that he was a married father of three.

He felt he had been given a second chance at life and was self-ishly determined to enjoy it in every way he could. If his public increasingly built his image up as that of a fearless gladiator, a swaggering, gunslinging cowboy who stared death in the face and laughed at its inability to claim him, then so much the better – it was all good for business. In fact, Knievel was quite happy to add fuel to the fire by telling wild tales about his past to anyone who would listen and he certainly commanded the attention of many. At this point, Knievel's stories were all fresh and new, and his audiences revelled in listening to his tales of derring-do as much as he enjoyed telling them. Few celebrities cherished the limelight as much as Evel did.

When he had been in a coma it was uncertain if Knievel would ever wake up again. He did. When he did awake, it was uncertain if he'd ever be able to walk again. He did. When he could hobble around, it was by no means certain that he'd ever be able to ride a motorcycle again; and when he did that it was still not known if he would ever be able to jump again. Having announced his atten-tion to jump again from his hospital bed, Knievel knew he had to capitalise on his newfound fame quickly before it dissipated. At the same time he realised there was little to gain by attempting another massive showpiece stunt like the Caesar's spectacle which carried such a high risk of injury, so Knievel decided on a return to his standard car-jumping routine, only this time the crowds would be bigger and the media coverage equally so.

After five months of recuperation, Evel returned to his roots and lined up a 13-car jump at the Beeline Dragway in Scottsdale,

Arizona for 25 May 1968. He may have thought it was a relatively safe option compared to the fountains of Caesar's Palace, but motorcycle jumping is never safe as Evel proved by wiping out again, this time breaking a leg and fracturing a foot. It may not have been as serious as the injuries he picked up in Vegas but for Knievel it must have been incredibly frustrating. His newfound fame gave him a licence to print money by simply doing what he'd been doing for the last three years, but his battered body would not let him do it.

He was forced into another boring and tiring period of recuperation, unable to work and unable to capitalise on his name. But he wasn't just losing out on the chance to *make* money, he was actually losing heaps of the money he had earned in paying medical bills. As he said, 'There's no hospitalisation insurance for daredevils.' That was to remain true throughout most of his career until he gained insurance through membership of the Screen Actors' Guild after starring in the 1977 movie *Viva Knievel!* Between 1965 and 1977, however, Knievel spent hundreds of thousands of dollars on his own hospital bills.

Just ten weeks after breaking his leg, Evel was back in the ring again at the Meridian Speedway in Idaho to attempt another 13-car leap, obviously undaunted by the number that had already proved unlucky for him. This time, however, he cleared the gap, and then repeated the feat in Spokane and Missoula before heading to the Tahoe-Carson Speedway in Nevada to jump a 'mere' ten cars. Despite seeming to have completely mastered the art of jumping 13 cars, Knievel crashed out yet again, having only cleared nine of his ten obstacles. This time he came down heavily and slammed into his own truck, which was parked just before the landing ramp. Not only did Knievel break his right shoulder, he also re-broke the left hip he'd smashed at Caesar's Palace just 10 months before. This was a serious setback aggravated further by his contracting a staph infection while recovering in hospital from his injuries. Staph infection is caused by the *Staphylococcus aureus* bacteria entering the body through a cut or wound. It can usually be treated relatively easily with antibiotics but it hampered Evel's recovery and was another irritation he didn't need. More hospital treatment meant more time off work, which meant more time making no money and more damned medical bills.

Knievel was becoming a very experienced hospital patient, and the more time he spent in them, the more he grew to hate them. Hospital food was a particular bone of contention. 'I don't like hospital food. If you are hungry enough I guess you can eat it but I'm a New York steak and lobster-tail man myself. You don't see much of that in hospitals. They don't seem to go much for oysters Rockefeller either.'

But Knievel wasn't always ready with an easy quote when hospitalised; after all, he spent an estimated total of three full years in hospital during his career, a horrendous amount of time by anyone's standards. But he remained staunchly philosophical about 'doing his time', simply putting it down to being 'the price you pay for being a risk-taking daredevil'.

Over the course of his life, Knievel would undergo 16 major open-reduction operations – where the body is cut open to have metalwork inserted. The result is that Evel has had around 40 screws and plates fixed inside him in order to piece him back together and hold him together, often needing to have some parts replaced as they were battered out of shape during further crashes and heavy, jarring landings.

Knievel's career injury tally makes for truly grim reading. As well as having a fractured skull and being in a coma for 29 days following his Caesar's crash, he also broke his nose, smashed out several teeth and fractured his jaw. He has broken both left and right collarbones several times and vertebrae in his upper back on two separate occasions. He has suffered a fractured sternum and broken all his ribs on different occasions, broken his right arm and his left arm at least twice each and has had both wrists broken. He has fractured vertebrae in his lower back and crushed his pelvis on three occasions as well as crushing his hip, which led to the total hip, ball and socket eventually being replaced with titanium in 1997. Below the waist he has broken both left and right femurs (the largest bones in the body) a total of five times, suffered a broken right knee and right shin and had both ankles broken. Not wishing to leave any part of his anatomy unscathed, Evel also broke several toes during his career. About the only major injury Knievel has successfully avoided is a broken neck.

He may have spent three years in hospital, but how many more years he spent healing from injuries outside hospital buildings is anyone's guess, and Knievel was notoriously short-tempered during any recovery process at home. Accustomed as he was to being a go-getter, he found it frustrating in the extreme to have to sit around doing nothing and having to be tended to while he waited for his body to heal so he could go out and have fun, make some more money and, ultimately, risk further injury.

Knievel was caught in a catch-22 situation: if he didn't jump he couldn't make money; yet if he did jump he ran the risk of injuring himself, which in turn meant he couldn't jump and therefore couldn't make more money again. Every time he jumped was a risk, but it was always a calculated one and he always accepted it when things went wrong. 'All my jumping risks were calculated . . . but anything can happen. You have to commit yourself to the jump 60 yards away. There are jumps [that] before you even take off you know you aren't going to make. Sometimes you find out in the air . . . and then you've got to make a decision. If you've got any chance at all, you grit your teeth and hold on. If you don't, then you relax and just roll with it.'

The latter part of this philosophy shows Knievel had an innate understanding of 'how' to crash. The first rule of being a professional stuntman or stuntwoman is to know that tensed-up muscles lead to more serious injuries, whereas relaxed, limp bodies tend to 'give' more and are less susceptible to injury. Even so, Knievel was well aware that his chosen profession/sport punished mistakes and errors of judgement more harshly than most others. 'Football players fall down on Astroturf or grass,' he explained, 'and rodeo riders fall down on nice soft dirt or cow manure. But boy, when you fall off a motorcycle at 60, 70 or 80 miles per hour on the asphalt, there's nothing in the world that compares with it. The asphalt bites back. It just murders your body; it tears you to pieces.'

Bizarre as it may seem, given his chosen profession and his refusal to retire from it despite the repeated injuries he suffered, Knievel actually did have a healthy respect for fear and by no means had a death wish. On the contrary, he used fear and nerves to pull the best from himself. 'Fear is a high-octane fuel for the possibility of success,' he often said. 'I have never subscribed to the "no fear" attitude. Those who truly feel they have absolutely no fear belong in a mental institution.' All the same, Knievel stops short of admitting to any specific fear or how it affects him personally. 'Do I fear death? No. Was I ever afraid to make a jump? If I was afraid, I was not going to tell you about it. I'm Evel Knievel. I'm not supposed to be afraid.'

Another fallout from the Caesar's crash was that Evel changed motorcycles again. Despite his enthusiasm for the Triumph T120

Bonneville he wasn't quite so enthusiastic about the support (or lack of it) that he felt he was getting from his Triumph supplier, Johnson Motors. He had already taken one last rash course of action in a bid to 'persuade' his supplier to increase its backing. 'Just before the Caesar's Palace jump I decided to cash in on some favours. I had loads of trouble with Johnson Motors out of California. They provided the Triumph motorcycle for me – one of the best motorcycles ever built – but did nothing in return for all the promoting I did for them. I threatened Pete Coleman, who was the president, that if he didn't put an attorney on the next plane to Las Vegas with a $20,000 check the Triumph would miss so badly that it would make it the laughing-stock of the motorcycle world. I told him I'd burn his cycle in front of Caesar's Palace. Can you believe he accused me of blackmail? But you better believe they sent an attorney and he had that check.'

This is another of Knievel's tales which should be taken with a pinch of salt. The last thing he wanted to do was miss such a big jump on purpose and risk life-threatening injuries; what's more, to the average spectator who didn't know a thing about motorcycles his missing the jump would suggest that Evel's skills were lacking rather than reflecting badly on the Triumph, which, to the majority of them, was just another motorcycle.

Whatever the case, at the end of 1968 Knievel parted company with Johnson Motors after Caesar's and hooked up with the rather obscure American Eagle company. Despite the patriotic-sounding name, the bikes were actually built in Italy by Laverda and sold in the States under the American Eagle brand. Knievel was introduced to the brand by former Honda America employee Jack McCormick, the man who coined the famous slogan 'You meet the nicest people on a Honda'. It may sound simple, even corny today, but the slogan went a long way in the 1960s towards convincing the American public that not all bikers were dangerous, greasy yobs – a campaign which Evel supported wholeheartedly.

Once Knievel decided to go with American Eagle he was allocated what was essentially a twin-cylinder Laverda 750S and again he stripped off all non-essential gear like mudguards, lights and indicators in a bid both to make the bike lighter and to make it look that bit more special. He also added a set of high, wide handlebars taken from a scrambler bike as they offered more control and leverage for pulling wheelies and controlling the bike on landings.

It was the Laverda which was first painted up in the now famous white Confederate stars on blue background stripes. Knievel would use a variation of this design for the rest of his career and to this day countless products are marketed (some licensed, some not) bearing a similar design. It was also while riding the American Eagle that Knievel's famous white-starred jumpsuit first appeared. He had switched to a white suit with stripes down the legs and sleeves while riding the Triumph, but it was only when he rode the Eagle in 1969–70 that the look he is now renowned for first appeared in full. The suit would continue to develop in the following years, becoming more and more outrageous, and would, somewhat inevitably, spark many comparisons with that other famous wearer of white jumpsuits, Elvis Presley.

It has long been debated which of the two men was the originator of the look and it is still a difficult matter to decide on since they actually appeared to develop along separate lines. While not exactly wearing a white jumpsuit, Knievel had been wearing white leathers (a growing craze among motorcycle racers at the time as they attempted to distance themselves from their greasy, black leather image) as far back as 1967 when Presley was still churning out dreadful Hollywood movies and had not yet returned to performing live. It was not until 1969, when he started his Vegas seasons, that Elvis appeared on stage wearing a fringed white jumpsuit, which had been developed from his interest in karate, hence the similarity to the standard white karate suit.

It was only when Knievel started adding flared bell-bottoms, high collars, large, initialled belts and, most blatantly, a jewelled cape in the early Seventies, *after* Presley had developed similar accessories, that he could be accused of copying the singer, of whom he openly admitted to being a huge fan. But at least Evel confessed he was influenced by Presley, saying he 'always loved the outfits that Elvis wore'. In fairness, the imitating may well have worked both ways to a certain extent: while Presley was never really associated with a walking cane, and certainly had no real need for one, he was photographed several times posing with one very similar to Knievel's. In this case, Knievel can definitely claim to be the originator. And it doesn't require a huge stretch of the imagination to imagine why Presley would take some styling cues from Knievel, for as the mid-Seventies approached, Elvis was piling on the pounds and was not attracting new young audiences. Knievel, however, was at the peak of his powers and hugely popular with American kids. Presley may well have taken a few styling cues from his fellow jumpsuited icon.

Knievel often went further than claiming to be just a fan of Elvis, once bragging that 'Elvis was a good friend of mine. He dated my sister Loretta, my half-sister, for a long time.' It is odd then that the two performed and often based themselves in Vegas, but no photograph appears to exist of the two 'friends' together, and none of Presley's major biographers make any reference to Knievel as being a friend of his. Despite this, Knievel once claimed in an interview, 'I used to go backstage at the Hilton Hotel in Las Vegas when he was done with his shows and we'd sit for two or three hours and talk together and have a drink or two with Colonel Parker. He was a wonderful guy; he always introduced me at his shows if he knew I was there.'

Knievel stands comparison with Presley on other fronts too: he was not referred to as 'Elvis Presley on a motorcycle' for nothing. Like Presley, Knievel had come from a poor background and had virtually created his own arena in which to become famous. If Presley became the king of rock 'n' roll, then Evel became the king of the daredevils. He even took to hiring an entourage, who he decked out in matching silk jackets and dark sunglasses, a clear reflection of Presley's famed 'Memphis Mafia'. By 1974, at the peak of Knievel's fame, this crew numbered 19 men. And although Elvis went on to win the battle of the bulge convincingly from Evel, the pair both added serious girth as the Seventies unfolded, making their jumpsuits look more like romper suits at times.

Knievel even went on to work with Marty Pasetta, the producer of Elvis's *Aloha from Hawaii* concert (the first ever worldwide satellite broadcast by an entertainer, which was seen by one billion people), for the ill-fated series *Evel Knievel's Death Defiers,* and also worked with movie director Gordon Douglas (who directed Elvis in *Follow that Dream*) when it came to shooting *Viva Knievel!* in 1977.

As much as Knievel admired Presley, he did point out that all Elvis had to do was go on stage and sing while he himself made a living out of breaking bones. Re-breaking his hip had put Evel out of action right through the winter of 1968–69. He broke it in October and was not fit enough to ride again until April, when he appeared over four days at the Los Angeles Memorial Sports Arena. That his longest jump was over a mere eight cars can be attributed to two factors: he was performing in a relatively small indoor arena which didn't allow enough room for big jumps, and he was obviously playing it safe, not wanting to risk further damage to his still-fragile hip.

Despite the fact that these jumps were far less of a spectacle and far less daring than his Caesar's leap, Knievel was now such a star that he could command big bucks for all his appearances. But he knew his audience would soon tire of watching easy jumps and, in an effort to maintain spectator figures and retain his own credibility, Knievel planned an indoor record attempt at the unglamorously titled Cow Palace in San Francisco on 23 January 1970. His aim was to jump eleven cars, but in the end the performance went down in the Knievel history books for all the wrong reasons: namely, that he finally came face to face with a group he had despised and badmouthed for years. They were called the Hell's Angels.

Although they prefer to call themselves a biker 'club', and steer clear of the word 'gang' to avoid any allusion to organised crime, Knievel had always seen the Hell's Angels and other motorcycle 'clubs' as being no-good thugs and criminals. He had repeatedly attacked them in the press as being bad for biking and bad for society as a whole. 'These guys are dogs – they belong in penitentiaries. They're murderers, they're thieves, they're drug dealers . . . I hate their guts and I hate what they stand for and I want everybody to know they are not accepted by motorcycle people. We don't like them. That's just the way it is.'

His hatred of the Angels prompted one of Knievel's finest ever quotes. Having stated that he was liable to shoot any Hell's Angel that ever got in his way, he added, 'God created all men, and Winchester made 'em equal.'

Much of what Knievel was about was a reaction to the biker gang-culture, which really took off in the 1960s and which was led by the Hell's Angels. The Angels had their origins in the immediate post-World War Two years when dispossessed and restless air crews came back to America and found they could no longer fit into society. The image went mainstream when, in 1954, Marlon Brando roared onto the silver screen as Johnny on his Triumph T120 Bonneville (the same make, though an earlier model, of the bike Knievel himself had used), looking for something, anything to rebel against. The film itself was inspired by the real-life Hollister incident of 1947 when a motorcycle gang rode into the small Californian town and terrified the locals with their drunken revelry. The press sensationalised the event but it caught the public's imagination and fear, and since then the motorcycling community had a tarnished name, which it still, to a certain extent, suffers from.

Scores of Hell's Angels movies in the 1960s did little to rectify the situation, and few were brave enough to speak out publicly against them. Knievel had no such fear and, to his credit, he did what he could in a bid to enhance the image of motorcycling in the eyes of the general public. As well as speaking openly against the Angels, he chose to wear white leather like a knight in shining armour, in contrast to the predominant black-leather look of the time. He also, somewhat hypocritically, always addressed his audience before his jumps and preached the benefits of clean living. He spoke out against the perils of drinking, the dangers of drug use, and the need to be a patriotic all-American citizen. It was very much a case of 'do-as-I-say-and-not-as-I-do', but since the kids he was addressing were unaware of his heavy drinking and extra-marital affairs, that mattered little. Knievel was at least *trying* to be a good, wholesome example, if only verbally.

The great irony is that while attempting to convince the mainstream public that motorcyclists were nice, normal, sensible

All hail the King of the Daredevils.
Knievel soaks up the applause after another successful jump.

Jumping his way to fame over the Caesars Palace fountains in Las Vegas on New Year's Eve 1967. Evel crashed and spent 29 days in a coma but upon awakening, he found he was famous.

'Yeah, just bring me up some Wild Turkey and some girls. Lots of girls.' Knievel had no qualms about admitting that he was an over-sexed alcoholic.

ABOVE: Jumping a record 19 cars at the Ontario Motor Speedway in California, February 1971.

BELOW: Evel once boasted that if kids could vote he'd be President. Judging by this picture he wasn't far wrong.

ABOVE: King's Island, Ohio, 1975. In preparation for his 14-truck jump. It was the longest successful jump Evel ever made.

BELOW: Even from a hospital bed the Knievel PR machine kept on rolling. Evel speaks to the press after crashing in a practice jump over a pool of sharks. Chicago, 1977.

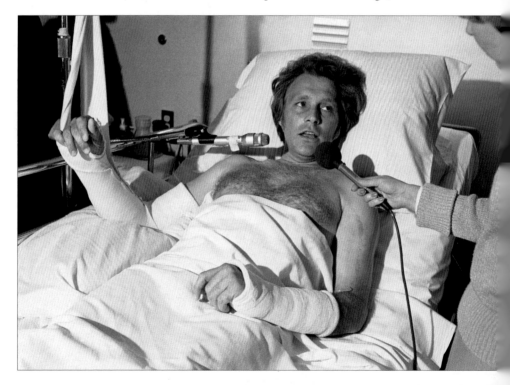

Pretty woman. Knievel was never too far from a beautiful woman.

[K]nevel, Linda and daughter Tracey [a]rrive at the Snake River jump site [o]n the morning of the attempt. [S]ons Robbie and Kelly were also in [a]ttendance. Note the famous cane.

ABOVE: 'God take care of me, here I come.'
Snake River Canyon, Idaho, 8 September,
1974.

BELOW: Woodstock on two wheels – but
without the love ethos. The Snake River
Canyon jump turned into a riot.

Blast off! Knievel attempts to
leap three-quarters of a mile
over a canyon in a 350mph,
steam-powered rocket. Surely
the maddest stunt of his career?

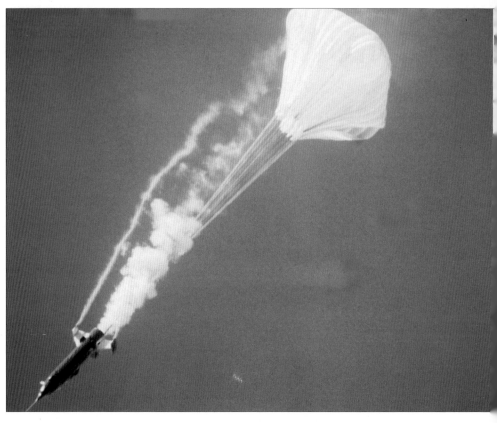

ABOVE: The defining moment in Knievel's career. Did he pull the plug or not?

BELOW: The X-2 Sky Cycle was easier to recover than Knievel's reputation after the Snake River attempt.

people, Knievel himself was coming within an inch of losing his life every few months. He appeared to be a man on a suicide mission, not a God-fearing do-gooder. As the head of the American Motorcyclist Association, Ed Youngblood, once said, 'Evel was a double-edged sword for us because the danger factor hurt but the safety speeches helped. With all the crazy jumps and broken bones and wild outfits, he did an awful lot to promote the idea that motorcyclists are crazy and that it's a terribly dangerous activity. In a way, Evel was saying all the right words but doing all the wrong things.'

Knievel has never fully explained how his deep hatred of the Angels originated, but it all came to a head at the Cow Palace in January 1970 in front of a capacity crowd of 12,000 people, although accounts differ on how events actually unfolded. According to the authors of *Evel Ways*, Evel was performing wheelies *before* making his big jump when a Hell's Angel appeared from the audience and threw what Knievel describes as a tyre iron at him (a metal tool for removing tyres). The Angels had heard and read about Knievel bad-mouthing their organisation and this particular individual had obviously decided to show his own hatred for Knievel. It was the wrong place to do so, as Knievel explained: 'I saw this little bastard standing in the middle of the floor giving me the finger and I always wanted to punch one of the bastards anyway, so I revved my motorcycle up and I threw it into a slide and I knocked this guy piss-over-tea-kettles. All of a sudden, about 500 people jumped out of the grandstand and they grabbed these four-by-fours and these two-by-fours [wooden planks] and they absolutely beat the hell out of these Hell's Angels. They beat those Hell's Angels to death.'

While not quite beating them to death, Knievel's fans did ensure that the Angels involved took quite a beating and three or four of the 15 or so members involved were reputed to be in intensive care for months. In *Evel Incarnate*, Steve Mandich has the near-riot taking place after Knievel has successfully cleared the 11 cars. He also claims Knievel took a swing at the Angel but was in turn thrown to the floor himself and only saved by his bodyguard, Gene Sullivan, who floored the Hell's Angel before hustling Knievel off to his trailer.

Whatever the scenario, in today's climate Knievel would probably have been charged with inciting a riot, but as it was he was later granted the Key to the City of San Francisco and made honorary mayor for a day for his actions. It seemed the people of San Francisco had had as much of the Hell's Angels as Knievel himself had. Once again, Evel had turned what could have been disastrous PR into another great publicity vehicle. He had shown that he was prepared to stand alone against the mighty Hell's Angels, even if he was made more secure in the knowledge that 12,000 of his fans were there to help him.

Renowned Hell's Angel and author of the autobiographical book *Hell's Angel*, Sonny Barger, recently put forward his feelings on the Cow Palace fight and the Knievel/Angels rift. 'He made a derogatory remark about the Hell's Angels and somebody threw a Coke can. There was a big fight with Evel and his crew, and since that time we haven't gotten along. Every chance that he has to say something bad about the Hell's Angels, he does. And every chance we have to say something bad about him, we do. But the reason I believe people like Evel Knievel say things about the Hell's Angels is to bring notoriety to their own names. People would rather hear things about the Hell's Angels than about Evel Knievel, so he says derogatory things about us.'

It is interesting to note that Barger claims it was a Coke can which was thrown rather than a much heavier and more dangerous tyre iron, but the fact remains that, 34 years after the event, Knievel and the Angels are no closer to being reconciled. And that's probably just the way both parties prefer it.

# 5
# Colour Me Lucky

**'I'm going to have the best clothes, the best boots, the best diamonds, the best cars, motorcycles, booze and women on the face of this earth.'**

One of the most significant benefits of the Caesar's Palace crash was that it caught the attention of certain parties in Hollywood, and, in particular, that of the actor George Hamilton.

Memphis-born Hamilton was just a year younger than Knievel and had his first movie role in the 1959 film *Crime and Punishment USA*. He had since garnered a reputation as a ladies man and throughout his career would be associated with a bevy of Hollywood beauties, including Elizabeth Taylor, but he was perhaps best known in the gossip columns for his mid-1960s relationship with President Lyndon Johnson's daughter, Lynda.

Hamilton's perma-tan has since made him something of a laughing stock with contemporary audiences, but in 1970 he still had enough clout and respect in Hollywood to produce a movie, and he decided he would make one about Evel Knievel's life story, casting himself in the title role.

The suave, smooth (and often cheesy) appearance and manner-isms of Hamilton were in sharp contrast to the gritty, tough-guy image Knievel had built up, but when Hollywood comes knocking, few refuse to answer the door and Knievel was no exception. Knowing that a movie about his life had the potential to make him an international rather than just a national star, Evel had no hesitation in signing up for the project. But for once his acute busi-ness sense failed him. Desperate for money to fund his increasingly extravagant lifestyle, Knievel agreed to a flat up-front fee of just $25,000 for the rights to his life story and, in his haste, missed out on the opportunity to earn any future royalties. But even if the film didn't make him quite as rich as it should have done, it was Evel's ticket to Hollywood and he wasn't complaining.

Hamilton managed to raise a budget of $750,000 for the movie, which was to be directed by Martin J. Chomsky who had several *Star Trek* episodes to his credit and would go on to direct the hugely successful made-for-television epic *Roots* in 1977.

While plans for the movie were being laid, Knievel continued jumping his way through 1970 with varying degrees of success and luck. His first gig after the Cow Palace riot was at the Seattle International Raceway on 5 April, where he attempted to leap over 13 Ford Cougars, but yet again he suffered problems. The run-up to the ramp was over wet grass, which caused Knievel's rear tyre to spin, which in turn meant he couldn't gain enough speed to make the leap. Once again he clipped the landing ramp and was almost thrown clean off the bike but somehow managed to steer it to a halt, despite having a punctured and buckled rear wheel.

Bitten but still not shy, Evel regained his composure and moved his ramps to a hard-standing surface where he would be guaranteed the traction he needed. Knievel had vowed never to jump over Tarmac again after Caesar's but his determination not to disappoint paying spectators now overruled any concerns for his own safety; he'd said he'd make the jump and he was going to keep his word.

Even more incredible was the fact that Evel added a further five Cougars to the line-up, taking the total number of vehicles to 18. This equated to a distance of 120 feet – further than Knievel had ever successfully jumped before. It was a brave move considering he had already come up short on the 13-car attempt but it was one that paid off as he cleared the gap comfortably and sent the 15,000-strong crowd wild.

But such moments of pain-free victory were always short-lived in Evel Knievel's world, and he was back on bone-crunching form at the Yakima Speedway near Washington one month later. Despite the fact that he was 'only' required to jump 100 feet, the obstacles he had to clear were 13 Pepsi-Cola delivery trucks, which were naturally taller than cars and therefore required a higher trajectory. Since Knievel never employed any scientific means to calculate the trajectories of his jumps there was always a very real risk that he would get them wrong, and at Yakima that's exactly what he did. Leaving too little room for error, Evel failed to gain the necessary take-off speed and fell short on the safety ramp yet again, this time smashing off the side of his American Eagle and suffering a broken collarbone, an extremely painful injury and one which normally takes two months to recover from.

Undeterred as usual, Knievel had his shoulder braced up in time for his next appearance six weeks later in Vancouver in Canada where he broke his own indoor jump record by clearing 12 cars. It is worth noting that there are no perfectly accurate measurements for Knievel's jumps and, although he continually boasted of break-ing world records, there was no professional body governing such feats at the time. There can be a significant difference in the distance covered in jumping 12 cars which are each parked either one foot apart or one inch apart, and the same goes for jumping 12 cars which are wider or narrower models than others. For the purposes of clarity therefore, the term 'record' is only used as a relative term to explain that Knievel is jumping more vehicles, either indoors or outdoors, than he has previously jumped. It does not mean that the record is officially recognised.

Seemingly falling into the pattern of a successful jump being followed by a crash, Evel broke several ribs and fractured two vertebrae in Seattle on 4 July – American Independence day – when falling off his bike several hundred yards after a rough landing.

His injuries forced him to cancel the jump he had scheduled for the following week, but Evel was back for more punishment in Pennsylvania in August where he once again fractured a vertebra and also broke his hand and shoulder. Knievel faced yet another boring and painful period of recuperation but he put his time to good use, as was customary, by hustling for deals on the telephone. During this period he managed to set up one of his more lucrative sponsorship deals – he signed to ride for legendary American motorcycle firm Harley-Davidson.

Formed in Milwaukee in 1903 by William S. Harley and Arthur Davidson, Harley-Davidson is the world's oldest continual manufacturer of motorcycles and today has a market value of $15 billion. But it has not always been so; the firm has had its share of lows and only recovered from certain bankruptcy in 1984 after floating itself on the stock market. The company's other big lull was during the 1960s, and until its merger with the bowling-ball manufacturer AMF, Harleys were really only valued by motorcycle groups like the Hell's Angels, who initiated a craze for customising the bikes, a craze which continues to this day. The Angels have long taken credit for keeping the Harley brand alive during those lean years, and, naturally, were none too pleased when one of their most out-spoken critics was chosen as the firm's new golden boy. But for Evel Knievel, the Harley link-up was a match made in heaven.

The all-American hero had, until late 1970, been riding a 'phoney' American machine in the American Eagle, made as it was in Italy. So when the brand folded due to poor sales (Knievel obviously wasn't inspiring quite enough bikers to rush out and buy one), Harley stepped in with an offer he couldn't refuse – and it would prove to be mutually beneficial to both parties. Knievel would finally have the backing of the biggest motorcycle company in the States and he would be riding an all-American machine to match his all-American image. For Harley-Davidson, Knievel finally represented a chance to break free from the biker gang image it had been tarnished with, even if Knievel was no real saint in his own private life. But as far as the public was concerned at that time – in an age before innumerable intrusive gossip magazines began revealing every sordid detail of celebrities' lives – he was evil in name only.

Naturally, Knievel did not let the opportunity to make some serious money pass by, and in fact would years later say that the cash Harley offered was the only real motivating factor in signing for the firm. Knievel certainly provided good value for money for his new sponsors and never missed a chance to sing the praises of Harley-Davidson and the XR-750 machines they had provided him with. He officially announced the link-up in 1971 at Daytona Beach, Florida by saying, 'My bikes are Harley XR-750s. I've got 60 horsepower to the rear wheel of the bike. It's the most powerful set of wheels going. I can go from zero to 60 in four-and-a-half seconds.'

Looking back now, Knievel still has fond memories of his time with Harley-Davidson. 'The people at Harley-Davidson were one of the finest families I ever did business with. They kept their word and stood by my side the eight years I worked with them. I was proud to be a part of the Harley-Davidson team.' The firm presented Evel with a 100th Anniversary Edition Road King Classic for his sixty-fifth birthday in 2003.

The iconic Harley-Davidson XR-750 had only come into being in early 1970 when race-team manager Dick O'Brien slotted a modified Harley Sportster engine into an old Harley KR racing frame. But by 1972 the bike was winning American national dirt-track racing titles and, in various forms, continued to do so over the next three decades, ensuring itself a place in the history of motorcycling.

But it was Evel Knievel who first enjoyed any real success on an XR-750 and brought the bike to the attention of the general public, not that many of them actually cared what make of motorcycle he was riding since they were largely non-motorcyclists themselves. His Harley-riding debut at the Lions Drag Strip in Los Angeles also happened to be his last appearance of 1970 and Knievel ended the year on a high (quite literally) with a successful leap over 13 vehicles.

Having beaten his own indoor record by twice clearing 13 vehicles at the Houston Astrodome in January 1971 in front of an incredible 99,000 people, Knievel headed to the Ontario Motor Speedway in California to perform another jump, and this one was to be filmed by Hollywood cameras as the set piece for George Hamilton's movie of Evel's life.

The first working title for the film had been *Color Me Lucky* – a phrase Knievel was fond of painting on the fuel tanks of his motorcycles. But it seemed simpler and a lot more self-explanatory (if rather uninspiring) to just call the movie *Evel Knievel*. At least then no one would be in any doubt as to what the film was about.

The Ontario gig didn't start well with Knievel fracturing his right hand during a rough landing after clearing 13 cars. Determined to get some footage in the can for the upcoming movie, however, Evel upped the ante the following day and made a spectacular and comfortable 129-foot leap over a record 19 cars. It was the furthest he had jumped to date and would provide a perfect climactic long-distance jump for the MGM film.

Supporting actors were lined up to appear alongside George Hamilton, most notably Sue Lyons (who had a role in the 1964 Richard Burton/Ava Gardner movie *Night of the Iguana*) as Knievel's wife Linda. Filming locations were authentic as the cast and crew headed for Knievel's hometown of Butte to shoot scenes representing Evel's early years. As one would expect, the movie portrayed Knievel as a bit of a rebel who came good and ultimately achieved the American dream as a man with no fear, a man whose 'death will be glorious', as Hamilton's closing voiceover predicts.

Hamilton was no stranger to biopics, having already played out the life of Country and Western star Hank Williams in the 1965 movie *Your Cheatin' Heart*, but he made a poor Knievel, and while the movie performed modestly well at the box office and still enjoys regular outings on various satellite channels, it's far from being an all-time classic. It would have worked much better as a gritty, realistic portrayal of Knievel's life, which had, even by 1971, seen many ups and downs.

At the time, Knievel was full of praise for Hamilton's portrayal, but he would later become bitter about the fact that he made so little money out of his own life story while Hamilton fared much better. 'George made a lot of money on the picture and he did a great job of playing me but this guy never even said thanks. I'm the one who got him out of his pretty-boy image, but now I still think he's a pussy.'

*Evel Knievel* opened in Los Angeles on 14 July 1971 and served the purpose it was intended to. Oversimplified and over-glamorised, as screen biopics tend to be, it nevertheless entertained the kids who made up the majority of Knievel's fans. In fairness it was typical of many of the easy-going, lightweight movies of the time and should be viewed as such.

Evel himself had no real cause for complaint. Few people can claim to be so famous that Hollywood commissions a movie of their lives, so while he may not have made too much in hard cash from the film itself, the publicity it generated for him in general guaranteed further earnings, even if they were to be indirect.

But it didn't seem to matter how much Knievel earned – he always ended up spending more. Reflecting on his acquisition – and eventual loss – of great wealth, Knievel said, 'Bobby Knievel never made me a dime . . . Evel Knievel made me about 60 million dollars . . . and Evel Knievel spent about 63 million dollars.' His lifestyle by the early 1970s had become as outrageous as any top Hollywood star and all the trappings were flaunted shamelessly. 'I wasn't the richest man in the world,' Knievel admitted, 'but for a cycle rider from Montana I was having a damn good time. I spent more money having fun than any man alive. Aristotle Onassis didn't know how to live. My philosophy is take one day at a time.' And if that meant spending way beyond his means, so be it. After all, his entire philosophy was built around the premise that he'd rather live a rich man than die a rich man. 'All the money in the world can't buy your way into heaven and it can't buy your way out of hell – it was meant to be spent right here and I'm going to have the best clothes, the best boots, the best diamonds, the best cars, motorcycles, booze and women on the face of this earth just as long as I keep going.'

Over the years, some of those cars included five Rolls-Royces, three Ferrari Spyder convertibles, three Cadillac pickups, a 1971 Ferrari Berlinetta Boxer, a 1984 Aston Martin Lagonda Sedan, a custom-built Sparks III convertible, a $129,000 white and gold Stutz convertible (which Evel claimed was the only one of its kind in the world and which featured 24-carat-gold plating inside as well as genuine sable carpeting both inside and in the boot), and another Stutz which he claimed was originally built for Prince Charles. He also claimed to have an Aston Martin which was made for Charles. Evel had apparently stunned the Stutz salesman who sold him the convertible by presenting him with a personal cheque inlaid with genuine gold embossments. It came from a series of cheque books which alone cost Evel $7,000 a year. And as well as his street cars he also owned three bona fide Indianapolis-style racing cars and up to 30 motorcycles at any one time. Knievel's list of cars changes every time he recites it, but all the cars he did actually have were hung with the #1 Montana Governor's licence plate in various forms, including '1–Evel', '1–1', and 'Stutz 1'.

Knievel's most famous mode of transport, however, was the massive liveried truck and trailer unit with which he used to go on tour. It was custom-built by Kenworth of Kansas City, Missouri at a cost of $100,000 and Knievel claimed it was the longest vehicle of its kind in the world. It featured a 14-speed automatic transmission and housed Evel's office, dressing room and lounge. It also boasted a colour TV, stereo, air-conditioning unit, heating and Olympia beer on tap. The trailer unit carried all of Evel's bikes and eight tons of ramps and equipment.

Knievel's motorised luxuries were not restricted to road-going vehicles; he had a fleet of yachts and boats which would have shamed a small country's navy. Moored in 300 yards of docking space in Fort Lauderdale, Florida, where he also bought a home, Knievel's boats were all called *Evel Eye 1* – a play on the 'evil eye' design which fishermen have long painted on their boats to ward off evil spirits. The fleet consisted of 11 boats, ranging from an 87-foot Broward to a 120-foot Fed ship complete with its own helicopter and landing pad, two motorcycles, two jet skis, two speedboats and a crew of seven. The Broward and the Fed boats alone cost him $5 million but there were many smaller craft including yachts and speedboats. By 1999, however, Knievel rued the day he ever started buying boats due to the vast amounts of money he was forced to spend on their upkeep. 'I'd never have another one . . . there's only one thing you can spend more money on than a ship and that's a woman. They're both bottomless pits you keep pouring money into. I'll give you a lesson in life. If it flies, floats or fucks – lease it. Don't be an idiot!'

When he had to take to the air, Evel was not short of private transport either. Having started out owning a small fixed-wing Cessna aircraft earlier in his career, he eventually bought two private Learjets and a helicopter, which, like his boats, were all emblazoned with the famous Knievel logos. Rumour has it that Knievel bought a second Learjet just so he could fly alongside the other and admire his name on its side. If he was close enough to read his name, however, he presumably would not have lived to tell the tale.

While he was actually pictured with his Learjets and helicopter, Knievel's later boast that he had owned 14 aeroplanes including a Golden Eagle, a Beech Duke, a King Air and a Bonanza seems rather far-fetched, as does his claim to have bought 16 aeroplanes in one day. He even boasted that he'd met the Shah of Iran – one of the world's richest men – who apparently told him, 'You bought more planes in one day than I've bought.'

Even more incredible is Knievel's claim that he flew around a million miles at the controls of his planes despite the fact that he never had a pilot's licence. 'I don't need a licence to fly an airplane,' he once bragged. 'I fly one any damn place I feel like it. The FAA [Federal Aviation Administration] can't stop me from flying an airplane. I'm not going to violate nothing. What's a licence mean? How are they going to stop me from flying around in the air up there? I mean, that's silly. I can fly a 747 – there isn't anything I can't fly . . . Evel Knievel is capable of herding an airplane round the sky.'

Knievel did admit to employing pilots so his boasts of being able to fly anything must once more be taken with a pinch of salt, certainly if the testimony of his favoured pilot, the dubiously named Watcha McCollum, is anything to go by. When asked by a reporter if Evel helped fly the planes, McCollum responded, 'No, he just sits. In the helicopter I took the dual controls out so he couldn't even play with it.'

Yet Knievel insists he once had a close call while flying his Cessna into the Continental Divide Raceway near Denver, Colorado on his way to a jump. He was aiming to land on the drag strip just 50 yards away from where thousands of spectators were already seated in a grandstand, but he hit a marker flagpole as he banked the plane round. 'I knocked a wingtip tank off going into Denver, to the racetrack there. My men forgot to take the flagpole down. I had a big twin Cessna. Knocked the wingtip tank right off. But I landed it, got out, did my wheelies, made the jump, jumped back in and took off again. Flew it right out of the racetrack and had 30,000 people standing right on the hill. They were afraid to come down on the track!'

Transport aside, in one of his most ostentatious displays of wealth, Knievel was once photographed literally shovelling heaps of cash into his own personal bank vault in Butte. The heavy vault doors had the initials 'EK' etched into them alongside an engraving of Evel pulling a wheelie on his motorcycle. On the inner door was the inscription 'Evel Knievel National Bank: Absolutely NO LOANS'.

But his money never stayed in the vault for too long. Knievel took great pride in blowing it as quickly as possible and sneered at rich celebrities who didn't enjoy their wealth. Speaking of the hugely successful country singer Garth Brooks he once said, 'I saw him on TV one time, he says, "I made so much money I couldn't spend it all." Garth . . . I wanna tell you something: you travel with me for 30 days, I'll bust you so quick it ain't even funny.'

Of course, the ultimate status symbol for any wealthy man is his house, and, naturally, Knievel didn't skimp on his own purpose-built $200,000 mansion in Butte. Built overlooking the sixteenth fairway of Butte Country Club, Knievel's house was set in 9.8 acres of land and featured a private putting green, a six-car garage, a helicopter landing-pad, an art gallery, stables and a lighted outdoor horse-riding arena.

Clothes were another way in which Knievel liked to flaunt his wealth, and even in an era as gaudy and shameless as the 1970s he still managed to stand out. As far back as 1969, *Parade* magazine had declared Evel Knievel and Liberace the best-dressed men in America, but as fashion became more outrageous in the Seventies, so did Knievel's wardrobe. Chequered trousers, impossibly large collars ('I looked like the flying nun'), satin jackets, snakeskin boots and $750 shirts were all favourites in the Knievel wardrobe, which he once boasted was 'better than most retail stores'. Only in the politically incorrect Seventies could he have got away with wearing a thigh-length coat made from chinchilla fur, or a silver mink coat worth $8,000, while lighting his cigars with $100 bills. Evel was not ashamed of being rich.

To complement his outlandish clothes, Knievel draped himself in expensive jewellery, never being seen without his diamond-encrusted 'EK' ring, his jewel-tipped walking cane and two medallions round his neck fashioned from solid gold $20 pieces. Other items included a 13-carat diamond ring shaped like a motorcycle, a 12-carat diamond ring and a 33-carat diamond watch, all of which he claimed were an insurance against hurting himself since no one would insure him as a daredevil. But his most extravagant jewellery purchase was the Papal Cross, which he bought and insured for $2 million. The diamond- and emerald-encrusted cross, accompanied by a ring, was given to the United Nations by Pope Paul VI to be sold for charity to help alleviate human suffering. When it came up for auction Knievel bought both items, keeping the cross for himself and giving the ring to Linda.

Looking back on his frivolous spending (he claimed he got through $100,000 every month on expenses and payments on his possessions alone), Knievel had no regrets. 'I didn't manage my money any better than any other kid who makes it real fast. I'm not ashamed of it – I've had a ball. If I were to drop dead tomorrow I've lived every minute of my life. Money to me is like Monopoly money ... Money's made to spend. You've got to spend, spend, spend. I enjoy life to the fullest. I *like* the idiots who put all their money in the banks, you know why? So I can borrow it. Who the hell wants a lot of money? I'd hate to get hurt and have a doctor tell me that I only had a few hours to live when I had five or six million in the bank.'

By the early 1970s Evel said he wasn't jumping for any less than $7,000 a time, a far cry from the $500 he'd been charging for shows just a few years before, but he was still getting through his money quicker than he could earn it, although that was all part of the plan. 'I hope the day I die I'll have spent all the money I earned. My greatest fear is for some guy who didn't have the guts to carry my shoes across the street to marry into my family and then inherit all my money.'

In July of 1971, Evel hit the road again to raise more capital. His four-night stint at Madison Square Garden in New York was designed to promote his forthcoming movie but the event was significant for another reason: it marked the public debut of Knievel's son Robbie as a motorcycling performer. Robbie may only have ridden round the stadium holding the American flag aloft but he was still just nine years old. It marked the start of a career which would not only better Evel's in terms of distances and obstacles jumped, but would also lead to some severe animosity between father and son, as Evel became jealous of Robbie's success when his own star began to wane.

Knievel senior cleared nine cars and a van each evening at Madison Square before moving on to perform three more success-ful shows in Buffalo, New York, in Wilkes-Barre, Pennsylvania, and in Philadelphia itself. All performances went off without a hitch and it was only after he had cleared 16 cars in Massachusetts that his luck ran out on a slippery landing ramp, causing him to crash. He was unhurt and moved on to Portland to better his own indoor jumping record by clearing 12 cars and two vans, although the force of the landing smashed Knievel's left hand into such a mess that a reporter reputedly vomited upon seeing it.

Knievel kicked off his 1972 jumping season with an appearance at the Tucson Dragway in Arizona where he showed a surprisingly caring side to his tough-guy image. After learning that a woman suffering from an undiagnosed disease wished to meet him, Knievel visited Linda Hudman in the University of Arizona Medical Center. On leaving the hospital, Evel asked doctors if it was possible to allow Hudman to attend the jump on a stretcher as long as medical personnel were present. When the doctors agreed, Evel paid for an ambulance and crew and gave Hudman the best seat (or rather, stretcher) in the house to watch him jump, made sure she was taken care of all day and kissed her farewell upon his departure. He could be kind when he wanted to be.

From Tucson it was off to the Chicago International Amphitheater before making a return to San Francisco's Cow Palace, scene of his run-in with the Hell's Angels in 1970 and a venue which seemed to be cursed for Knievel. Spectators who could see the landing area from their seats could have been forgiven for thinking Knievel was completely insane to even attempt the jump. Facing him from the top of his ski-jump-style ramp, which stretched right to the top of the stadium seating, were two massive concrete support pillars. To avoid hitting them, Knievel would have to steer his Harley-Davidson sharply to the left or right immediately upon landing or face smashing into either one – or both – of them.

During the first night's show, Evel sped down his three-foot-wide ramp, soared over 12 cars and appeared to negotiate the pillars with relative ease, but on the second night it all went wrong. Having added three more cars to the line-up, Knievel also needed to add some speed on to his take-off and that extra speed led to such a hard landing that he was thrown from his bike, which then slammed hard into the concrete pillars, spinning and grinding its way out of the arena amid a shower of sparks. Knievel himself was lucky to miss the pillars and the wildly spinning bike, and he only suffered a broken ankle and bruising to his hand and ribs. It could have been much, much worse. Just three weeks later he was back for more, and, all too predictably, he crashed again, this time breaking a collarbone at the State Fairgrounds Coliseum in Detroit.

It was the sheer regularity of Knievel's injuries and his complete willingness to accept them without complaint which set him aside from any other sportsman, no matter how dangerous their chosen sport. In dangerous sports like motorcycle racing, competitors can expect to suffer several crashes during a season, but more often than not they escape unhurt. In an unlucky year they may break an arm or a leg, but with the amount of mileage they cover at racing speeds the amount of crashes per mile is relatively low. Of course, fatalities do occur but they are relatively rare, at least when the races are held on modern, purpose-built racetracks and not on closed public-road circuits like the Isle of Man TT.

Knievel, on the other hand, was spending just seconds on his bike each time he jumped and yet he managed to crash with alarming regularity. There were periods when he seemed to stand no better than a 50/50 chance of escaping from a jump uninjured, and yet he always came back for more, knowing full well that any one of his jumps could prove fatal. Fellow motorcycle jumper and stuntman Gary Davis – who would stand in for Knievel in the 1977 movie *Viva Knievel!* and go on to become stunt co-ordinator for Hollywood blockbusters like *Terminator 2: Judgment Day* – summed up Knievel's special type of courage: 'He was certainly the most courageous jumper among all of us. If I had had as many bad wrecks as he had I would not . . . absolutely not, have continued jumping motorcycles. He always came back; he always said he would and he always came back.'

The drive, desire and determination required to put oneself in great physical danger so soon after recovering from serious injury is not an easy thing to understand for most people but it is undoubtedly the key to Knievel's success. While he could (and has been) criticised for many things, no one can ever doubt the courage he displayed every time he mounted a motorcycle and sped down a ramp. He may have been partly, or even largely, motivated by money, but that does not detract from his courage. Most people would not attempt a 140-foot leap on a motorcycle for any amount of money if they could expect to be in a coma or suffering from multiple fractures just seconds afterwards. Knievel himself insists he always went through with his jumps for no other reason than to keep his word. 'I was on a schedule and I had an obligation to meet as a performer to the public and the promoter of the jump. I made a commitment and always kept my word. Hell, what was I supposed to do – give them their money back?'

Once a deal had been made it was perhaps understandable that Knievel would want to honour his commitment, but that doesn't explain why he never retired *after* one of his big crashes when he had already proved his honour by going ahead with the jump. The grim reality is that he had been given a taste of fame and fortune and he wanted more. As he said, 'I've been rich and I've been poor – rich is a lot better.' The only way he could maintain those riches was to jump. It was all he could do. And the thought of slipping back into obscurity and poverty scared Knievel much more than broken bones ever did. It was a simple trade-off: Evel Knievel was quite happy to take the pain of repeatedly smashing his body up if his public were willing to pay to see him do it. Seldom have the sacrifices required in the pursuit of fame and fortune been so simply yet graphically illustrated than in the case of Evel Knievel.

For his own part, Knievel attempted to answer the question of why he continued risking his life in a self-penned poem simply called 'Why?', which he first read out on *The Dick Cavett Show* in 1971 and which formed part of his spoken-word LP *Evel Knievel,* which was released on the Amherst label in 1974. The poem finishes with the words:

> *For you, what I do is not right –*
> *But for me, it's not wrong.*
> *What I have been trying to tell you all along*
> *is that it's got to be.*
> *You ask why?*
> *Well, just like you, I've gotta be me.*

But sometimes even the great physical sacrifices Knievel made were not enough. His public were by now taking his ability to withstand pain for granted and felt cheated if he had to miss a show due to injury. To give Knievel full credit it must be stated that if there was even the slightest chance of being able to make a jump no matter how badly hurt he was, then he would try it. Unlike pampered football players who roll around in feigned agony after a mere tap on the shin, Knievel never used his injuries as an excuse; and, in any case, if he didn't jump he didn't get paid and that would have hurt Knievel's sensibilities even more.

At the Lakewood Speedway in Atlanta on 11 June 1972, Knievel's audience shamed themselves. Having crashed during a rare practice jump the night before he was scheduled to appear in public, Evel suffered a broken lumbar vertebra and extensively damaged both hands. He was taken to hospital and told to rest as damaging his back further could cause paralysis. Knowing he was due to perform the following evening, anxious doctors had Knievel sign papers swearing to stay in hospital, but Evel told his friends to sneak him out the following day and take him back to the Lakewood Speedway in time for the show. Knievel's friend, Joe Delaney, explained, 'The motorcycle crowd back in those days was, I mean, a rough crowd. So we roll him [Knievel] out of the ambulance . . . Well, they think he's a chicken. They think he's scared to jump. They start hootin' and hollerin' at him, booin'.

There's about 5,000 people there. So he got pissed off and called for his motorcycle. He did a wheelie in front of the grandstand at 80 or 90 miles per hour with a broken back – standing up! I mean, crazy. You could see tears in his eyes. We put him back in the ambulance and took off. But that saved the promoter. And that told me the sonovabitch Knievel ain't got no sense.'

Knievel had become a victim of his own success. Having defied doctors so many times and having come back from so many horrific injuries, his public now thought of him as nothing less than a real-life superhero, immune to pain and the shortcomings of the fragile human body. Every jump he made had to be bigger and further to keep his audience amused, and he was expected to jump no matter what kind of pain he was in, because he was Evel Knievel and Evel Knievel didn't care about pain. In essence, he had set himself an impossible task, and even he was aware of the ghoulish element growing in his audiences. Early in his career, Evel believed his spectators were all rooting for him. He once said, 'These people are my friends. They don't want to see me miss a jump, they want to see me make it.' That sentiment changed as Knievel began to realise that at least some of his audience were not so supportive and he modified his earlier statement. 'I feel that five per cent of the people want me to die, 45 per cent want me to make it, but want to be there in case I don't, and 50 per cent are behind me all the way.'

Just one week after his crash in Atlanta, Evel set out for Oklahoma City to defy the pain and danger again, this time wearing a back brace to help him jump five cars and two vans before clearing ten cars the week after that in Illinois. He may have set himself near-impossible standards but he was determined to keep meeting them or die trying.

# 6
# Sins of the Flesh

## 'I didn't sleep with seven women in 24 hours for a bet – I slept with eight.'

'Women wanted me for my fame or my looks, or because of the danger thing, but mostly they just wanted to do it. I just had a sexual appetite for many women and I couldn't help it. I mean, you don't think when you're born that you're gonna be oversexed or that you're gonna have many women or that you're gonna be gay. You just don't do that. You are what you are.'

Evel Knievel claims to have slept with over 2,000 women, even though he was married for 38 years of that time. Born with rugged good looks and a flair for self-promotion, Knievel already had the makings of a serial seducer before he became famous, but the fame and fortune he found through jumping motorcycles cemented his status as a womaniser with few peers.

Knievel fulfilled his need for women at every given opportunity – and there were plenty of them – even though he knew word would often get back to his long-suffering wife, many times through pictures and stories published in newspapers. Despite the fact that he also had three children to think about, Evel had his own bizarre way of justifying his infidelity to himself and anyone else who would listen. 'I think if a guy's married and he has a little sex with another woman he can kinda compare her with his wife, and I've done that . . . and I still got the same wife. That means she's pretty goddamn good.'

But Evel's liberal attitude to marriage did not work both ways. Asked how he would feel if Linda had an extra-marital affair, he said, 'I wouldn't like it. I think if a man is a good-enough man, his wife wouldn't want to do that.'

Everywhere Knievel went he was hounded by women, and the stories which sprang up about his sex life have become the stuff of legend. Perhaps the most famous is Knievel's claim to have slept with eight women over a 24-hour period in Puerto Rico for a $1,000 bet. The legend has it that he got his thousand bucks.

At the height of his fame, Evel said he was forced to hire bodyguards just to keep over-keen women at bay. 'I was very promiscuous in those days. Hell, I had to hire guards to stand out-side my hotel room just to keep women away. I mean, everywhere I went I had to hire guards to fend them off. I even had two women fighting over me in a bar once, pulling each other's hair and every-thing. I thought it was funny as hell so I ordered a beer and just watched them. I took the winner to my room but I had to kick her out because she scratched my back too much – and that's not easy to explain to your wife.'

Knievel was such an icon to men and women alike in the 1970s that some men, quite incredibly, would send their wives or girl-friends to sleep with Evel just to be able to say they had done it. And the sexual daredevil was powerless to help himself, believing as he did that 'If God made anything more beautiful than a woman, He kept it to himself.'

That compliment to the fairer sex did not, however, extend to what Knievel saw as the scourge of Seventies society – women's liberation groups. He positively hated them, representing as they did everything Knievel thought a woman should *not* be. The Butte that Knievel was brought up in had been a man's town, somewhat lacking in any form of feminist movement and a place where women were the homemakers (or prostitutes) and men were the breadwinners. Knievel's views seem terribly sexist in today's liberal climate but he was very much a man of his time – and place – when it came to his outlook on feminist groups. 'I treat women the way I always did, except I treat the women's libbers different: if I catch one, I try and screw her a little harder. A woman's place is in the bedroom and in the kitchen and taking care of her kids. I think the ones making all the noise are the ones who've had problems with men.'

Even in the late 1990s Evel still felt a deep dislike for feminists and could be easily encouraged into a verbal tirade against them. 'Women's lib groups are a pain in the ass. I just don't like 'em. Most of them are gay and they're ugly. They look like truck drivers – like tacklers in a football team.'

Presumably the six erotic dancers (three for the afternoon and three for the evening) once supplied by the owners of a strip club for Knievel's pleasure did not count themselves part of the feminist movement; nor did the six ladies dressed only in red, white and blue Harley-Davidson T-shirts who were strategically positioned on the bed in Evel's boat on one occasion when he entered his cabin. Nor were the strings of nurses he says he conquered during his three years in hospital. 'I was pleasured by nurses more than once,' he confessed. 'We would get real friendly and one thing would lead to another, especially with the ones who gave me a bath.'

Perhaps such easy access to women affected his attitude towards them; an attitude which at times could border on paranoia. 'You know, women are the root of all evil, and I know – I am Evel. Look at Adam and Eve; it wasn't Adam who picked up the apple, was it? Genghis Khan – brought down by a woman. That ain't going to happen to me.'

Evel claims his sexual appetite eventually became so uncontrollable that he had to seek professional help, and while consulting a therapist he took time out to massage his own ego by asking why women found him so attractive. 'It got to be a real problem. I had to see a psychiatrist. I asked him why it was that women kept throwing themselves at me and he explained it like this. He said, "Look, to start with you are not a bad-looking guy. Secondly, your identity is danger; women, their chemistry, are attracted to danger. Then, you are Evel by name but not by nature, so you won't harm them. Women unhappy at home looking for an affair are just drawn to you like a magnet. You stick out like a sore thumb." I guess he was right; I'm not bragging, it was true.'

While Knievel was happy to boast that he'd slept with more than 2,000 women, he took great offence at anyone who claimed to have bettered his tally. When a reporter reminded him that Harlem Globetrotter basketball legend Wilt Chamberlain claimed to have slept with 20,000 women, Evel snarled, 'Use the mathematics. How do you get to 20,000? He's full of shit. He's a liar. Wilt Chamberlain is a fucking liar.'

Through all his womanising, Evel's wife Linda remained loyal and continued to bring up their children back home in Butte, however humiliated she must have felt about her husband's infidelities. Although Linda made a habit of shying away from any media attention, she did occasionally explain her feelings about her relationship with Evel. 'I used to be bitter and resentful . . . I always had a smile on my face, but inside I was really hurting so

I came to a low point in my life. I had not a good self-image of myself – I felt like I couldn't do anything right. I used to pray "Oh God, please change my husband", and He says, "No, Linda, *you* change."'

For his part, Evel always sang Linda's praises in public, making it more difficult to understand why he continued to humiliate her with his actions. 'I was always very proud to enter any place with my wife on my arm,' he would say. 'I always thought she was the most beautiful woman in the world.' Yet clearly she was not beautiful enough to command his loyalty.

Knievel also loved to boast about how domesticated Linda was and how well she looked after him and would often come out with comments like, 'She says she has only one job in life – to serve me.' Today, such a comment would produce guffaws of laughter – not to mention outrage in our climate of sexual equality – but Evel's attitude was quite typical of the time, a fact which he himself realises. Looking back on his infidelities and chauvinistic attitude, he shows no remorse, only admitting that 'That's the way it was back then. What's done is done.'

Sadly for Linda, she had more to worry about than her errant husband as 1972 drew to a close. Having done all within his powers to stop her marrying Knievel, Linda's father, John Bork, had grudgingly grown to like the daredevil to the point where the pair enjoyed hunting and fishing trips whenever Evel's hectic schedule permitted. It was on such a trip in Montana on 18 November that tragedy struck. Evel had taken Kelly and Robbie along with the 63-year-old Bork to the Madison River in Ennis, Montana to hunt duck. As the water turned rough, Bork instructed Knievel to head for shore, but before they could make it the raging river capsized their boat, spilling the party into the water. While Knievel desperately held on to his youngest son Robbie, Bork bravely managed to haul Kelly to safety but was then immediately carried away by the raging river and drowned. 'It's the most helpless feeling in the world,' Knievel later confessed, 'to see somebody that you love floating away from you in the river and there's nothing you can do.'

Bork's drowning must have been particularly heartbreaking for Knievel. Here was a man prepared to risk his own life on so many occasions, but in this instance nature took over and there was simply nothing he could do but watch helplessly and save his own sons. It is safe to assume that Knievel would not have thought twice about risking life and limb to save his father-in-law but that would have meant putting his sons at too great a risk. It must have been an agonising situation and one that played on his mind for many years to come. With Evel also having lost the grandfather who raised him earlier in the year, there were no celebrations in the Knievel household that Christmas.

Prior to the boating tragedy, Knievel had enjoyed a particularly successful run in the latter half of 1972. His last jump of the year was an attempt to break his own outright record by clearing 22 cars. While a lack of speed forced him to land on the safety deck on top of the last car, the 21 vehicles that he did manage to clear was to be the most he ever would – at least with the cars being placed end-to-end. For his first big jump of 1973, Evel announced he was going to leap over 50 cars at the Los Angeles Memorial Coliseum, but there was a catch – the cars would be crushed together two- and three-high and not laid out in a consecutive line, so the total distance equated to no more than that of about 18 cars placed end-to-end.

More than 23,000 people turned out to witness the event after Knievel spent a good deal of time in Los Angeles promoting his jump on television and radio. While there he had also agreed to help promote the wearing of crash helmets by filming a short piece with *Easy Rider* star Peter Fonda, which featured the two men riding around road cones in the Coliseum. Evel was not, however, overly concerned with his own safety if reports of him speeding down the Hollywood Freeway at well over 100mph were to be believed. But to his credit, Knievel was always willing to help promote the 'ride safe' message, for the benefit of both kids on push-bikes and older fans on their motorcycles.

What proved to be more dramatic than the distance covered at the Coliseum were the ramps Knievel employed to reach the necessary speed. As he had done at the Cow Palace, Evel built a huge 200-foot ski-jump-style ramp down from the uppermost reaches of the stadium's seating area, but unlike the set-up at the Palace he also employed another ski ramp at the other end of the stadium to allow him to slow down – or at least that was the plan. In the event, Knievel was travelling so fast that, despite deploying his drogue parachute from the rear of the bike on landing, he flew right up the landing ramp and over the top of it, effectively making a second jump before coming to rest against a barrier, unhurt.

For anyone who has ever ridden a motorcycle, the prospect of riding one up or down either of those narrow ramps would be terrifying enough, not to mention doing so at the speeds required to make the jump successfully. Riding up it in the rain would be an even more daunting task and it was one that caught Knievel out too. While testing the ramp before his big jump, Evel's bike slipped near the top before his helpers 'Big Bob' and Mike Draper could catch the handlebars. Evel and his Harley toppled backwards over five rows of seats, and when he came to rest Knievel found he had broken a finger. He remained undaunted as usual and the show went ahead as planned.

Overall, the jump was a runaway success and, somewhat amazingly, 1973 remained almost injury-free with Knievel's only real damage being a fractured hand, bruised back and bruised kidneys, which were all sustained in a crash at the Wisconsin International Raceway in Kaukauna on 7 October. He successfully cleared all of his other jumps in some 14 events during the year.

By now, Evel was more acutely aware than ever that his routine jumping tours needed to be backed up by the promise of something bigger, something more outrageous, and since he'd been talking about it since 1967 he decided he had to start making firm plans and even set a date for the most daring and hyped event of his entire career – he was going to jump over a canyon.

Evel's plan to jump the Grand Canyon may have been foiled but he was still determined to jump *a* canyon, and throughout 1973 the momentum continued building towards that goal. Knievel had found a suitable replacement for the Grand Canyon in the Snake River Canyon, which, for part of its length, runs close to Twin Falls in Idaho. He had visited the area as a child with his grandparents and knew that, while it was nowhere near as famous or iconic as the Grand Canyon, it would serve his purpose – and would even make things easier for him. While the Grand Canyon ranges from two to 18 miles wide and can be up to 5,700 feet deep, the Snake River Canyon was less than a mile wide and just 600 feet deep at the spot Knievel planned to jump. It was a formidable gap nonetheless, and a full 1,459 feet further than any jump Knievel had attempted before, at least on a conventional motorcycle.

Because the Grand Canyon plan had been scuppered over rights to use the land on either rim, Knievel made sure he would have no such problems in Idaho. Although he often boasted that he had 'bought a canyon' to make sure the jump would go ahead, he actually just leased 300 acres of land on either side from local landowners at a price of $37,000, thus ensuring he would at least be allowed to jump, should he be able to organise every other aspect of the ambitious plan. Knievel had organised a three-year lease, which ran from October 1971 until September 1974: if he hadn't jumped by then he would have to part with even more cash. The pressure was on.

Having secured the land, Knievel's attention turned to transport. Just what sort of motorcycle could get him across the 1,600-foot gap he had to bridge? Certainly no ordinary production motorcycle. Early wild ideas revolved around some sort of standard motorcycle fitted with additional propulsion, such as a steam-powered booster rocket. Evel did have a few unconvincing lash-ups made to promote the event, the most laughable being a mock-up Harley-Davidson three-wheeler trike with what looked like a jet engine mounted precariously on the back. Knievel envisioned building a massive run-up ramp measuring 740 feet in length and angled at 40 degrees, allowing him to attack the jump like he had all others but with the addition of a jet boost at the take-off point. But simple laws of physics soon proved this to be an impossible dream and Evel eventually realised he would need nothing short of a rocket to make the attempt, which was now beginning to look more like a short flight than a long jump.

Knievel received a letter from a rocket engineer called Doug Malewicki offering his services to design and build a small rocket that would be capable of launching Knievel across the canyon. Evel took an interest and asked Malewicki to put in some groundwork on the idea and get back to him. The result was the X-1, a 12-foot-long contraption looking like a mini jet-fighter, with no wings, two wheels and a set of stabilisers. The two wheels were where any comparison with a motorcycle ended but by now Knievel had accepted that the jump was simply not possible on a real bike, however heavily modified.

The X-1 had been revealed at the proposed Snake River jump site in 1972 – the year Knievel had first proposed to make the jump there. He had, due to so many unforeseen problems, been forced to postpone the attempt and set another provisional date for early 1973. This too was cancelled and Knievel would then not be drawn on a date any further than saying, 'I'll jump the canyon when I'm ready to do it. And I'm not ready to die yet.'

In fairness, much of the credit for the Snake River attempt must go to Malewicki as it was he who suggested the rocket idea, the nature of the near-vertical take-off ramp and the use of steam to power the X-1 (because it was cheaper, safer and more reliable than liquid fuels). But working with Evel Knievel was never easy, as Malewicki found out, and, after a series of arguments, he walked away from the project leaving Knievel with a basic plan for the attempt but no one with the necessary experience to develop it and make it happen.

With America's space programme still in full swing in the early 1970s, it was to Apollo 13 astronaut Jim Lovell (played by Tom Hanks in the 1995 movie *Apollo 13*) that Knievel turned to for advice. Lovell recommended a rocket specialist called Robert C. 'Bob' Truax, who Knievel boasted had worked with NASA on 'all the big space stuff right from the start'. Truax was a rocket and water-propulsion specialist, having once been president of the American Rocket Society and having been involved in the development of the Polaris missile with the Naval Research Laboratory, but he had never actually been employed by NASA. Even so, Truax was accustomed to working with sufficient budgets to see his projects through, but was soon to find out that getting money from Knievel was a tougher job than rocket science. The issue would lead, rather predictably, to more arguments and confrontations.

Truax's first priority was to arrange a test shot of Malewicki's X-1 to get a basic understanding of what he was dealing with, and whether or not the concept held any promise, which Truax already doubted. A massive earthworks project had long been underway on the rim of the Snake River Canyon to construct a base, angled at 40 degrees, for Knievel's take-off ramp. On top of this, Truax and his crew built a 740-foot ramp angled at 22 degrees for the test launch of the X-1. The unmanned craft blasted off the ramp safely but then spun round and headed nose-first down into the murky green Snake River.

If anything, the test served to prove just how brave Knievel was and just how dangerous the stunt was going to be, but it was only a half-hearted attempt, as Truax was fully aware. Although he used steam to power the craft, he only applied 1,300 lbs of thrust instead of the 5,000 lbs he had calculated as being necessary to clear the canyon. The angle of the launch ramp too would eventually be adjusted to a much steeper 56 degrees. The first test may have been a failure but it was certainly not an end to Knievel's dream, and, while the X-1 lay at the bottom of the riverbed for several months, Truax went back to the drawing board and worked on a second craft, which he naturally enough dubbed the Sky Cycle X-2.

Truax set to work in his premises in Saratoga, California building two Sky Cycles, one for an unmanned test and the other for Knievel's bona fide attempt on the canyon. The basic shape and principles of the X-2 were the same as Malewicki's X-1, but it was in a host of small modifications that the two designs differed. The new craft had three wheels and an open cockpit as opposed to an enclosed one, and, rather than being laid flat on his stomach, Knievel would sit like a regular pilot, though he would have a set of handlebars to hang on to, even though they served no steering purpose. The aerodynamics were improved for stability and efficiency and Evel would have a very small amount of steering control via two foot pedals which operated two small flaps on the X-2's nose.

Despite the fact that Knievel would eventually brag that the building of the X-1, two X-2s and the construction of the launch pad had cost him $1 million, Truax was still forced to use very basic technology to stay within Evel's tight budget. According to author Steve Mandich, the X-2 was built around a Navy bomber fuel-tank and was, in places, held together with nothing more than bailing wire. Mandich even reports the use of a lid from a can of dog food as part of a valve mechanism. Knievel himself seemed perfectly aware of the lash-up nature of the X-2, cheerfully referring to it as a 'tin can'.

The craft was 13 feet long and weighed in at 600 kilos, about the weight of three average sports motorcycles. Because Knievel would have so little control over its flight, the X-2 was actually registered with the FAA as an unmanned rocket, while the State of Idaho considered it an aeroplane and registered it as such.

With the Snake River jump date finally being confirmed as 8 September 1974, Knievel allowed Truax to continue his work as he himself embarked on yet another tour of the country to perform more jumps, rake in some much-needed cash, and promote the canyon attempt. Throughout 1974, Knievel would use every last ounce of the considerable promotional talent he possessed to hype the jump, and he was so successful that by the time 8 September came around he was the most talked-about man in the United States. Knievel mania was about to reach new heights.

The roller-coaster ride began on 17 February when Evel cleared 11 Mack trucks at the Green Valley Raceway in North Richland Hills, Texas. The event was covered by ABC for its *Wide World of*

*Sports* programme and viewers saw Evel almost completely over-shoot the landing ramp and slam down hard at its furthest end, just managing to avoid a crash.

The Knievel steamroller then moved on to Portland's Memorial Coliseum on 29 March, where Evel officially announced the Snake Canyon jump date of 8 September. Incredibly, with so much at stake over the canyon he also announced he would be making a further seven jumps leading up to the big day with the last being just nineteen days before the canyon attempt. It was accepted that Knievel never missed a chance to make money but it must have been obvious even to him that if he was badly hurt in any of those later jumps then everything he had organised for the canyon would have been for nothing. But then every jump carried risk, both financially and physically, and, to a mentality like Knievel's, the canyon was just another jump. If it happened to be more danger-ous than the others, well, he'd better make what he could now and spend it all the quicker.

Knievel had an unlikely ally in his quest for world domination in 1974 – rubber dolls. Rubber dolls in his own image, to be precise. First released in 1973, sales of the Ideal Toy Company's Evel Knievel action figures and toy motorcycles went through the roof as Evel mania swept the States and started spreading further afield once news of his outrageous canyon plan was broadcast round the world.

The toys were such a success that to this day many people remember the Evel Knievel toy they had as a child as much, if not more, than they remember the man himself. Such was the ingenu-ity of the toys that they were bought and enjoyed by kids who had never even heard of Evel Knievel, just because they were so much fun. The first model to be released was the standard $10.97 Stunt

Cycle, accompanied by a seven-inch bendy action figure with removable helmet and hands moulded into a grip-shape to clutch the bike's handlebars. The bike itself was mounted onto a 'Gyro-Powered Energizer' which, when turned furiously, wound up such momentum in the rear wheel of the bike that the bike sped off the device when a release button was pushed. After that, a child's imagination was the limit when it came to choosing obstacles to jump. Toy cars, flights of steps, Airfix models, scraps of burning twigs at the bottom of the garden . . . anything which came to hand was fair game. The thrill of seeing Evel losing his grip on the bike (which, like the real thing, happened more often than not) and wiping out was to be cheered as enthusiastically as any safe landing, in true parallel with Knievel's own real-life audiences.

Recognising the potential gold mine it was sitting on, Ideal quickly followed the Stunt Cycle with more increasingly bizarre models as they cashed in on the craze they had engineered. The Evel Knievel Dragster car, complete with working parachute, was released in 1974, as was the Stunt Stadium which included a ramp and an audience painted into the grandstands. There was also the Stunt World Set, which actually featured three-dimensional obstacles for the action figure to negotiate, but the strangest of the play sets had to be the Escape from Skull Canyon Set, which included a werewolf doll, lots of rocks and boulders and a plethora of skulls hanging in the trees. Quite what Evel was supposed to achieve in this set remains a mystery.

But there were more down-to-earth items released over the next three years. The Evel Knievel Chopper may not have been very practical to jump in real life but it still made for a collectible toy, and the Stunt and Crash Car was designed to break into segments upon impact. The Super Jet and Canyon Sky Cycles were nods to the Snake River attempt, and the Strato Cycle (which would be released in 1977) was based on a bike used in Evel's movie from the same year, *Viva Knievel!* Ideal even made a Scramble Van based on Knievel's own touring rig, and a Road and Trail Adventure Set, but the firm really began pushing the envelope with the totally bizarre Evel Knievel Arctic Explorer Set, and the Rescue Set that saw Evel dressed in his star-spangled jumpsuit and equipped with a fire extinguisher and radio!

Sadly, one toy Evel dreamed up never actually made it into production, as he explained with his tongue placed firmly in his cheek. 'One toy I'd like them to make is my own idea; I think it's the most super toy in the world. You wind it up, it goes like a little bugger, goes across the floor, grabs this little Barbie doll, throws her on the floor, gives her a little lovin', jumps back on the motorcycle and goes whizzing out the door screaming "GI Joe is a faggot!"'

However tenuous some of the links between Knievel and the products, both he and Ideal made a fortune from their sales, which outstripped sales of all Barbie and GI Joe dolls put together. It has been estimated that the branded toys grossed beyond $300 million over a ten-year period, and they unquestionably became one of the most popular toy lines of the 1970s.

Knievel claimed he was the first to have a toy made in his likeness and he seemed extremely proud of the fact. 'I was the first real person to be the subject of a successful action figure and toy line. To those youngsters, Evel Knievel was Batman, Superman and Captain Marvel rolled into one.'

As Ideal ran out of ideas for action figures and play sets, they began churning out other Knievel merchandise, including four-inch, die-cast precision miniatures of Knievel on various motorcycles, some based on his real bikes, some purely fantastical. The firm also produced a board game called the Evel Knievel Stunt Game in which players performed different stunts with an action figure and Stunt Cycle as they worked their way round the board.

Rival companies were not slow in trying to grab a slice of the market either, and the Addar model company jumped in with plastic scale-model kits of Knievel on various bikes, including the Sky Cycle. As well as this, no Seventies star was truly a star unless they had a plastic lunchbox made in their honour, and Alladin Industries were only too happy to oblige on this front, while the Ben Cooper company even marketed an Evel Knievel Halloween costume for kids, complete with a rubber Evel mask.

In an age before computer games had taken over amusement arcades, the pinball machine was king, and the Bally Manu-facturing Corporation would cater for Knievel fans and pinball aficionados alike by launching the Evel Knievel pinball machine on 27 September 1976. Knievel became only the third individual to have a pinball machine named after them: while rock groups like the Rolling Stones and Kiss already had themed machines, only country singer Dolly Parton and legendary ice-hockey player Bobby Orr could claim the honour as individuals.

The Knievel machine was the first fully electronic commercial pinball game ever produced, and, like the Ideal toys, it was a run-away success. It became the first Bally game to sell over 10,000 units and went on to sell 14,000 units in total. A scaled-down version for home use was also designed and built, but, for reasons that will later become clear, it never actually went on sale.

Various other firms, too numerous to mention, jumped on the bandwagon to produce Evel Knievel pillowcases, bed sheets and matching curtains, rubbish bins, tyre-mounted radios, T-shirts, baseball caps, Thermos flasks, belt buckles, bicycles, bedside lamps, beach towels, drinking straws, key-rings, and even a Sky Cycle electric toothbrush with the toothbrush mounted on a replica of the ramp built at the canyon. For a time in Knievel's heyday it was harder to find a product without his name on it than one with. And as far as he could keep track of them all, Knievel made sure he got his share of the profits. By 1974, as Evel prepared for the most audacious jump of his career, the money was simply rolling in.

# 7
# Million-Dollar Drunk

**'If you think Jesus had a Last Supper, wait until you see mine. I plan a party that will leave mankind breathless.'**

Evel Knievel liked to think big. A crazy idea like jumping over a canyon is always guaranteed to receive some coverage in the media, whoever attempts it, but there is no way that the Snake River Canyon event would have created anywhere near the amount of public interest that it did, had Knievel not been a natural-born showman and promoter.

He wasn't just content for television cameras to capture the event and show it on the evening news, nor did he plan to settle for a few hundred live ticket sales at the remote location of the jump site. Evel wanted nothing less than to make his jump the biggest pay-per-view sporting event in history, hoping that punters all over the world would buy tickets to attend movie theatres where they could watch the jump live on closed-circuit television.

Knievel planned to sell 200,000 tickets at the jump site itself, turning the sleepy neighbourhood of Twin Falls, Idaho into a latter-day Woodstock on two wheels. Knievel was already a huge name but Snake River was set to make him a living legend, as well as a truck-load of cash from the TV rights, ticket sales, appearance fees and related merchandising.

Knowing his star was shining at its brightest, Knievel kept up his public appearances and his jumping, determined not to let the momentum slip. After clearing 16 vehicles (nine cars and seven vans) in Portland in March 1974, he cleared 10 Mack trucks in Fremont, Irvine, Kansas City, Tulsa, and in West Salem, Ohio. These jumps were risky enough, given that the canyon attempt was just months away and any serious injury could have seen it cancelled at huge financial loss, but Knievel's very last jump – just three weeks before his big day – seemed completely unnecessary and insanely risky. He headed north to Canada in a bid to break his own record by jumping 13 Mack trucks at the Canadian National Exhibition in Toronto.

As a warm-up to Evel's jump, Robbie and Kelly (now 12 and nearly 14 respectively) both performed wheelies round the stadium, all decked out in mini Evel-style suits and capes. The 21,500 audience loved it, and, at that point at least, Evel seemed to love it too, sounding very emotional as he introduced his sons over the PA system. After addressing the crowd and reminding them that this was his last performance before the canyon assault, Knievel easily soared over the 105-foot gap between the ramps and left Canada triumphant, ready to focus his thoughts entirely on the big one.

Earlier in the year, the huge organisational effort required for the canyon jump meant that, for the first time in his career, Knievel had been forced to bring in some outside help to promote the event. It's not that he lacked the ability to deal with such a task (he once claimed, quite accurately, that he was better than P.T. Barnum and Colonel Parker put together), he simply didn't have the time. Evel brought in Bob Arum, who owned 75 per cent of the biggest boxing promotions company in the world, Top Rank Inc. Arum also acted as Muhammad Ali's attorney and manager and was the recognised king of closed-circuit television promotions. Arum in turn brought in a certain Sheldon 'Shelly' Saltman to help with promotional duties. It was a move that would have grave consequences for Knievel some years later.

The trio arranged an exhausting, non-jumping, promotional tour during the summer of 1974, which would see Evel take in 62 cities in just 15 days at a cost of $350,000. It was rather sensationally billed as the 'Evel Knievel says Goodbye Tour', and Knievel, Arum, Saltman and a select band of others flew by Learjet to all the venues, starting with the Rockefeller Center in New York on 24 June.

It was during this tour that Knievel released more detailed plans of the upcoming event to hundreds of journalists all over the United States, as well as revealing how much money he expected to make from it. In New York, Arum presented Knievel with a cheque for $6 million – supposedly his guaranteed advance on royalties for the closed-circuit television rights alone. It was later revealed that the cheque was simply a publicity stunt and Knievel's actual advance was more in the region of $250,000. Arum was still expecting to gross $32 million all-in from the deals relating to the jump, with Evel claiming a $10 million share, though, as optimism gave way to reality, that figure was eventually downsized to $20 million.

Arum boasted that there had been a demand for 200,000 tickets to watch the jump live but that he'd been forced to limit sales to 50,000 by Idaho state officials. On the final day of the promotional tour on 14 July, Knievel claimed all 50,000 tickets had been snapped up the first day they went on sale, though his boast quickly proved hollow when it was revealed that the $25 tickets hadn't even gone on sale yet.

But the real big audience figures were expected to come through closed-circuit ticket sales. Knievel and Arum expected around two million people would pay $10 apiece to watch the show live in a two-hour broadcast to be shown in cinemas and theatres around the world – and Knievel expected a 60 per cent share of the profits, netting him $1,200,000.

And there were so many more ways of cashing in on the jump, and Evel always made sure he never missed out on his cut of the profits. He would receive 60 per cent of camping charges (ranging from $2 to $7.50 per head); 30 per cent of the profits from the sale of T-shirts, burgers, popcorn, hot dogs and beer; and a slice of all the action going on in Twin Falls itself, where everything from Evel Knievel posters, albums, toys and baseball caps, to EK underwear and radios were being sold. If it said Evel Knievel on it, the man himself demanded a piece of the action.

On 31 July, Knievel flew to the jump site to unveil his completed X-2 Sky Cycle to the press. He hadn't done himself any favours by using the word 'cycle' to describe his bizarre creation, as many people were disappointed when they saw it bore no resemblance to a motorcycle. It could have saved a lot of criticism if Knievel had just called it what it was – a rocket.

Bizarrely, he had become increasingly paranoid about anyone discovering the 'secrets' of the X-2. He employed security guards to stop anyone getting too close to the craft and told one reporter, 'There are hundreds of guys who want to know how this Sky Cycle works, and if they found out, everyone will be into the canyon-jumping game.'

While Knievel had sat in the extremely confined cockpit of the X-2 before, he hadn't done so with the craft in its launch position, a position of 56 degrees, which made his entry infinitely more difficult. It took the assistance of three workmen to hoist him into the machine, which would, he prayed, successfully carry him over the canyon. Sitting exactly as he would on launch day, Evel's nerves seemed to start getting the better of him. He was probably only half-joking when he shouted to Arum from the cockpit, 'Hey Bob. I don't wanna do it!', but he was deadly serious when a sponsor asked him to smile for a photograph, replying, 'Can you think of anything funny enough for me to smile about being up here?'

Following the press call, Bob Truax and his team performed a static firing of the X-2's power-up system. The engine fired on the third attempt and a massive burst of steam spewed from the tailpipe, so powerful that it blasted rocks and rubble for yards in all directions, forcing Evel to take cover behind a tree. He was reported to have emerged looking pale and saying, 'And I'm going to ride that thing? Over there?'

The next logical step was to fire the test model X-2 over the canyon in order to assess the chances of Knievel surviving the leap. For reasons never adequately explained, the press were not informed of the test and it was carried out in secret on 25 August, just two weeks before the jump date. Like the X-1 before it, the X-2 plummeted straight down into the canyon, but there was at least a reason for this: it was only fired at half power using around 2,500 lb of thrust. Truax claimed he was more interested in testing the parachute recovery system which would help the craft glide down to a gentle landing. Had the team already decided it was mission impossible? Were they testing the chute because they suspected the craft had no chance of making it across the gap and that Knievel would inevitably drift into the canyon? It seems odd that out of two tests with two different craft, neither one was given its full head of steam to see how far it would go. Rather, with Knievel's budget already spent and no more test rockets to fire, the team concentrated on the get-out clause – the parachute system.

Significantly, the parachute whipped out before the X-2 had even cleared the launch ramp. There were still two weeks in which to make modifications but there could be no more test shots. Knievel had already spent his allocated budget and was unwilling to commit any more money to the project, so the next craft to be fired over the Snake River Canyon would be the last remaining X-2 – and Knievel would have to be in it.

Bob Truax insisted that, while both craft may have plummeted into the depths of the Snake River, neither test had been a failure. 'Well, those two didn't really fail. We fired the first one at one-third power in order to discover if the ramp could take the punishment. The second one was fired over the rim and into the canyon on purpose. One-half power was used and we were looking to test two things – how the drag chutes would function and to see how efficient our recovery team was.'

Successful or not, Truax admitted the jump was still a huge risk. Knievel himself obviously thought that if he was going to die in the attempt he might as well go out with a bang. During his promotional tour he had revealed his plans for a 'last supper' in the week leading up to the canyon jump. 'You know what? I'm gonna try and spend a million dollars in Butte, Montana and Twin Falls, Idaho the week before I jump the canyon. A million-dollar drunk. I'm going to have the biggest party you ever saw at the Freeway Tavern in Butte. I'm going to drop one million dollars. I'm inviting Liz Taylor, the Pope, whatever the Greek husband of Jackie Kennedy calls himself, and the entire city of San Francisco. If you think Jesus had a Last Supper, wait until you see mine. I plan a party that will leave mankind breathless. I want the Pope to come. In fact, I'd pay for His Holiness to bless me before take-off time.'

As well as inviting the Pope, Knievel extended the invite to anyone else who wanted to come along. 'The Governor of Montana is already planning on calling in the California National Guard just to help him. The big party's going to start at a tavern in Butte, Montana called the Freeway, and that's where it's gonna go – right down the freeway. I spent 25 or 30 thousand dollars in Butte when my motion picture was made there. Partying and fighting. I left town because I broke both hands. Got in lots of fights, lots of 'em. You know, come back, do a picture, some guy's jealous, says something to you. Anybody say anything to me, I'll knock their goddamn head off. I knocked the heads off the Hell's Angels. I'll knock the head off any son of a bitch who opens his mouth to me.'

But Knievel's most outrageous promise was that he would bring along an armoured Brinks truck filled with $250,000 in cash and tip it out among his fans and fellow revellers outside the Freeway tavern. Those who were familiar with Knievel's often idle boasts knew better than to believe him, but the more gullible were taken in and many turned up in Butte for Knievel's last supper hoping to make it rich. Naturally, the truck never did turn up – a fact which makes a mockery of Knievel's code of living, which was always, 'if you say you're gonna do something, you do it'. That was, after all, the reason he kept giving when asked why he was going to risk his life jumping the canyon; not for the money, but because he'd *said* he was going to do it. Knievel once claimed that the thing he was most proud of in his entire life was that he'd kept his word in attempting to jump the canyon. His word about throwing $250,000 in cash to his fans was obviously less important.

Nevertheless, the party did go ahead, though on a much smaller scale than Evel had promised. Instead of throwing out cash, Knievel tossed out cans of beer from behind the bar in the Freeway Tavern to a few hundred revellers; spirits and wines were not on the house. The party moved on to the Acoma Lounge and Supper

Club, Knievel and his entourage being driven in a police car to the venue, leaving everyone else to follow by whatever means were at their disposal. Again, Evel climbed on top of the bar and tossed out free beers, but there was still no sign of any free money and disappointment was beginning to show on the faces of more than a few who had turned out. The last supper then moved on to the Met Tavern and finally the Elmar, just a few blocks from Evel's house. By three in the morning he had slipped off home and the party to end all parties was over. It was far from being a million-dollar blow-out, as Evel admitted years later. While he says he 'tried' to get through a million, he'd actually only managed to blow a few thousand dollars. It was to be the first of many disappointments surrounding the canyon jump.

Knievel continued to promote his big moment right up until the day of the event itself. As well as his jumping tour and his promotional tour, he had appeared on every television chat show that would invite him (and most did) and had spoken to every reporter who was prepared to spread the word about what Knievel was calling the sporting event of the century.

Finally, after seven years of dreaming and planning, boasting and bragging, people began turning up at the Idaho jump site in the days leading up to the event. But it was no family fairground audience that began to converge upon the canyon; the first arrivals were a motley band of bikers, and the locals began to fear the worst. The quiet town of Twin Falls (population 21,914 at the time) was situated just three miles from the jump site, and while some locals appreciated the boost for local business the event would surely provide, others were wary about reports of 50,000 wild motorcycle fans descending on their town. Situated 132 miles east of Boise, Twin Falls was founded in 1904 and by 1974 was a peaceful and relatively prosperous little town where the main concern that year had been the damage to local potato crops following a bout of frost in August. Agriculture had always been the chief source of income for those living in the fertile 'Magic Valley' and potatoes were generally of much more interest to the inhabitants of Twin Falls than Evel Knievel. But by jump week that had all begun to change as wild rumours began to circulate about the influx of people into the town. Hell's Angels would be arriving in their thousands; it would be like Woodstock but without the atmosphere of peace and love; it would just be full of drugged-up, long-haired beatniks out to cause trouble. And what was even worse for some residents was that jump week clashed with the Magic Valley Fair and Rodeo.

Despite the fact that no more than 50,000 were to be permitted at the jump site, rumours persisted that more than 200,000 people would turn up anyway, and who was going to stop them if they did? Twin Falls County Sheriff, Paul Corder, tried his best to play down the rumours and denied that huge numbers of biker gangs were camping just out of town, that two young girls had been raped and that hippies had been walking around town naked. He was, however, forced to admit that there had been some incidents of petty theft, although there was no proof that these had been committed by out-of-towners.

It must have been some consolation for the residents of Twin Falls to hear that joining the hordes of rowdies would be some of the biggest celebrities in the world – at least, they would if Knievel was to be believed. He boasted that he had invited scores of celebrities along, including Elvis Presley, John Wayne, Steve McQueen, Burt Reynolds, Dustin Hoffman, Ali McGraw and Andy Williams; and that was on top of his invite to the Pope. Unsurprisingly, none of the above-mentioned were spotted cruising the streets of Twin Falls in the week leading up to the jump, or on the jump day itself for that matter. It was simply more P. T. Barnum bravado from Knievel, the ultimate shyster.

Knievel himself was flying between Butte and the canyon site daily in the lead-up to 8 September, checking out the organisation, making last-minute refinements to the Sky Cycle, and attending to a multitude of problems which were thrown up by the scale of the project and the lack of funds which he had invested in it. It was bad enough that 50,000 people might turn up, but Knievel was still boasting of 200,000 and yet there were only 200 portable toilets built on-site and a laughable 15 public payphones. Even worse, only 65 policemen were to be brought in to keep the peace among a crowd which many feared would turn nasty. If 200,000 people did turn up, it would mean just one toilet for every thousand people, one payphone for every 13,333 people and one policeman per 3,076 people.

Sheriff Corder seemed unconcerned, however, claiming he had 600 National Guardsmen on alert as a back-up force, 250 of which would have full riot gear should things turn nasty. Knievel himself had organised his own security crew, but his overheard description of them as his 'goon squad' seemed more apt than the term 'security', given their credentials. The squad was made up of ordinary people who had arrived at the site early, had little else to do, and wanted to get closer to Knievel. Several more were hired through an advertisement in the local press. They were paid $2.50 an hour and many carried guns until Sheriff Corder stepped in and pointed out it was illegal.

Knievel was ultimately responsible for everything that happened on-site, from security to fencing and from TV rights to fast-food stalls. He had never found it easy to delegate responsibility, and, while he should have been concentrating on what was to be the most important jump of his career, he was on-site daily trying to

deal with what seemed like a thousand things at once. Rock promoter Don Branker, who was involved in promoting the event,
explained the situation. 'Top Rank aren't exactly running the
show. Evel is. All of it. Every single detail. He doesn't trust anybody about anything. He wants to do everything himself and his
response to everything is money. That's his only concern – money.
How many dollars will it cost? And how many dollars will it
bring in?'

One particular problem Knievel had to face was the growing
fear that thousands of people straining for a better glimpse of the
event could end up being pushed over the canyon rim to plummet
to their deaths. A fence had been built to counter such an event but
it was woefully inadequate. The six-foot-high chain-link fence
stood some 40 feet back from the canyon rim and ran for 1,500 feet
along it, but as its posts were not anchored in concrete it would
have been all too easy to push over, despite the planned presence of
security guards to protect it. Branker soon became horrified by
Knievel's tightfisted approach to security. 'I tried to talk him into
putting another fence along the rim for Sunday but he won't go for
that. "One fence is enough," he says, and he keeps talking about
the security men who'll be up here. "The fence costs too much," he
says. I tried to argue with him, told him that it should be carte
blanche for security, but he just said, "It's my show, not yours."'

There were other aspects of Knievel's character that Branker
objected to, and he wasn't shy in admitting it. 'After I'd worked
with him a while, though, I started noticing certain things. He has
a real tendency to exaggerate, more than any person I've ever met.
In addition to that, he himself believes everything he says. Where
I come from, that's a pathological liar.'

Knievel was even responsible for hiring people to pick up
rubbish and pulled off one particularly humiliating stroke to

humble one of his motorcycle-jumping imitators. Bob 'Wicked' Ward idolised Knievel and had stood in for him at a jump in Georgia two years previously when Knievel was injured. Knievel had always despised any form of competition, believing that since he had practically invented the 'sport' of motorcycle jumping it was his domain and his domain alone. When Ward approached his hero wide-eyed, asking for a job at the site, Knievel obliged – by paying him $2 an hour to pick up litter.

Gleefully, Ward took up the post, and in between bouts of litter-picking wasted no opportunity to tell people he was Evel Knievel's understudy; that he was ready to take over from the master should the master be killed. These boasts seemed to have escaped Knievel's ears for a time, but when Ward went one step further and painted 'Wicked Ward: Evel Knievel's Understudy' on the side of his car and cruised up to the jump site basking in his imagined glory, Knievel went crazy. Spotting him in the crowd, Knievel stormed up to Ward waving his cane and yelling, 'You sonofabitch! I want your ass out of this town by sundown. Don't ever let me see your face in a town where I'm working again!' Ward reportedly left town in tears.

By the Thursday before the jump approximately 5,000 people had gathered in and around Twin Falls. Many of them had come to take part in or watch the motocross races organised as an extra attraction, since the jump itself, however it went, would be over in a few short minutes. Further entertainment was planned for launch day itself, though only those watching on the closed-circuit tele-vision coverage would have any hope of seeing it, since all the acts would be performing near the canyon's edge, out of sight of the paying live spectators.

Bob Arum had always said that there were only two ways to watch the canyon jump: live at the site or on closed-circuit in a cinema or theatre. There was to be no coverage on network television, not even weeks after the event. Various members of the press, however, had noticed television broadcast trucks belonging to Evel's long-standing collaborators ABC parked at the jump site, and suspected another con. It looked like Knievel and Arum were trying to force people into buying theatre tickets or live gate tickets by claiming it was the only way to see the event of the century, when there had actually been a television show planned all along. As it turned out, Arum had indeed struck a deal with ABC, in which the firm would provide the cameras and team to film the event for the closed-circuit coverage free of charge and would then be allowed to use the footage one week later to air on television. Between them, Arum and Knievel never missed a trick.

Another television channel, CBS, tried to get in on the action by offering the Idaho Land Board $50,000 for use of the opposite side of the canyon to film the event. They argued that national interest in the jump was so great that it had become a news story and not just a performance, and therefore they had a right to film it. But when Bob Arum threatened to cancel the event if CBS went ahead with filming it the firm backed down, realising that there was nothing to be gained by anyone in a non-event.

ABC tried to further encourage anyone who wasn't already on the Knievel/canyon bandwagon to hop aboard by screening a new documentary, *One Man . . . One Canyon*, as well as re-running the George Hamilton movie, *Evel Knievel*, in the days leading up to the event.

As the big moment drew ever closer, the strain on Knievel began to show, and it reached a peak when he had a run-in with an NBC cameraman called Jim Watt. During a pre-jump press conference in Knievel's massive personal trailer, Watt requested that the daredevil stand up during the question-and-answer session in order that the assembled media would be able to get better pictures. Knievel, obviously nearing breaking point, exploded, 'If I wanna sit down I'm gonna sit down,' before telling Watt to get out of his trailer. After some further heated words on Knievel's part and a refusal to be humiliated on Watt's part, Knievel jammed Watt's camera into his face and struck him with his cane, knocking the diminutive cameraman to the ground and sending his camera reeling. Watt later attempted to sue Knievel for $1.1 million in damages, but nothing ever came of it and Knievel refused to back down or even apologise, simply saying of the offending cane, 'The cane is worth 20,000 dollars and I wouldn't want to waste it on an NBC cameraman.'

It was an ugly incident, but not as ugly as things turned around the jump site on the eve of the main event. Around 500 of those camping in the area embarked on a rampage, burning fast-food stands and breaking into any vehicle or trailer that contained booze, further fuelling their riot. Drunken, helmet-less bikers (Idaho had a mandatory helmet law, unlike some American states) tore up the land on their motorcycles and rode through the camp bonfires. A fire engine was also vandalised, and the only thing which prevented the Sky Cycle from being torched before the big show was the armed guards on the fenced-off launch pad. The carnage didn't cease until dawn and for many 8 September was a day to sleep off a thumping hangover in the Idaho sun, oblivious to the main event.

But for Evel Knievel it was to be the biggest day of his life. There was just one last thing he had to arrange before he tried to get some much-needed sleep. 'The night before the canyon jump I made a deal with my son Kelly. I said, "Tomorrow, when we get in the car to go the airport I want you to pretend that you left your little shaving kit in the house and you gotta run back in for it," and

I said, "I got a picture I had made for your mother here and if I get killed at the edge of the canyon I wanna make sure that this is hanging on the wall over the bed in this bedroom when she comes home." What I had done was gotten a picture of the Snake River Canyon without the Sky Cycle or the ramp or anything in it and I had written in the sky, "To my darling wife Linda – I love you" and signed it Bob.' According to Knievel, Kelly carried out his duties to the letter.

# 8
# Rocket Science

*'I think that man was put here on earth to live,
not just to exist.'*

The Idaho sun rose over the Magic Valley accompanied by a stiff 20mph wind, which not only fluttered the Old Glory flag on top of the launch ramp but coated everyone present with the dusty, dry sand of the Snake River Canyon rim. There could be no more talking, no more hype, no more planning and no more excuses: Evel Knievel was finally going to face the canyon. But there were going to be far fewer people there to see his attempt than he had imagined.

After the initial predictions of a 200,000-strong crowd had been downsized to 50,000, it was estimated that only 15,000 people turned up on jump day to witness the event live. In fairness, the remote location of the site probably contributed to the disappointing crowd figures, but given that there are few major cities with canyons running through them there was little Knievel could do about that. The show had to go on, despite the added headache of a New York congressman who was kicking up a fuss and wanted to ban the closed-circuit television coverage of the event. Republican

John M. Murphy was concerned that Knievel's antics would inspire young children to emulate him and put their lives at risk. He complained, 'I have received newspaper reports and photos from concerned parents in Idaho which already show youngsters on bicycles and jerry-built ramps trying to perform Evel's stunts over local streams . . . One of the phone calls to my office came from a parent who felt the promotion of this event was having a bad effect on young people and that Mr Knievel was a sick individual.'

Murphy claimed he had received hundreds of letters of complaint, and in a completely over-the-top statement called Knievel a 'modern-day pied-piper of suicidal mayhem'. The Federal Communications Commission, to whom Congressman Murphy complained, refused to get involved, and the whole protest eventually fell on deaf ears. It was one problem solved but there were plenty more to contend with on jump day.

As the temperature soared above 80 degrees, the shortage of food and beer on-site, due to the looting of the night before, became ever more apparent. And there was a shortage of security men too at first light as many had left in disgust at the rioting campers. Knievel hired more, even more goonish than his first batch, selected as they were from some of the hordes of troublemakers who had that very morning been threatening to break down the fence which enclosed the launch site, the press area, Knievel's truck, the ABC television trucks, and the prototype X-1. The latter had finally been retrieved from the depths of the canyon and put on display, a grim reminder that there really was a genuine chance of Knievel meeting his doom this very day. A further reminder of the dangers – albeit an unintentional one – was the one-ton, six-foot-high granite 'monument' which had already been erected by the canyon's edge to commemorate the event, whatever the outcome. Many commented that it looked more like a tombstone than a monument, and while it bore the words, 'From this point on September 8th, 1974, Evel Knievel attempted a mile-long leap of the Snake River Canyon', it had been left with enough space to carve an epitaph should the need arise.

Evel Knievel finally made his appearance at the jump site by helicopter at around 1.45 p.m., along with Linda, Kelly, Robbie and Tracey. He made straight for his trailer, waving to the gathered and impatient crowds on the way, then was hidden from view again, determined to spend some quiet time with his family before he had to do what he'd come to do; what he'd waited seven years to do.

After a quick glimpse of their hero there was once again nothing much more for the crowd to do or see. They certainly couldn't see the sideshow acts that had begun on the canyon rim. Acts like the Karl Wallenda family who performed pyramids on a tightrope; the Sensational Parker who would swing out over the canyon on a flexible pole; the Great Manzini who would wriggle out of a straitjacket while being suspended 150 feet above the crowd by a burning rope; and Gil Eagles, who was to ride a motorcycle blind-folded along the rim of the canyon between obstacles. It was pure big-top hokum and of no more interest to those in closed-circuit theatres who could watch it than to all the ticket-paying live fans who couldn't. Even so, at least it would have given them *something* to do as they waited for their hero to reappear.

The rougher elements of the crowd took the time to make their own entertainment, most of it inspired by drink and drugs. Upon seeing a handwritten sign held aloft by one hopeful young man pleading, 'Chicks – Show Your Tits', a certain young lady obliged by removing her T-shirt. She got more than she bargained for as the crowd immediately hoisted her aloft and began stripping the remainder of her clothes off as she was passed around by mauling, desperate hands. Eventually she was stripped completely naked and was thrown over the fence into the press compound, her flesh scratched, bruised and bloody but her vacant eyes signalling that she didn't know much about what was going on.

This was the side of the Knievel Woodstock that the closed-circuit coverage choicely ignored, preferring as it did to focus on the Butte High School marching band's procession and all the other wholesome all-American carnival acts.

Finally, Knievel strutted out of his trailer, decked in his jump-day finest: the lucky red rabbit's foot attached to the zip of his leathers, the zip itself being largely undone; famous cane in hand. With his huge Elvis-style collar, the flared trouser-legs and the Harley-Davidson Old Glory Number One logo, Knievel looked more like a Las Vegas entertainer than a rocket passenger. The only giveaway was the custom-painted jet-fighter-pilot helmet he carried under his arm.

He made his way up to a platform on the launch mound over-looking the spectators to be interviewed by David Frost, who was hosting the closed-circuit television show (and would later use much of the material for the benefit of British audiences on *The Frost Interview*). Looking strained and talking much quieter than usual, Knievel told Frost, 'I think my chances now are 90 per cent. I've got a team behind me, Mr Truax and all the boys, that are 100 per cent and I think we'll do it. I wish the wind wasn't blowing so hard but I think we'll do it.'

Despite the fact that he was breathing heavily just from walking up the launch mound, Knievel insisted that he was in top shape for the jump. 'I've kept myself in good physical shape. I don't drink very much and I've never taken a narcotic and I'm ready to go. I'm in good physical shape and mentally, right now, I'm 100 per cent. I'm ready to go.'

He added that if he was going to die, then smashing himself into a canyon was about as good a way to go as any. 'I've never been afraid in my life of dying under any circumstances . . . As far as the dying goes, if I have to hit that wall over there on the other side I think that maybe I would rather do that than be the victim of a senseless tragedy. I'd rather be busted into the wind like a meteorite and not become just dust. I think that man was put here on earth to live, not just to exist, and today is the proudest day of my life.'

One of Frost's guest commentators on the broadcast was Apollo 13 astronaut Jim Lovell, who, interestingly enough, had some concerns over the X-2's parachute recovery system. Having checked over the craft on the morning of the launch and had a last-minute discussion with Knievel, he told Frost, 'We did tell him to make sure to hold the lever back on lift-off because we don't want to pre-release the drogue chute. At one time in the vehicle we had an automatic system that would release the chute. This did not work too well, as a matter of fact it released it prematurely on the last [practice] launch. So now Evel has a switch, which he must hold back with 45 pounds of pressure, and when he wants to release the chute he leaves the lever to go forward. If something happens to him and he blacks out he'll release the lever automatically and the chute will open. Of course, we don't want the chutes to be released prematurely because it would slow down the trajectory and he'd land in the river. And so that's the main thing he has to do is to hold back the lever until the proper time, which is about 10 seconds after [the launch].'

For once in his career, Knievel and his team had actually calculated the forces, distances and trajectories involved in a jump. Instead of simply eyeing up a ramp, twisting the throttle on his motorcycle and hoping for the best, he had spent many hours with his crew, calculating in great detail what was needed and how the whole thing would work. So, in theory at least, the X-2 would be launched up the take-off ramp at a 56-degree angle and would reach its maximum speed of 394mph five seconds after lift-off. By that point the engine should have burned itself out but the craft would continue soaring upwards until it reached its peak altitude, 15 seconds after the launch. The X-2 should then slow to 227mph as it levelled off. At that point, 3,000 feet up and almost a mile from the launch site, a preset gyroscope would trigger the parachute recovery system, then a drogue chute would be deployed which in turn would pull out the main parachute. The entire 'recovery' sequence should take just eight seconds but would give Evel a series of three-G jolts at each separate stage of the sequence. Twenty-three seconds and 4,700 feet after lift-off, the X-2 should be at 2,200 feet altitude and should begin floating back down to earth at a rate of 15mph, landing two minutes and three seconds after its launch. On paper at least, every last detail seemed to have been worked out, but if history has taught us anything it's that theory doesn't always translate smoothly into practice.

There really was only one way to find out if the calculations had been correct and if all would go to plan, and that was to climb into the Sky Cycle and activate the launch button – but not before asking for God's blessing. In the absence of the Pope who had mysteriously failed to respond to Knievel's invitation, Father Gerry Sullivan, reputedly a cousin of Knievel's, led a prayer asking God to deliver Evel safely across the canyon. As he finished, the national anthem was played, and, as a last attempt to tug on the heartstrings of all present, John Culliton Mahoney's 'The Ballad of Evel Knievel' blared out over the PA system, followed by Evel's recorded recital of his poem 'Why?'. His parting words to Frost as he prepared to mount the Sky Cycle would appear to have inspired a young Arnold Schwarzenegger; for as he turned his back on Frost he simply said, 'I'll be back.'

As the last words of his poem rang out, Knievel was finally hoisted up to the Sky Cycle in the 'Liberty' crane, looking for all the world like the king of the daredevils in his red metal throne as the chair he sat in swayed and twirled gently. He waved to the throngs below who waved, yelled and cheered back, some positively and others jeeringly. But whether he was eagle-eyed enough to take in one particular tribute among all the hustle and bustle is unknown. As he was being hoisted up, one man in the crowd grabbed his lady companion by the hair, forced her to her knees, popped out his manhood and 'encouraged' her to perform an indecent act. As she did so, he shouted out, 'For you, Evel – for you, man!' What benefit the act was expected to bring to Knievel is unclear.

Naturally, the television cameras avoided this incident, as they did all the other undesirable happenings in the rowdy crowd, and concentrated on Knievel's struggle to enter the cockpit of the Sky Cycle, aided again by three of his crew.

The countdown began as 700 lbs of water reached boiling point, ready to launch Knievel skywards with 5,000 lbs of thrust. Finally, after a week of milling around in hundreds and then thousands, the collective attention of the crowd that had gathered on the banks of the Snake River was fixated on whatever their vantage point allowed them to see of the flimsy-looking craft that was the X-2. Many were rooting for Evel; others were hoping for a gory crash-and-burn spectacular, but even the cynical were now captivated.

Knievel himself, though surrounded by thousands and with many hundreds of thousands more watching in cinemas all over the United States, was now completely and utterly alone. He had said goodbye to his family and it had not been a pleasant task.

'I hope that no one ever sees in their wife's eyes and in their children's eyes what I saw in my wife's eyes and my kids' eyes before that jump. My wife was petrified. And I hope nobody ever has to say a prayer like I said when I punched that fire button. I just said, "Three seconds to go. God take care of me, here I come." I know what men felt like when they stood in front of an executioner. I was a dead man. I never thought that I had a prayer. I didn't think I would get 10 feet in that thing.'

With a final countdown of 10, 9, 8, 7, 6, 5, 4, 3, 2, 1, there was then an almighty whhhooooosh as if the lids of ten thousand boiling kettles had been blasted off simultaneously. Knievel had punched the fire button, and the immense rush of pressurised steam blasted him upwards and sent huge chunks of earth, stone and debris flying 100 yards all around with tremendous force as Knievel's crew ducked for cover.

The X-2 flashed up the ramp at tremendous speed, pinning Evel back hard into the cramped cockpit seat as the crowd gasped, yelled and cheered in equal measure. He had done it. The madman had actually gone through with his promise of seven years and the X-2 looked easily fast enough to reach the other side of the canyon. Or at least it did for two seconds. Confusion reigned as the craft started twisting to the right just after launch, eventually performing a 360-degree roll while still rocketing forwards and upwards. Then it happened. The crowd were puzzled, scared and disappointed as they saw the Sky Cycle's parachute open and the craft started slowly drifting down into the canyon.

With the benefit of slow-motion replays it was clear to see that the craft's much smaller drogue chute had opened the very instant the steam was released and the rocket was thrust up the ramp. But the whole thing happened too fast to be caught by the naked eye in real time, and Knievel was already about 1,000 feet in the air before spectators realised something was wrong. As the full chute opened, the wind started blowing Knievel back into the nearside canyon wall, and Knievel, sensing the danger he was in, began struggling desperately to break free of his harness and helmet. The helmet might have helped if he was to crash into the canyon wall but it could prove lethal if he should fall into the Snake River itself.

The X-2 and Evel disappeared from sight, down into the canyon, and the once-rowdy crowd was hushed as everyone waited for news. The television commentators feared the worst, as did Knievel's family and friends and the majority of the gathered spectators. Perhaps only the Hell's Angels were rubbing their tattooed hands with glee at the prospect of ridding themselves of one of their most outspoken critics.

Two helicopters hovered low, churning up the 18-foot-deep waters of the Snake as several rescue boats honed in on the stricken daredevil. No one above the rim could yet see if he had struck the canyon wall and landed on a ledge or if he'd sunk straight into the river. Then suddenly, out of the underhang of the canyon wall, a white figure standing upright on a boat, waving up at the gathered thousands, told the story – Evel was alive and relatively unscathed. The crowd, which had been so hushed, erupted with approval at the sight.

The Sky Cycle had drifted down into the canyon at around 15mph, bounced off a rocky ledge and continued down until it had come to rest on another ledge just 20 feet from the river itself. Had it bounced just 20 feet more, Evel Knievel would almost certainly have drowned, strapped into the cockpit as he was in a five-point fighter-pilot seatbelt. He was extremely lucky to be alive.

The first man to reach Evel was an old personal friend called John Hood. He had scrambled down a rope from a helicopter onto the small canyon ledge into which Evel had crashed and helped the star into a boat, then he himself waited in turn to be retrieved. Knievel was lifted back up to the canyon rim by helicopter while the unfortunate Hood waited patiently to be rescued. By nightfall, help still hadn't arrived and it seemed that Hood had been completely forgotten amid all the furore surrounding his more famous friend. Shamefully, he was forgotten about all the following night and was forced to wrap himself in the X-2's parachute for warmth until morning, when, apparently still unmissed, he somehow managed to scale his way more than 500 feet unaided up the canyon wall to safety. Sometimes it helps to be famous.

As Knievel was set down by the helicopter back up near the launch site he was completely swamped by reporters, spectators, fans and security men. He seemed genuinely dazed and his face was bloodied from the impact of the crash landing. David Frost, professional as ever, was the first to thrust a microphone in the star's face to ask what had gone wrong. 'I don't know what happened. The machine, it turned sideways. I tried to steer and then I felt, like a brake. I didn't know the chute was open . . . the jolt I got . . . I couldn't get my seatbelt undone. Thank God I didn't go into the river. Boy, I could have never gotten out of it. It hit the shelf of rocks and then bounced into another shelf of rocks. Shit, I don't know what happened; it went sideways, it turned. Bob [Truax] told me if I saw the canyon wall and not the sky, for Christ's sake to let it go. When it turned, I let her fly. It just about knocks you out. They came and got me out down there and put me in the boat . . . I couldn't get my safety belt un-harnessed. If I'd a [sic] gone in the river I'd a [sic] never got out of it. Never.' When another reporter asked Knievel if he was going to try to jump the canyon again, he replied, 'I don't know what I'm gonna do. I sat in it and gave it my best, and . . . I don't know what to tell you.'

Evel retired to the cool sanity of his air-conditioned trailer to greet his long-suffering family, who had clearly responded to the event in very different ways. His daughter Tracey said, 'We were certain he was dead. He had prepared us for his death. When we discovered he was alive, it was more of a shock to get that news than any other.' Robbie, on the other hand, seemed to believe his father was invincible. 'I was so used to him surviving every jump that this event was no different for me. I think I would have been more shocked if he had failed.' Linda was overwhelmingly relieved and cried for joy at her husband's safe return.

Dazed and confused as he undoubtedly was immediately after the jump, Knievel could have had no idea of the far-reaching consequences of his failure to leap the Snake River Canyon. It wasn't the failure as such – after all, his audience had always thrilled to see him wipe out as much as seeing him make a perfect landing – it was the nature of the failure, in that many suspected foul play. When it became common knowledge, through pictures in the press and the television coverage which was eventually shown, that the Sky Cycle hadn't even left the launch ramp before its drogue parachute blew out, many people thought Knievel had planned it all along; that he knew he'd never make the jump (after all, the first two test shots didn't) and had decided to go along with the sham, make as much money as he could, and pull the chicken switch as soon as the rocket was fired.

To this day, Knievel seethes with rage when anyone dares to mention such a possibility. 'I waited seven years and then had an engineering mistake made, a malfunction, and the parachute blew out on take-off because of an electrical malfunction. The engineer didn't know what the hell he was doing.'

Despite all his impressive qualifications, the blame was to fall on Bob Truax – at least as far as Knievel was concerned. He claims he himself hired parachute specialists in the early days of the project and that Truax replaced them with his own people. 'That idiot fired my parachute team. He got his own parachute guy. It malfunctioned on blast-off, nearly cost me my life, cost me making it across. I should have made it a half-mile across that thing.' He added that he would 'never put my life in his [Truax's] hands again'.

It seems unfair to blame Truax, since his credentials were impeccable and Knievel had forced him to work on a shoestring budget which itself was not forthcoming. Further, Truax stood to gain a $100,000 bonus if Knievel made it across the canyon, so it seems certain that he did the very best job he could with the limited funds he was given. Even so, Knievel was so incensed about his reputation being under threat that he later appeared on a US television show called *Lie Detector* and took a lie-detector test in a bid to prove that the failed canyon attempt had not been his fault and that he hadn't copped out. For what it was worth, he passed.

Those who blame Knievel for a cop-out need to consider several issues, the first being that releasing the chute early was actually more dangerous than attempting to go all the way. A gentle 15mph landing on the opposite canyon rim – or even halfway across, down in the river – would have been much less dangerous than being blown back into the canyon wall where he could have been knocked unconscious before dropping down into the water, or even killed as the flimsy X-2 smashed into the wall. And if the chute had not opened so early, the X-2 would not have spun so dangerously as it left the ramp. It is debatable if Knievel even *could* have released the chute so instantaneously with the blast-off. Slow-motion footage shows the chute literally blowing out simultaneously with the blast of steam that sent the rocket on its way. Perhaps the tremendous force of the blast-off jolted the parachute release lever out of Evel's hands. But the one overriding factor, which Evel's critics seem to forget, is the man's reputation for having a go at anything. After all, aborted attempt or not, it took a lot of courage to be strapped into an under-developed, prototype rocket, press the fire button and be launched 1,000 feet into the air above a deep, craggy and watery canyon.

In a sense, Knievel couldn't have won either way, as he often admitted. 'If I had made it across that canyon, people would have said, "See, that was easy." If I had died, they would've just said a daredevil died – Evel Knievel – it was his last big jump. But excuse me – I'm still alive.'

If Evel had proved anything in his career it was that he wasn't afraid of getting hurt and he wasn't afraid to get back up and try again. There is no reason to think he did not also give the canyon jump his best shot. Knievel is the only man who will ever know if his courage left him at the crucial moment, and he will never admit to it if it did. Even 30 years after the event he values his reputation too much to damage it by admitting to any weakness. It seems that in the case of the canyon he must be given the benefit of the doubt. He did, after all, *attempt* to jump it, and that's what he'd always promised he would do. That fact remains his proudest achievement – the fact that he had kept his word after seven years of promises.

The Snake River attempt made worldwide headline news on 9 September, overshadowed only by the news that President Ford had pardoned former president Nixon over the Watergate scandal. Estimates as to how much money Knievel actually made from the attempt vary greatly. Certainly the $6 million cheque was proved to have been a mere publicity stunt, but he still claimed to have made between $2.5 and $3 million from the jump.

The crowd on the day had been disappointing, and closed-circuit television sales had returned much less revenue than expected. The event was only broadcast in 250 venues, not the 400 that had originally been envisioned, and at least one showing had to be cancelled due to poor ticket sales. Even Bob Arum declared the response to Snake River very disappointing, and admitted that the overall gross was in the region of $4 million rather than the $32 million he and Knievel had been hoping to make.

Whatever anyone's personal opinion on whether or not Evel Knievel faithfully attempted to jump the Snake River Canyon, one fact remains: no one else has ever been mad enough to try the stunt, despite there being a wealth of Evel imitators out there, and it's a fact not lost on the man himself. 'There's all kinds of guys said they wanted to jump that canyon. And God hasn't moved it one inch. Not one inch! And I don't see no big long line of daredevils standing out there wanting to try it.'

# 9
# London Calling

## 'I was a mess after Wembley. I was hurt bad.'

If notorious American gangster Bugsy Siegel had not had the vision to create Las Vegas in the mid-1940s, Evel Knievel would probably have done it for him. Never was a city more suited to an individual than Vegas was to Knievel. The glitz, the glamour, the gambling, the hustle, the shows, the bars, the girls, the sheer unashamed gaudiness of the city captivated Knievel more than any other place on earth.

He had already been making regular trips to the Nevada oasis to watch world championship boxing matches before he turned himself into a star in Vegas by jumping over the fountains at Caesar's Palace. As he made more money, so he made more and more trips to Vegas, often flying in a group of friends in his Learjet to party for days and weeks on end. Knievel considered himself the biggest gambler that Vegas had ever seen, not because of the amount of money he threw around the craps tables, but because he felt he had gambled his life there in 1967 when trying to jump the fountains.

At the heart of his fascination with the city was his love of gambling. Throughout his adult life Knievel was a compulsive gambler who would bet on practically anything, the more bizarre the better. Legend has it he once bet the tip of his own finger on a single putt in a golf match, and having lost the stroke he chopped the end of the finger off with a shovel, it being the only sharp object at hand. The finger was later, according to the legend, sewn back on.

On another occasion, while heavily under the influence of his favourite poison, Wild Turkey, Knievel bet his friend Wayne Newton $10,000 that the reclusive multi-billionaire Howard Hughes was dead because no one had seen him for so long. The bet stuck for several months until, according to Knievel, Hughes chartered Knievel's Learjet to fly to Houston, Texas and was found dead on arrival, proving that he had actually been alive at the time the bet was placed. Knievel found the circumstances so incredible and darkly amusing that he happily coughed up the ten grand, which was easily covered by his charter fee anyway.

Knievel had even bet the famous tennis hustler Bobby Riggs that Riggs could not set out from Las Vegas on a Harley-Davidson under 200cc (Riggs had never ridden a bike before) and arrive at the Snake River Canyon, which was 616 miles away, within 72 hours and in time for Knievel's jump attempt. Riggs immediately took, and passed, his motorcycle test and turned up at the Snake River jump site a day early. Knievel was forced to stump up $25,000, which Riggs later donated to charity.

Playing golf offered Knievel almost endless opportunities to bet and he took every one of them. Rules would be set before the start of every round: if your ball went in the water you paid all the other players $100; if you landed in a bunker it cost $250; if your ball landed in the rough it cost you another $250, and so on. But there were ways to win back lost money too – if any player managed to hit a duck or bird and kill it, for example, he could expect to receive $1,000 from each player.

The tales of Evel's gambling have become part of the myth that surrounds him and only he knows for sure how many of them are true, how many are exaggerated and how many are complete figments of his talent for spinning tall tales: 'I once won $50,000 on a round of golf, beat this guy one up.' 'I lost $250,000 at blackjack once. Didn't hurt though, cos I had $3 million in the bank at the time.' 'I won $100,000 betting on football in one year alone.'

But the stakes weren't quite so high when one particular journalist joined Knievel and his friend Chuck Cosgriff for a round of golf shortly before the Snake River jump. Having heard all the tall tales surrounding Knievel's gambling, the journalist was extremely disappointed to report that Evel only 'won $5 from Cosgriff on the afternoon, an afternoon in which the betting ran to hundreds of dollars but finally cancelled out nearly even. So much for those $1,000-a-hole golf matches that have entered the legend.'

While he always maintained he was a man of his word, Knievel was never averse to stacking the odds in his favour when it came to gambling. For years he carried a silver dollar with heads on both sides. Not surprisingly, he claims to have never lost a coin toss in his life. Yet despite his apparent recklessness, Knievel believed he was a 'sensible' gambler, if there can be such a thing. 'I like to gamble and I am good, but I am no maniac. If I had just a dollar left I would bet 50 cents but not the whole dollar. That kind of gambling is for snivelling failures.'

It is no surprise that Knievel was so fond of gambling, given the nature of his chosen profession. No matter how many safety measures he took before a jump (and they were few), when he twisted the throttle of his motorcycle and aimed for a take-off ramp or the edge of a canyon, the end result was always a gamble. If he landed his bike safely it was counted as a win and he was suitably rewarded financially. If he wiped out he still got paid, but his penalty for 'losing' was a whole lot of pain and weeks or months spent recuperating. Almost everything Evel Knievel ever did was a gamble to a certain extent, and in 1975 he took a new gamble with his career in deciding it was time to try a new market: Knievel flew to the UK for his first-ever performance outside the United States.

While he was still massively popular with the kids in America, his Snake River failure had taken its toll on Knievel's reputation with his older and more cynical followers. The UK promised a fresh, new market where he figured he might possibly meet with less cynicism. It also promised to be a lucrative visit as his planned eight-venue tour was set to net him $250,000. But there were reasons other than money that tempted him across the Atlantic, as he explained: 'I'd never been to England and wanted to go. In Europe, I'd only been to France, with Jackie Stewart and Princess Grace's brother for the French Grand Prix. I wanted to tour all of Europe because my great-grandparents were from Germany and I wanted to jump the Berlin Wall. I also wanted to jump the River Thames but political bullshit put an end to that.'

The original plan had indeed been to restore the Sky Cycle and launch it over the Thames from Battersea Park with the aim of landing in the grounds of the Royal Hospital in Chelsea, an idea which now sounds quite absurd. If Knievel had organisational headaches in such an isolated spot as the Snake River Canyon they were going to be multiplied a thousand-fold in central London, and so it proved. Instead of simply being able to lease a stretch of land on both sides of a canyon, to jump the Thames Knievel would have needed permission from various authorities including the

Port Authority, the Water Authority, the Department of the Environment, the Pollution Authority and the Metropolitan Police. It clearly wasn't going to happen in bureaucratic Britain but happily there were other obstacles that could be jumped and in more convenient places too.

Working with British television stalwart David Frost on the canyon jump had clearly paid dividends for Knievel as the relationship indirectly led to his UK trip. Frost owned a promotional company that was handled by British promoter John Daly, and, having commentated on the canyon coverage, Frost suspected the brash American could be a hit in the UK – if only the team could decide on a suitable spectacle.

Aside from the River Thames and the Berlin Wall, Knievel ludicrously talked of jumping the English Channel, having presumably never seen it and thus not realised that the only way he could 'jump' it would be in his Learjet. It was finally decided that a standard motorcycle jump in a controlled environment would be the only realistic option in the centre of Britain's capital, and where better to stage it than the then-home of English football, Wembley Stadium.

With the venue having been decided on, Knievel then announced in a superb promotional flourish that he would not be jumping cars, vans or Mack trucks in the capital's stadium, but 13 traditional red London buses, before moving on to perform in Birmingham, Sheffield, Glasgow, Bristol, Portsmouth and Southend, then winding up the tour, very appropriately, in Blackpool – England's seedier seaside version of Las Vegas.

To jump London Corporation red buses – a very symbol of the city itself – in the world famous Wembley Stadium was an inspired touch of marketing, but there was one slight problem which no one had anticipated: the great British public didn't seem to know anything about Evel Knievel, apart from the fact that he was some nut who had failed to jump a canyon in America. Knievel was going to have to make himself famous all over again and he only had a few weeks in which to do it.

Evel arrived in the UK in early 1975 to begin his whirlwind promotional tour and to make the as-yet-unconverted Brits sit up and take notice of him. He was filmed being given a guided tour of London and looked utterly bemused as a Beefeater at the Tower of London gave him a history lesson concerning the decapitation of Henry VIII's wives. He showed his contempt for the various authorities governing the River Thames by driving scores of golf balls into the river and he caused traffic chaos in central London by refusing to drive on the left-hand side of the road in his custom-built Cadillac pick-up.

Bizarrely for a supposedly fearless daredevil, Evel had a row with a London cabbie who he felt was driving too fast and ended up storming out of the Hackney cab and hailing another. Knievel also cycled round the capital carrying his famous cane and stopped to talk to anyone who would listen, all for the benefit of television cameras and all in the name of selling tickets. Knievel condensed ten years of self-promotional experience into three short weeks and used every trick he knew to draw attention to himself – and it worked. From having sold just 7,000 tickets prior to Evel's promotional activities, the event became completely sold out by show time as 90,000 people booked tickets to discover for themselves what the madcap phenomenon of Evel Knievel was all about.

Knievel seemed to appreciate his new fans as much as they took to him and he seemed to genuinely enjoy his time in England making new friends – and new conquests. 'The English crowd and people were great to me. I spent three weeks in London and made a lot of friends like Henry Cooper and Graham Hill. And I dated a pretty little English girl who worked in a golf shop . . . and a French girl.'

Behind the scenes, John Daly had been having his share of headaches with the Wembley authorities. Accustomed as they were to staging football matches and the Horse of the Year Show, the officials expressed all manner of reservations about Knievel to Daly. 'They were about to put on a show which quite honestly they became more and more terrified over. Let alone filling the stadium, they were also concerned as to whether the people would get full value for money. What about the turf? What exactly does this Evel Knievel do? Is there any chance we could change his first name?'

Eventually Daly and co-promoter Bob Arum, veteran of the canyon jump who obviously thought there was still some mileage left in Knievel, soothed the nerves of the Wembley officials and the jump was given approval to go ahead. Even though Wembley was Britain's biggest stadium at the time there was still insufficient room for Knievel to make a fast-enough run-up to clear 13 buses and he reverted to building yet another ski-jump-style ramp reaching up into the highest seats of the stadium. But when Knievel first set eyes on the ramp and the 13 buses he knew it still wasn't enough, as ABC commentator Frank Gifford – who was present when Knievel first saw the Wembley set-up complete with the 13 buses – explained: 'The first time he looked over and he saw the buses he said, "Hell, I can't do that." I said, "Can't do what?" and he said, "I can't jump that far."' Gifford suggested that Knievel remove one or two buses but Knievel was adamant: 'I said I'd jump 13.'

During some practice runs before the big day, Evel discovered that he had the wrong gearing to reach the required speed for take-off and knew he would never get the correct parts shipped over from Harley-Davidson in the US in time for the event. But with all the hype he had struggled so hard to generate, Knievel decided to go ahead with the jump rather than risk his reputation in the UK to add to his now rather tarnished image in the States.

The day of the jump was, somewhat unusually for Britain, scorching hot, and the capacity crowd stripped off to enjoy the May sunshine and watch majorettes, high-wire motorcycle performers and a man setting himself on fire and diving 50 feet into a tank of water, while they awaited the appearance of the main man. By the time Knievel was ready to make his appearance they had worked themselves up to fever pitch, eager to get their first glimpse of the all-American hero in the flesh.

Knievel had brought his growing collection of branded trucks and vehicles and displayed them on the hallowed turf alongside the doomed Sky Cycle. The tunnel which led onto the famous football pitch had been fitted with microphones to capture and amplify the noise of Knievel's Harley-Davidson as he revved it up. After a rendition of both the British and American national anthems, Knievel gunned the bike into life and revved it wildly to work up his audience. Then, as the screams and cheering reached a crescendo, he roared out into the stadium, one hand in the air, and rode round the circumference of Wembley, waving to his new-found adoring audience.

In another touch of marketing genius, Knievel had – for the first time since making it his trademark – abandoned his white jumpsuit and replaced it with a navy blue outfit, mimicking the colours of the Union Jack while still keeping his American stars. When it came to working an audience, Evel Knievel never missed a trick, and with his own personal tribute to all things British he sent the Wembley throngs into a frenzy. Whatever happened afterwards, Knievel had cracked the UK. For one man to attract such a massive crowd for a show that would last only a matter of minutes was a real tribute to his talent for self-promotion and a true measure of the popularity of Evel Knievel in the mid-1970s.

What did happen next cemented his fame in Britain in a way that a successful jump could never have done. After two practice runs to gauge his speed and play to the crowd, Evel came storming down the flimsy, narrow ski ramp at around 80mph, raised his body slightly off the seat of his Harley and took off smoothly to rapturous applause and the flutter of thousands of camera shutters. The jump was long and low (Knievel was actually jumping single-decker buses and not double-deckers as is commonly believed) and all looked to be going well, but his analysis of the gearing proved accurate and Knievel landed roughly and slightly sideways on the safety deck covering the thirteenth bus. The resulting crash footage has since become almost as famous as the Caesar's Palace wipe-out which had first made Knievel's name eight years before.

Evel was thrown high into the air, almost performing a hand-stand while still desperately struggling to hold on to the Harley's handlebars, and, as the bike bucked and tossed at high speed, Knievel was finally forced to let go, and his body was slammed onto the Wembley turf, where he rolled end over end, churning up dust. The rogue bike eventually caught up with Knievel and slammed into him hard, chasing him down until both man and machine gradually ground to a halt in front of a terrified, and now silenced, audience. 'I tried to hang on to that motorcycle all the way down that ramp, just like riding a bull, but I just couldn't hang on to it. It finally threw me off and I went over the handlebars and when I landed it caught up with me and got right on top of me and just burned the hell outta me. And of course I was unconscious for several minutes after that jump. I didn't know where I was.'

Just as he had blamed Bob Truax for his failed attempt on the canyon, Knievel wasted no time in pointing the finger of blame for the Wembley crash, and this time it was his mechanic, John Hood, who copped the flak. 'I just didn't have enough speed to make the jump. I needed to be doing 90mph at the bottom of the ramp but I was only doing 80mph. I shifted gear three times but I knew at the bottom of the ramp I wasn't going to make it. My idiot mechanic didn't get the gearing right. He was a complete idiot – he didn't know what the hell he was doing. In the end we couldn't get the right gearing from Harley-Davidson in time so we just had to go ahead with the jump. The crowd had paid their money.'

Knievel's injuries were bad. He had fractured some vertebrae, broken his pelvis, and broken his right hand and one finger as well as suffering a concussion. Yet, with pure Knievel bravado – still pumped full of adrenalin and in too much shock to feel just how bad his injuries were – Evel asked to be helped to his feet so he could address the crowd. Battered, bruised, cut, bloodied, and covered in dust from rolling end-over-end on the parched Wembley turf, Knievel shocked the stadium with his announcement. 'Ladies and gentlemen of this wonderful country, I've got to tell you that you are the last people in the world who will ever see me jump because I will never, ever, *ever* jump again. I am through.'

The crowd applauded wildly, feeling relieved that their new hero was still alive, and feeling that little bit special in having witnessed what was to be the great Evel Knievel's last-ever public performance. With that, Knievel was laid on a stretcher and whisked off in an ambulance, his career apparently over but his sense of humour still intact. As he apologised to John Daly for wiping out and ruining the planned UK tour, he excused himself by saying, 'My grandma always taught me to catch the last bus.'

But 24 hours is a long time in the motorcycle-jumping business, and, speaking from his hospital bed the following day, Evel declared that it had only been the pain talking when he announced his retirement and he wished to withdraw his statement.

No matter how willing he was to carry on jumping, he certainly wasn't able to do so, at least in the short term, and the seven other dates on his UK tour were cancelled, much to the disappointment of all those who had not made the trip to London. Flying back home to the USA, Knievel might well have intended to return to the UK in the future to capitalise on what was essentially a whole new market, but his Wembley appearance was to remain his only-ever performance outside America and Canada.

Back home in the States, Knievel was reunited with Linda and his children who had not travelled to England with him. It was only then that he discovered the true extent of his Wembley injuries. 'Doctors in the UK made some mistakes after the Wembley jump. They took an X-ray of me and said, "Well, there's nothing wrong with you." I didn't say anything but I'd split the whole of my pelvis. They couldn't see it on the X-ray though, so they told me to take these Percodans [painkillers]. I couldn't walk. I knew my pelvis was busted and a week later I was sitting on a motorcycle and I almost passed out because the pain was so terrible. It turns out there were two cracks as wide as your finger up the back of the pelvis. I was a mess after Wembley. I was hurt bad.'

Battered and broken once more and having lost out on the chance to make some serious money with his eight-date tour, Knievel began another process of recuperation, nagged by the constant worry of how he was going to keep himself and his family in the manner they had become accustomed to. His gambling and extravagant lifestyle had begun to take its toll on Knievel's bank balance and Evel was realistic enough to know that the only way he could earn more money was to jump yet again. He hadn't performed in the US since the canyon fiasco more than eight months previously. Maybe his American audience would be ready to receive him now the furore over the canyon had died down?

His mind troubled by the constant need to make money and his body racked by pain once more, Knievel was not a good patient when recovering from injury. He gobbled down painkillers in a bid to gain some respite from the constant hurting, and, unable to play golf, fly to Vegas, to gamble or even womanise, Evel turned to his life-long companion, Wild Turkey, for solace. 'I had my share, and everybody else's, of beer, whisky and major painkillers.'

For a man who thrived on action and the adrenalin rush of performing dangerous stunts, being cooped up at home was hell itself and he often took out his frustrations on those around him, which usually happened to be Linda. Despite all Evel's infidelities, Linda still very much wanted her marriage to work and wanted, more than anything, to put an end to her husband's suffering. She had almost lost count of the times she'd had to nurse Evel back to health and, at 36, Knievel's body was not healing as easily as it did when he was a younger man.

Evel did everything within his powers to keep Linda sheltered from the press, perhaps fearing she might reveal more than he wanted known about his private life. Yet on the few occasions when she did speak to the media she always stood by her man while admitting that she lived in constant fear of losing him – if not to another woman, then to a fatal accident while performing. 'It was always scary from the very beginning. His first jumps I know I would kind of hang on to his arm. I think I bugged him a little until he finally told me to leave him alone because it was hard enough to make the jump without somebody bugging him. So I finally kept my mouth shut and let him do what he wanted to do, and this is the only thing that's ever made him happy.'

The pressure on Knievel to retire must have been immense, both from himself and from those who cared for him. But in his mind the pressure to make money was even greater. He was far too proud to lose the status he had suffered so much to attain, and his expensive tastes simply couldn't be catered for if he took a regular job or even managed to dream up a way of cashing in on his name without actually having to perform.

It seems strange that Knievel was unable to turn his marketing genius to anything other than jumping, and, try as he might to come up with a viable alternative to leaping a motorcycle, he drew a blank and eventually announced his plans to jump again on home soil. This time he would attempt to leap over 14 buses in Ohio, almost five months to the day after his horrific Wembley crash. In his willingness to trade pain and discomfort for cold, hard cash, it appeared that Knievel would happily have sold off limbs and organs if the price was right. The decision to attempt 14 buses when he had failed to clear 13 in London appeared to be optimistic in the extreme, but with a longer run-up area Evel believed it was possible, and, besides, as he said, 'I wasn't going to jump 13 buses – that's an unlucky number. I decided to jump 14.'

Knievel's Wembley crash – which was televised in the States on ABC – seemed to have gone some way to winning back his American audience. Ironically, it was the very fact that he crashed which persuaded at least some of the offended populace that he *was* still prepared to pull the trigger that he *was* still prepared to get hurt and that he'd shown those Brits what true American heroism was made of. An easy landing would simply have added fuel to the fire that Knievel couldn't hack it any more and was simply churning out con trick after con trick to make money.

Certainly, ABC seemed happy enough to continue their partnership with the daredevil; the channel showed no fewer than three Knievel-related programmes over a one-month period in the build-up to Knievel's 14-bus leap at the Kings Island Family Entertainment Center in Cincinnati, Ohio. A one-hour documentary called *Evel Knievel: Portrait of a Daredevil* was followed by an appearance by Evel on *Saturday Night Live with Howard Cosell*, in which the stuntman goofed around with Muhammad Ali, a man he had met on several occasions through their joint associations with promoter Bob Arum.

Knievel had first met Ali before the Snake River Canyon jump at a party in New York, and the clash of egos must have been audible for miles, though the two did get on well together. When Ali turned to Evel and proclaimed, 'You know what you are? You're the white Muhammad Ali!', Knievel readily responded, 'Then you're the black Evel Knievel.' Years later Knievel would boast, 'I was prettier and just as great as Ali. Every time I saw him I used to kid him and give him one of my pictures, autographed. He is still my champion . . . I will always admire him because he is the greatest even to this day.'

While he didn't actually make an appearance, Knievel was clearly the inspiration for a two-part episode of ABC's hit show *Happy Days*, which starred Henry Winkler as the Fonz, another Seventies icon and one who was the very epitome of cool. Although often repeated, the two-part show was originally screened just before Evel's 14-bus attempt, and, in a bid to prove his cool, the Fonz attempted to clear 14 trash cans on his motorcycle, proclaiming as Evel himself had done that '13 is unlucky'. He may have fallen from grace at the canyon but, at least judging by ABC's listings schedule, Knievel appeared to be as popular as ever once again on the eve of what was to be the longest jump he would ever make.

# 10
# Unhappy Landings

### *'I fear dying but I can't quit because the banks won't let me.'*

It's a fact that Evel Knievel is better known for his failures than his successes, and no jump proved this more than his perfect leap over 14 Greyhound buses at Kings Island, Ohio on 25 October 1975.

Most people with even the slightest passing interest in Knievel have heard of the Caesar's Palace crash, the failed Snake River Canyon attempt and the horrific Wembley wipe-out, but few have heard of Kings Island, the scene of Knievel's greatest success. This has largely been due to the media who, while repeatedly screening Knievel's horrific crashes, seemed to ignore the many times he did manage to make safe landings; although, to be fair, the media is at the same time pandering to what viewers want to see and read about – and, more often than not, that's blood and guts.

Evel arrived in Dayton, Ohio on 13 October to visit the Kings Island jump site and perform some practice jumps before the main event. He had already completed a seven-city, non-jumping pro-motional tour to publicise the event, taking in Cleveland, Akron, Columbus, Indianapolis, Louisville and Cincinnati.

A jump stadium had been specially built for his attempt just outside the Kings Island Family Entertainment Center. Able to hold 70,000 people, it was hailed as the largest temporary-seating arena in the United States. Even so, there were fears that it might not be big enough as word started getting around that up to 100,000 people might turn out to see Knievel's longest-ever jump. The attendance record in the entertainment park itself was 43,000, and everyone involved fully expected this to be broken. The centre-piece of the arena was a 400-foot-long ramp leading up to where the 14 Greyhound buses would eventually be placed, but Evel built up to that number slowly during the week, initially jumping just five, six and seven buses.

When the first five buses were lined up for his initial practice leap, Knievel complained they were not close enough together and that he wanted them 'so close together that the paint would rub off'. The drivers then parked them just eight inches apart but Evel still wasn't happy until a local friend called Pete Ankney suggested he bring in two fork-lift trucks to lift the buses into place so they were actually touching. Knievel obviously wasn't taking any chances on this one. As Ankney commented at the time, 'Eight inches may not sound like much, but when you multiply that 13 times you're talking about more than eight feet.'

Unusually, and perhaps showing a new-found caution after one crash too many at Wembley, Knievel continued making practice jumps throughout the week before taking a day out on Friday to celebrate his thirty-seventh birthday. The mayor of Dayton, James H. McGee, presented Knievel with the keys to the city, and Montgomery County officials commissioned a six-foot birthday cake designed to feed 300, which featured 14 buses and a model of Knievel on his bike suspended above them. A reception was held in Courthouse Square where Knievel cut the cake and distributed it to onlookers and officials.

Knievel explained to gathered reporters that, after a week of practising, he was mentally ready for his record-breaking attempt. 'I've never been in a better frame of mind for a jump than I am now. I was scared to death at the Snake River but I think the greatest thrill I've ever had in my 10 years of jumping was hearing the countdown by 5-4-3-2-1 and pushing that button.'

In view of his Wembley disaster, Knievel also explained that he had switched to taller gearing which would allow a greater take-off speed, and that he had extended his approach area by some 85 feet in order to build up as much speed as possible.

On the morning of 25 October, exactly five months and two days after announcing his retirement at Wembley, Evel Knievel was back in the arena once more and ready to risk everything again. The show kicked off at 2 p.m. with eleven skydivers plummeting 13,500 feet into the arena in the shape of the initials 'EK' before hot-air balloons were released and biplanes performed stunts, all adding to the carnival atmosphere. In the arena itself, live bands churned out music and the usual circus-style acts attempted to keep the crowds entertained. As usual, Knievel's continually growing array of vehicles were on display, this time being joined by a new Formula 1 race car and a 'crash car', both full-size versions of the toys which were on sale.

Despite all the efforts of building a 70,000 capacity arena, only 25,000 spectators turned out on the day, paying $8 a head to watch the jump alone or $12 if they also wanted admission to all the rides in the Family Entertainment Center. It was still a healthy crowd for one man to be able to command but Knievel's act often suffered on the crowd-pulling front because it was over so quickly. In 1975, $8 was a lot of money for a show that would be over in a few minutes, and more and more people were waking up to the fact.

Contributing to the lower-than-expected attendance figures was

ABC's decision to show the event live in a one-hour-broadcast special. It was a wise decision on the channel's part. While just 25,000 turned up to see Knievel in the flesh, an incredible 32 million television viewers switched on at home to watch the comeback of the greatest daredevil of all time. It remains ABC's highest-ever viewing figure with a 52 per cent audience share. The Snake River Canyon failure had quite obviously been forgotten.

Those who did make the effort to attend the live show went wild with excitement as Knievel finally entered the arena and made his usual round of wheelies before addressing the audience and explaining his decision to jump again after he had announced his retirement. 'You can't be the best in the world and fall off and get up and say, "I quit." Not if you're an Evel Knievel you can't. And I'm not gonna quit that way. I will try it again: if I make it, I'll continue, if I don't . . . if *I* don't . . . I'm gonna pack it all in.'

Set against a spectacular backdrop of roller coasters and Ferris wheels, Knievel was back where he belonged; back in carnival land, only on a much grander scale than his early county-fair days. For his biggest-ever jump Evel had come full circle, and his son Robbie, now 13 years old, made his real performance debut pulling wheelies round the arena in a miniature pale blue version of his father's famous suit. Evel rode alongside, his huge cape billowing in the wind, looking more than ever like Elvis Presley on a motorcycle. But Robbie remembers the Kings Island jump for very different reasons. With Evel still in great pain from his Wembley crash, Robbie explained his concern: 'You know, he was in a lot of pain cos the doctor wouldn't shoot the Xylocaine into him to numb him up cos he was busted from the jump before. I held his hand while he shot the Xylocaine in himself . . . so every time he went off that ramp it scared me – it scared me pretty good.'

Pumped full of Xylocaine to numb the pain signals being

emitted from so many parts of his body, Knievel finally made his approach to the ramp that would take him into orbit over 14 ten-foot-wide Greyhound buses. The approach was fast, nearing 100mph, and, as usual, Evel stood on the footrests of his bike just before take-off and eased his body into a semi-standing position to gain better control of the bike in mid-air. Thousands of camera flash-guns exploded in the audience as the deep, guttural roar of the V-twin Harley-Davidson reached a crescendo before the split second when Evel left the ramp. Then, with traction left behind and the rear wheel spinning freely, the revs fell away in an eerie, limp silence as the back end of the bike dipped, as Knievel intended, ready for a rear-wheel landing. As he soared down onto the safety ramp covering the fourteenth bus the bike was approaching the near-vertical, and it looked for one chilling moment like Evel was going to wipe out again. Instead, the rear wheel slammed hard down onto the landing ramp followed almost impossibly swiftly by the front wheel. The crowd erupted. He had done it.

Speeding out of the arena, Knievel glanced back towards the ramp, apparently unable to believe he had actually bridged the gap; that at 37 years old, battered and broken, he had jumped 133 feet – further than ever before – and executed a safe, almost perfect landing. There was life in the old dog yet.

While he may have travelled a further distance in the air at Caesar's Palace (141 feet), his crash-landing back then meant there was little glory in the achievement. After all, as Evel himself said, anyone can jump a motorcycle, the problems begin when you try to land it. Jubilant and more than a little relieved, Evel rode back into the arena and up the landing ramp to accept the wild applause of his audience; of those who still believed that they were looking at the last of the gladiators; a man whose spirit simply refused to be broken; a man who defied age, gravity and pain. But his post-jump speech to the crowd revealed that, in a sense, his spirit was broken, or at least not as wildly optimistic as it had been hitherto. Sounding emotionally drained, he announced, 'I am going to continue to perform throughout this country and throughout the world, and I hope that I'll meet success while doing it, but as far as I'm concerned, I have jumped far enough.'

It was only in later years that Knievel admitted he had actually wanted to retire after Kings Island. 'I really wanted to quit then. It was the first jump that I made that was successful where I thought, "Yeah, I might hang it up – I did this." But, of course, I went on from there.'

Knievel had admitted that this was the end of the line, at least as far as distance went; that his bike 'didn't have wings' after all, and that he had to be wise enough to know when to stop before he really did kill himself.

Once, while en route to a performance in Austin, Texas, Knievel had heard two locals talking about him in a Mexican café in Deming, New Mexico. They were – unwittingly – grossly exaggerating Knievel's achievements while fully believing they spoke the truth. Evel had jumped 152 cars, not to mention the Grand Canyon itself. Unrecognised, Knievel listened in and realised that the myth and legend which had grown up around him had got out of hand; that people fully expected the impossible from him and that his real achievements were always going to pale in comparison. 'I'm going to get killed,' he thought, 'living up to what people want me to be. I've got to quit.'

The other major problem was that in a very real way he could never actually win, at least among the cynics of the world. If he wiped out he was no good; he didn't make the jump stick. Yet if he did land safely then the jump must have been too simple. A journalist covering the Kings Island show expressed this very opinion all too clearly. Bucky Albers wrote of the event, 'The descending ramp was built in such a manner that it began with plywood stretching from the centre of the tenth bus. So, despite the implication that he would crash if he did not clear 14 buses, Knievel had to clear only 10 to come to a safe landing.'

Evel was extremely relieved to be able to admit to himself that the big jumps were over; that the big risks were over. 'After missing 13 buses in London, England and then coming to Kings Island and jumping 14, don't think I wasn't nervous. There was never anybody gladder in the world than me when that jump was over.

'People said I wasn't scared before a jump; that's bullshit, I was scared. I'd have a shot of Wild Turkey whisky before each jump to calm myself. I'd get this knot in my stomach and this lump in my throat every time. People who go around wearing "No Fear" T-shirts now are full of shit.'

Fear or no fear, Knievel would continue to perform as he had stated, but his performances in the future would be more like exhibitions mixed with personal appearances, with much shorter jumps being attempted. His philosophy from that point on was to 'Put on the shows and try and provide the best entertainment possible and try and stay alive and not get hurt any more.'

This statement showed a fundamental lack of understanding as to why people flocked to see him jump in the first place. Was it any surprise that Knievel's popularity went into decline when he had actually publicly admitted that he wouldn't be taking risks any more? That he wouldn't be making long jumps any more? And that he wasn't prepared to get hurt any more? Knievel himself had long been aware that a certain percentage of his audience came to see him crash, get hurt or even die. To deny them any of those possibilities was to deny them a show. It was tantamount to Frank Sinatra announcing that, while he would still be staging concerts, he wouldn't actually be singing any more, just making a walk-on public appearance. Effectively, Knievel's various statements to this effect marked the beginning of the end of his career.

But while his career as a serious stunt performer may have been all but over, Knievel was still popular enough to attract the attentions of Hollywood, and he spent much of 1976 preparing for, and filming, the second Knievel-related film, *Viva Knievel!* In the hoopla following Snake River, Warner Bros. had signed Evel to a three-picture deal, and the first was to be *Viva*. It was not to be an updated biography following on from George Hamilton's 1971 *Evel Knievel* movie, but rather a fictional action-adventure with Evel starring as himself. His list of co-stars was fairly impressive, if at times miscast. Most notably miscast was legendary dancer Gene Kelly starring as Knievel's alcoholic mechanic, but other star names in more suitable roles included supermodel Lauren Hutton as the love interest, with roles also for Leslie Nielsen (later of *Naked Gun* fame), Red Buttons and Cameron Mitchell. Frank Gifford, Evel's long-standing crony from ABC, also made a cameo as himself.

The rather lame plot (although to be fair it was like Hamilton's movie, fairly representative of many films being made at the time) revolved around Evel trying to foil drug smugglers who were using replicas of his trucks and trailers to bring cocaine from Mexico into the US. While Knievel played himself he was not permitted to perform any jumps for the movie for obvious reasons: if he was hurt it could cost the studio hundreds of thousands of dollars in downtime. Warner Bros. turned to another respected stuntman, Gary Davis, to stand in for their star performer. Davis explained why Knievel had to take a back seat when it came to the riding segments in the movie: 'Evel Knievel was the star of the movie, he was not Evel Knievel the daredevil. If, for any reason, Evel would have gotten harmed . . . all he needed to do was catch a cold and it shuts down the show. During one of the sequences I was out riding, getting the crowd excited – they [the production team] wanted to shoot the crowd. Evel decided he was gonna come out and entertain too. Something went wrong and he fell off the bike; it flipped over on a wheelie. That was it. Warner Bros. [had] a lot of money invested in him at that time and they said, "You're done, you will not ride." It's not that he couldn't have done the stunts, it was that they couldn't afford to allow him to do it.'

The film was directed by Gordon Douglas, who had enjoyed considerable success with a string of movies dating back to 1931 and starring such big names as Frank Sinatra, Elvis Presley, Bob Hope and Jerry Lewis. The film's producer, Irwin Allen, had also enjoyed remarkable success, albeit more recently with smash hits like *The Poseidon Adventure* and *The Towering Inferno*.

Initial interest in *Viva Knievel!* seemed encouraging as Evel was swamped by fans during filming in Los Angeles. Things eventually got so out of hand that Warner Bros. had to post a line of security guards around the perimeter of the East Los Angeles College Stadium where some of the opening scenes would take place. Allen was quoted in the local press as saying he had never seen anything like it in all the movies he had made, even when he was working with top-flight movie stars.

The movie had a rather modest budget of $5 million (compared to the $15 million spent on *The Towering Inferno* for example) and was scripted by Norman Katkov and Antonio Santilla, although Knievel claims to have had a hand in the process. It would certainly seem so, given that the movie seemed at times to serve solely as a vehicle for portraying Evel as a nice guy; one who visited kids in hospital and dished out – surprise, surprise – his own Ideal Knievel toys; and one who would always take a stand against drugs. Ideal toys also benefited from the movie tie-in by releasing a wind-up version of the film's futuristic bike, the Strato Cycle.

His involvement in *Viva Knievel!* took up much of 1976, and when Evel wasn't on set he'd enjoy hanging around Hollywood's bars, mingling with the rich and famous, just as he enjoyed doing in Las Vegas. Knievel's favourite LA bar was Filthy McNasty's, which, like so many other bars and clubs in the city, had a neon sign outside advertising the evening's entertainment. What distinguished it from all the others was that when Knievel was holding court the sign outside proudly announced 'NOW – Drunk Inside – Evel Knievel'. Unlike some stars, who go to exceptional lengths to protect their privacy, Knievel announced his presence wherever he went and thrived on being the centre of attention. While filming *Viva Knievel!*, Evel stayed in the Sheraton Universal Hotel in Hollywood where he was next door to *Kojak* actor Telly Savalas, whom he considered a good friend. 'We were room-mates for a couple of years at the Universal. We used to drink together, play golf together at the Lakeside Country Club. He was a great guy, we had a lot of fun together.'

Knievel had, in fact, spent much of the last few years living in the hotel where he could mingle with Hollywood's finest, and, along with his hotel suite in Las Vegas, he counted the Universal as very much a home from home.

With Linda back in Butte looking after their three children as usual, Evel was free to enjoy himself in any way he saw fit, and LA offered as many temptations as Las Vegas, if not more. But the fine foods and increasing dependence on alcohol were taking their toll on the once well-built figure of Evel: he was getting fat, and by the time October rolled round he hadn't performed a jump for a whole year. He was becoming dangerously idle. With money continuing to be a problem, Knievel announced he was going to don his jumpsuit yet again and this time it would be in Worcester, Massachusetts on 11 October 1976, but, just as he had stated back in Kings Island, he wasn't jumping for distance, just for show.

Despite initially promising to jump 13 vans, Evel broke his word on the day, claiming there wasn't enough room for such a leap. Instead he performed two jumps over a mere four vans, three jumps over seven vans, and one not-so-climactic jump over ten vans – a distance of just over 70 feet. The only real bonus for those watching was that Robbie Knievel, now aged 14, made his first ever public jumping appearance instead of just popping wheelies in his father's wheel tracks. Even so, only 9,000 people turned out to see the show, a sure sign that Knievel's popularity was on the wane and that he was losing his credibility.

Had he hung up his flared jumpsuit and cape after Kings Island he could have retired with his reputation intact, notwithstanding the lingering Snake Canyon critics. At that event he had pulled off his biggest-ever jump masterfully in front of record television audiences and a healthy live gate, and had introduced his son into the arena he himself had created. In fact, keen to forget his final few disappointing appearances after this jump, Knievel has in recent years often cited Kings Island as his last performance.

The obvious next step for Knievel would have seemed to be in guiding and managing Robbie and capitalising on his famous name in whichever non-jumping way he could. With some wise investments he might even have managed to find some long-term financial security, but it was not to be.

Evel had originally intended to retire after his Snake River jump, but had carried on when the pay packet for that event had not turned out to be what he had expected. Then, after his Wembley crash, he actually did announce his retirement, albeit in a rather affected state of mind. He had once again considered packing it all in after Kings Island, but, as far as he was concerned, it was not an option available to him for one simple reason: he owed too much money and jumping was the only way he could think of to make more of it, even if his fear of dying was becoming more acute with age. 'I don't want to die,' he admitted. 'I get very nervous and afraid when I perform now and I'd like to retire. The older we get the more our way of thinking changes. No man likes to admit that he isn't as good as he once was and it's hard to quit any business. But when I get hurt now I don't heal up like I used to. And I fear dying. But I can't quit because the banks won't let me. I borrowed a lot of money from them and I've got to pay them back. I've got a lot of obligations and investments. People went into investments with me because of my earning power. If I didn't need to earn big money I'd retire. If I'd bought just one less Learjet or one less yacht I'd have another million or so in the bank and I wouldn't have to keep on working.'

Knievel often referred to himself as 'the last of the gladiators', but he had never been more like one than he was now. Here was a man risking his life to win his freedom; his freedom from the very profession he had chosen. The fact that Knievel was also risking his life for financial freedom while gladiators fought for literal freedom mattered not – the principle, and possible outcome of death, was the same. He had fought himself into a corner he couldn't get out of and his almost desperate confession of fear and concern is all the more touching for that. Like a prostitute trying to buy her way out of the trade, Knievel was going to have to keep on working the streets for the foreseeable future just to be able to survive.

Two weeks after his Worcester appearance the Knievel road-show rolled into Seattle for a two-night performance in the city's new Kingdome. Despite promising he would jump 10 buses at the indoor venue (obviously in an attempt to draw a larger audience),

Evel went back on his word again and only jumped seven buses over the two nights, a decidedly unspectacular feat considering he had jumped twice that many at Kings Island just one year before. For devoted fans and those who had never seen Evel in the flesh before, it may have been enough to satisfy, but the non-risky nature of the jumps meant the media were little interested and only 15,000 people showed up at the venue, although ABC did once more cover the jump for television. Significantly, it was to be the last time Knievel would work with ABC and his last time on the network after 17 appearances over the last decade. But there were other television channels and Knievel hooked up with one of them to plan a spectacular new stunt.

Finally realising that short leaps over a handful of vans or buses were not going to be money-spinners, Knievel resorted to his earlier genius for gimmicks and came up with one of the best of his career when he announced that he would jump over a pool of live sharks. With the smash hit movie *Jaws* having been released just the year before, shark fever was still consuming the States, just as it was the rest of the world, and Knievel once again showed his marketing genius by cashing in on the fact, even though the sharks in question were relatively harmless lemon sharks rather than the Great White featured in the movie (of which there are none in captivity). While lemon sharks have been known to attack people on rare occasions, the 14 specimens flown in from Marathon in Florida were so heavily sedated that they probably wouldn't have noticed if Knievel and his Harley-Davidson had plummeted straight into their tank. As one wry observer pointed out, the sharks were probably more scared and in more danger than Knievel was.

Still, it was a great gimmick which offered plenty of headline-grabbing potential and Knievel's new television allies, the CBS network, didn't miss a chance for advance publicity. The jump was to take place inside the Chicago International Amphitheater, which claimed to house the world's largest saltwater pool, and it would mark Knievel's first live show on prime-time television as the first in a string of episodes called *Evel Knievel's Death Defiers*. Each week, various performers would attempt bizarre and often dangerous stunts in the first part of the show as support acts to Knievel's headlining performance. On paper at least, the show appeared to offer the perfect way for Knievel to stay in the limelight by performing oddities and novelty jumps without having to take the huge risks inherent with long-distance jumping.

Despite the more lax attitude to animal rights that existed in the 1970s, there were still certain groups opposed to the jump on the grounds that it was cruel to the sharks – and the evidence supported their fears. Although 14 sharks were captured in Florida for the jump, one died in transit and several others were close to death by the time of the show. Never one to let the facts get in the way of the hype, Knievel boasted that he was going to jump over the world's largest saltwater tank which would be filled with deadly, man-eating sharks. In reality, the leap would only measure 90 feet, which was far shorter than Knievel was capable of jumping, and the sharks were so drugged and unwell that they represented little more danger than a tank of goldfish.

But jumping a motorcycle always carries a risk, no matter how safe the leap appears and how experienced the rider is. In this case it was the unforeseen danger of a slippery landing ramp that caused Evel problems. He had decided to make a practice jump on the afternoon before the live special because 'the jump was so dangerous I couldn't bring myself to do it cold turkey'. While he easily sailed over the tank of water, Knievel landed on his front wheel, slipped on the upward-reaching ski-jump ramp and smashed into

29-year-old Mobile Television Services cameraman Thomas Green.
It was the first time in his career that a bystander had been involved
in one of Knievel's many crashes, and initial reports indicated it was
serious. Word started to spread that Green had lost an eye in the
incident and those rumours have now entered the Knievel legend
and have become accepted as fact, even though contemporary
newspaper reports stated that Green was only 'treated for minor
injuries at the hospital and released'.

Knievel himself was not so lucky. He had broken his right fore-
arm and left collarbone and suffered serious bruising. Speaking
from the Michael Reese Hospital in Chicago, he insisted the jump
was doomed to failure in such an enclosed environment. 'I knew
when I saw it all squeezed together that it wasn't going to work.
When we put it all together, the ramp, the tank and the ski slope,
it was too cramped.' And while he claimed the landing ramp was
also too steep to be safe he took full responsibility for his failure,
claiming, '. . . the pressure started to build up in me'.

Knievel had originally intended to make the jump at either
the Kingdome in Seattle or the Astrodome in Houston, both of
which were larger but too cost-prohibitive, given that a tank would
have needed to be built in either venue. The crash obviously ruled
out Knievel's headlining performance on his new television show,
but at least he had taken the precaution of having his practice
run filmed should anything go wrong. 'I asked for camera coverage because I knew it wouldn't work and at least they'd have
something on film.'

Unfortunately that something was not enough and both the
live and television audiences were grossly disappointed that
the star of the show was lying in a hospital bed instead of being
out there entertaining them. Knievel spoke to cameras from his
hospital bed and the practice crash was shown repeatedly as part of

the show, but it was not enough to guarantee the show's future. Apart from Evel's absence – which had prompted the 3,000-strong live audience to boo loudly – the show was panned by critics who felt that any live show which risked televising someone being seriously injured or killed was in the utmost bad taste, and all plans for the series were cancelled after critics voted the pilot episode the worst programme of the year.

The shark jump was to be Knievel's last high-profile performance, and while he would continue churning out the odd performance over the next few years, none was spectacular enough to merit any kind of media hype or attention.

Sadly for Knievel, who desperately needed to find a less risky profession as the years caught up with him, his film, *Viva Knievel!*, bombed at the box office when it was released in Los Angeles on 13 July 1977. For Knievel it led to a lasting resentment of Hollywood, which he described as '. . . that place on earth that God will insert the tube if he ever decides to cleanse the world by giving it an enema'. The other two Knievel movies were, unsurprisingly, cancelled and Knievel never worked in films again, although he did go on to star as himself in an episode of the massively popular series *The Bionic Woman* in November 1977.

Knievel was becoming little more than a carnival act, living off his famous name and performing well within his capabilities. But while he was as good as washed up professionally, he was still capable of making worldwide headline news; though this time for all the wrong reasons.

# 11
# Hear no Evel,
# See no Evel, Speak no Evel

## 'Skinny little, rotten little bastard.
## I shoulda killed the little prick.'

Sheldon Saltman is not one of Evel Knievel's favourite people. A Hollywood promoter, he worked with Knievel on the Snake River Canyon jump and was by his side throughout the 62-city promotional tour leading up to the event itself. It was during this time that he gathered information through personal experience to write a book called *Evel Knievel on Tour*, and in August of 1977 it was published. Evel was not at all amused by it. 'He said I was a drug-taker and that I hated my mother. He said I'd fucked every girl in Butte, Montana. My kids even had to quit high school over that book. And it broke my mother's heart. I've never taken a drug unless it was prescribed by a doctor. That guy was just a filthy, stinkin' little liar.'

In truth, while Saltman (along with co-author Maury Green) did not paint a particularly glamorous picture of Knievel, he didn't actually reveal anything which avid readers of newspapers and magazine articles about Evel would not have already known. He detailed Knievel's heavy drinking habits, which were well known to all despite Evel's constant 'do as I say and not as I do' pre-jump speeches; he told of Evel's use of painkillers and tranquillisers, which was to be expected of someone who had suffered as much pain as Knievel, and none of the substances was illegal anyhow. As for Knievel's womanising, while he may not have managed to sleep with *every* girl in Butte, Montana he had made no secret of the hundreds of women he *had* slept with over the years, and therefore had little right to complain when someone else committed this fact to print. And while Evel cursed Saltman for saying he hated his mother, all Saltman actually said was that Evel had refused to stay overnight in Denver on one occasion because his mother lived there. There may have been any number of reasons for Evel wishing to avoid his mother at that particular time which had nothing to do with 'hating' her.

Knievel's outrage was a typical overreaction on his part and may have had more to do with the rumours that he had initially co-operated on the book but had fallen foul of either the publishers or Saltman himself and now stood to lose out financially. Whatever the case, little more would have been heard of the matter had Evel not decided to administer his own justice – Butte style.

Saltman at this point was vice president of the Fox Telecommunications Group, and on 21 September Evel tracked him down to the Twentieth Century Fox studio lot in Los Angeles. An accomplice, who Knievel still refuses to name, then grabbed hold of Saltman (who later claimed there were two accomplices) while Evel repeatedly beat both his arms with a baseball bat. The beating was so fierce that it left Saltman with a compound break (where the bone breaks through the skin) to his left arm and a broken right wrist, along with the expected bruises, aches and pains. Saltman's left arm was so badly broken it required surgery to insert a metal plate to piece it back together.

But if it was Butte justice in Evel's eyes, it was Butte justice with a difference – two (possibly even three) against one was not accepted in Knievel's hometown. Knievel has always insisted that he needed help because both his arms were in plaster, but since his last recorded jump was over the tank of sharks in Chicago eight months previously, this does not stand up. To further justify his actions, Evel also said the accomplice was necessary so that he could 'very carefully' break Saltman's arms without missing completely and killing the hapless promoter. And the reason for wanting to so carefully break Saltman's arms? 'So he don't write any more goddamn books.'

The moment may have proved satisfying for Knievel, but even by his standards he must have known that this time he had overstepped the mark. While he himself viewed broken limbs as little more than an inconvenience, and while he had every right to mangle his own limbs at will, the law took a very different view when it came to wilfully breaking someone else's, as Evel became all too aware.

Leaving the scene of the crime with his unnamed accomplice(s) – and leaving Saltman in a great deal of agony – Knievel made straight for the West Los Angeles Police Station to turn himself in. He had known the consequences of his actions before tracking down Saltman and was fully prepared to pay the price. After being charged with assault with a deadly weapon he was released on $1,000 bail and even found it within himself to joke with the press that 'I've jumped everything else, but I won't jump bail.'

But beneath the bravado Knievel must have known his life was spinning out of control. Overweight and approaching 40, his career had practically halted with the disastrous shark-pool affair and now he was facing a possible custodial sentence. But whatever his true feelings, he still had to live up to the image of Evel Knievel, and Evel Knievel could not show any signs of weakness, be it in the face of danger and pain or in the face of the judicial system. Yet he had no regrets about his actions and if anything wished he had gone even further, saying Saltman was '. . . a filthy little leprechaun user of people. Skinny little, rotten little bastard. I shoulda killed the little prick.' In a more humorous outburst Knievel said, 'If I catch him in Los Angeles I'm gonna slap him so hard they'll pick him up for speeding in San Francisco. That's how hard I'm gonna hit him.'

Three weeks after the assault, Knievel appeared before Los Angeles County Superior Court on 12 October 1977 after reportedly having drunk half a bottle of Wild Turkey, which was considerably more than he used to consume before a jump and a real indicator of just how nervous he actually felt about the whole legal process. The judge was forced to grant an overnight delay since Knievel and his lawyer, Paul Caruso, could not agree on how to plead. Knievel, still feeling he had done the right thing, wanted to plead guilty, while Caruso wanted to plead not guilty. True to form, Knievel sacked Caruso and defended himself, pleading guilty and insisting he had done the right thing and could still count on the support of his family and friends back in Butte because he had been honest and admitted to his crime.

It may have been how things were done in Butte, but, unfortunately for Evel, it's not how things were done in Los Angeles, as Judge Edward Rafeedie explained. 'We long ago abandoned frontier justice in California. No affront justifies such retaliation. It sets a terrible example.' Rafeedie sentenced Evel to six months in Los Angeles County Jail and ordered three years probation (Knievel often boasted that he was sentenced to three years but only served six months). His sentence would start in one week's time. On leaving the courthouse, Knievel addressed the gathered

media who finally had a new and sensational angle on the stuntman they had become progressively bored with. But there was to
be no avalanche of sound bites from the usually quotable Knievel
on this occasion, only a solemn acceptance of his sentence. 'I only
have one thing to say about this day in court. That judge is a good
judge and he's a fair judge. I have nothing more to say.'

The judge had recommended that Knievel be given work
duties on weekdays but should return to the prison each night
and at weekends. It didn't seem too harsh a deal and in fact there
were many who complained that he had been shown preferential
treatment because of his celebrity status.

Knievel didn't care and, as always, found a positive side to his
situation on which to capitalise. With the spotlight fixed firmly
back on him, he used the week before he was due to start his
sentence to announce the most outrageous stunt of his career. Evel
arranged a press conference at the Sheraton Universal Hotel in
Hollywood – where he was still living – to announce the details. He
would be strapped to the underside of an aeroplane flying at 30,000
feet and would release himself with the intention of hitting one of
13 massive bales of hay placed in the car park of a Las Vegas casino
– without a parachute. With hindsight it seems too ridiculous
for words but Evel at least appeared to be taking the plan seriously
and even displayed some detailed drawings of himself strapped to
the undercarriage of an aeroplane.

Ridiculously far-fetched the plan may have seemed, but, given
the fact that Knievel had actually gone ahead and attempted the
canyon jump when many thought it was suicidal, there was a
growing sense that Knievel might just actually be mad enough to
attempt this one too. He boasted of having signed up a veteran
World War II bomber pilot who would fly the plane, while he
himself would have a homing device surgically implanted in his

chest to help guide him to one of the hay bales. Knievel drew further gasps and looks of utter disbelief when he announced he would voluntarily have his spleen – one of the body's vital organs – removed, because it could rupture upon landing, though why he only considered that his spleen could be damaged and not his head, neck, back, or any other part of his body was anyone's guess.

Again, Evel announced that this jump would mark his retirement, and again he promised it would be a massive money-spinner which would net him around $20 million. He set the date for 4 July 1978 and headed off to jail. At least the media would have some fuel to keep the Knievel name going for the six months he would be absent. In the event, Knievel's sanity was never put to the test as the Las Vegas Gaming Commission threatened to slap a restraining order on Knievel as soon as they got wind of the plan. Las Vegas didn't need a public suicide on its hands.

Knievel remains convinced the stunt could have worked with the help of the US Army's Golden Knights parachute team. 'The Golden Knights were gonna fall right in with me to about 1,000 feet on a laser beam that was being shot [upwards] from the middle of the haystacks, and then let me go in, but I was gonna come all the way down with oxygen and no parachute, just free-falling. And believe me, someday that will be done. It will be done.'

On 21 November, Evel turned himself in at the Santa Monica County Courthouse, wished a simple 'good morning' to the gathered press and was driven off in a bus to begin his sentence. But it soon became clear that even prison could not subdue Evel's flamboyance or dampen his spirit. Each morning he made his way to the offices of Ralph Andrews Productions in Toluca Lake to continue making plans for his suicidal aeroplane drop, having not yet been threatened with the restraining order. But unlike the other work-release prisoners who were dropped off at their respective workplaces by a prison bus, Evel had a chauffeur pick him up in his Stutz. It was a touch of pure Evel and conveyed the message to the outside world that he wasn't doing regular time like the other convicts but was being treated according to his celebrity status. He was, after all, Evel Knievel, and even when in prison he was going to play by his own rules, at least as far as the law would allow.

In January 1978, in an even more outrageous display of contempt for the authorities, Knievel kept a promise he had made to his fellow inmates. He had said that if he won a particular bet on a football match he would rent an entire fleet of limousines to ferry those inmates to their work details. Evel won the bet and, true to his word, on 4 January a fleet of 20 limousines pulled up outside Los Angeles County Jail to take Knievel's cronies to work. They did so for the next four days. 'Aw, what the hell, you know? They had to catch a bus so I got 'em all limos. I won some money on a Rose Bowl game so I spent it on them. I got limousines from Carey Limousines at the Beverly Hills Hotel. I had a good time.'

The use of limos to travel to work was not in itself in breach of any prison regulations so long as Knievel reported back at the prison each night – on time. To be more than a few minutes late could, in the eyes of the law, be considered a breakout attempt, so when Knievel turned up several hours late on one particular occasion Judge Rafeedie was not amused. Evel might have got away with his breach of regulations had it been a one-off slip-up, but his public displays of contempt for his sentence and his continual signing of autographs for guards and prisoners had already angered Rafeedie and he now had the excuse he was waiting for to punish his celebrity inmate.

There were rumours that Evel had been spotted in a bar with a mystery woman, and while these were never confirmed, Evel had still been late in getting back to the prison. He even had the audacity to play a few rounds of golf when he should have been working. 'They caught me playing golf . . . My buddy brought the clubs up for me, a guy named Jack Swank. He brought them out, and my yellow shoes and my green, red and white bag, and I was out in the field hittin' balls and people were stopped along the freeway saying, "What the hell's the matter with this God-damn nut? He's out here thinking it's a country club."'

At his disciplinary hearing, Judge Rafeedie said, 'The spectacle of an inmate signing photographs and autographs I find very offensive. You are not Evel Knievel, you are Robert Craig Knievel with a booking number. Do your time like a man. You are in jail. You ought to spend the rest of your time in jail and spend it in self-examination.'

Knievel had no option this time but to obey the judge's orders and finally got a taste of what a real prison sentence was like, and it was not to his taste. 'It was degrading. I mean, I was allowed privileges like using a telephone and I played a lot of basketball, but it was degrading. The guards were pretty good to me though – I never had to do any work. In fact, I spent a lot of time in solitary so nobody bothered me. It was a lot better than being out in the general population.'

The solitary that Knievel speaks about was actually the high-power hold of Los Angeles County Jail, usually reserved for particularly dangerous prisoners but a place where Evel says he chose to be held. 'I was in there cos I chose to be in there. I wanted to do my time, I didn't want to be bothered and I didn't want to listen to all the bullshit in jail. I found time went by faster in the cell. The sheriff wanted me to be a "keep-away" prisoner; he didn't want nothing to happen to me in the jail. So they let me do that, that's where I stayed. There were only six cells in there. You couldn't see your hand in front of your face when they locked the door.'

It was in the high-power hold where Knievel claims to have been neighbour to the notorious serial killer and cult leader Charles Manson. 'Guess who they put in with me? The first fuckin' guy they brought in – Charles Manson. I about shit. Right in the cell next to me. He was in there with me for 63 fuckin' days.' Knievel added that 'Manson was being evaluated by a psychiatrist for the trial of Leslie Van Houghton. He was as skinny as he could be and he looked just like a rat. He never said a word to anyone and there's no doubt in my mind that he's insane. God made that dirty bastard – let Him deal with him.' Then, bizarrely, in the same outburst Knievel seemed to change his mind about letting God deal with Manson and felt a more earthly form of justice would be appropriate. 'Let's kill him,' he snarled. 'Hang him by his nuts from Hollywood and Vine.'

Knievel served out the remainder of his sentence in the county jail without the privileges of a work detail, and was released on 12 April 1978 having served just four months and 22 days of his six-month sentence. But if he thought that was an end to his problems he was wrong – it was only the beginning. Despite his own initial efforts to make light of his jail sentence, few other parties viewed his disgrace in the same way and Knievel was soon to discover that many fans, sponsors and associates had turned their backs on him.

Knievel's fan base was made up largely of young, impressionable kids, and while Evel continued preaching that they should live a good life, avoid narcotics and be God-fearing Christians most parents were happy enough to indulge their kids' worship of Knievel, even if he didn't quite live by the principles that he preached and even if his chosen profession was ludicrously dangerous. What they were not prepared to accept was having their children look up to a common criminal who had savagely assaulted a man, and neither were Knievel's sponsors, including Harley-Davidson and the Ideal Toy Company who both decided he was no longer a suitable role-model to be in partnership with. They withdrew their endorsements immediately.

To Evel, such rejection must have been puzzling in the extreme. Hadn't he done the honourable thing by seeking out vengeance on someone who had slurred himself and his family? After all, that's how the situation would have been handled in Butte, Montana. He had said upon leaving prison, 'I have no regrets. I feel the majority of society understands the reason for my action.' Clearly, society did not, so what was the problem? The problem was that mainstream Americans did not think the same way or follow the same moral code as the people of Butte, the eye-for-an-eye and tooth-for-a-tooth system of the old Wild West having been long since replaced by a faith in the American judicial system. At least some of Knievel's old friends back in Butte remained loyal and understood his actions. His long-time friend Paddy O'Boyle said, 'If somebody tells lies about you and your family round this town, they're gonna get a thumpin'. And that guy [Saltman] that came up here was trying to exploit Knievel's family . . . and I think the guy got everything he deserved. But it's too bad that Bob had to go to jail over that. He probably wouldn't have here in Butte but out in California it's a little different.'

As late as 1998 Knievel was still fuming with rage over the incident, telling the BBC that 'There's some people on this earth that deserve killing. They're not good human beings. They're worse than the rottenest apple in the barrel.'

Evel may have done what he thought was the right thing, but in doing so he had alienated most of those who had previously supported him, and it was not until 1999 that he finally admitted he had perhaps overreacted to Saltman's 'insults'. When asked to list some of the major lessons he had learned in his life, he cited one as being, 'When you're mad at someone, it's probably best not to break his arm with a baseball bat.'

What made this financially threatening situation even worse was the fact that after six months without earning any money, Knievel had already been forced to sell off many of his more luxurious belongings just to pay bills and loans and keep his family in the manner they had become accustomed to. Of his 16 boats, Evel sold all but three speedboats and one 80-foot yacht. He also sold two of his four houses, five mink coats and piles of valuable jewellery, keeping only what he referred to as 'the big stones'.

Harley-Davidson had been Knievel's main sponsor and the Ideal toy sales represented the largest single source of income he had. Without their endorsements the stuntman was facing complete financial ruin as well as disgrace, so he headed for the only place he knew he could seek refuge – Las Vegas. With a typical gambler's mentality, Evel figured he could win back his fortune in the casinos and simply ignored the possibility that gambling what little he had left would very probably land him in even deeper financial trouble.

By 1979, after the best part of a year of gambling, drinking and trying to ignore his problems, Knievel finally saw the error of his ways and declared Las Vegas 'A city that ruins lives. A city that has a licence to steal from you. A city of sin, of rot and heartbreaking false pretences.' Of the casinos themselves he added, 'They rob you. It's the worst gambling in the world. They have a licence to steal from you. People who gamble there are perfect examples of fools being born every minute.' Upon finally realising this, Evel drove to the airport to head back to Butte. En route, he tossed away his last $5,000 gambling money and vowed never to return to Las Vegas. It goes without saying that the money could have been better spent, given Knievel's predicament.

While he had woken up to the perils of gambling in Vegas, Evel didn't stop gambling on the golf course, where he was spending more and more time working on his handicap of 12 as his career and reputation floundered. At least there he could 'even the odds' for a win more readily. One famous story has Evel turning up at a golf course first thing in the morning with two bottles of vodka. Knowing his opponent would never dream of drinking neat vodka so early in the day, Evel commenced drinking on his own, one bottle after the other, all the way round the 18 holes. By the time he neared the end of the game he appeared to be roaring drunk and was missing easy shots. With his opponent suckered in, Knievel bet big-time money on the last hole and played it perfectly, winning the cash. It was only then he revealed that he had been drinking water all along and had only feigned his drunkenness.

It was, however, one of the few occasions that Knievel had to feign drunkenness; he had been drinking heavily for years and the downward trajectory of his career had led him to seek solace in ever-increasing quantities of Wild Turkey. Knievel's blotchy, bloated appearance betrayed the fact he had a drinking problem and he himself admitted that the late 1970s and almost all of the 1980s was a very dark period for him. 'Yeah, I was a hard drinker. I wouldn't pass up a bar, pal.'

While golf allowed Evel a means to relax and perhaps even earn a few thousand in bets, he also gave back to the sport he loved by playing in many pro-am charity matches. As far back as 1975 he had been awarded the 'JFK Man of the Year Trophy' by the PGA for his donations and personal appearances at charity events. Former president Gerald Ford presented Evel with the award.

Throughout the Seventies Knievel also hosted the 'Evel Knievel Labor Day Golf Tournament' in Butte to raise money for local charities. Evel would invite celebrity pals like Mickey Rooney,

Leslie Nielsen and Joe Louis to attend, and used to fly them down in his Learjet before he was forced to sell it off to help pay his mounting debts. Over the years he played with some of the biggest names in golf, including Lee Trevino, Jack Nicklaus and Arnold Palmer.

But it was Knievel who needed charity now, and, with the best will in the world, playing golf was not going to earn him enough money to stabilise his accounts. In a last-ditch attempt to cash in on his famous name, Knievel became involved in what was to be a shambolic tour of Australia, though in a strictly non-jumping role. He was set to act as compere on the 'Evel Knievel Thrill Spectacular' and would perform a few wheelies but would not jump, even over short and relatively safe distances – it would be left to his son Robbie to do the jumping. In truth, Knievel should have known that the public – even a new Australian one – would not be interested in seeing Knievel if he wasn't going to be performing, but with so few options available to him he accepted the invite and flew to Australia in February of 1979.

The tour had been organised by an Australian promoter named Michael Edgley, who had experience in touring with circuses and ballets but not with stunt performers. He had arranged 50 stunt acts ranging from high-wire motorcycle teams to high-fall specialists, with Knievel being the only famous name among them. The plan was to perform 40 shows over a nine-week period, covering most of Australia, but the tour seemed doomed from the off as Knievel was clearly only interested in getting paid for the use of his name to promote the show and had no real interest in the show itself. He mysteriously refused to answer questions at his first press conference and instead disappeared to the comfort of his hotel. Things only got worse as the tour kicked off in Orange, New South Wales. After making a grand entrance and pulling a few wheelies,

Knievel disappeared again, disgusted with the poor amenities at the venue and with the totally unorganised show in general, which was suffering from technical problems and a lack of equipment that had been held up in transit. After the eighth stop on the tour, Knievel had had enough and decided to quit. He told Edgley he could no longer use his name to promote the tour, which was subsequently changed to the 'World's Greatest Thrill Spectacular'. It limped along unnoticed as a disappointed Knievel jetted back home to the States, no closer to solving his problems.

If there was any consolation for Evel in 1979 it was the birth of his fourth child, Alicia, on 14 May. He was delighted with the arrival of his second daughter but another mouth to feed only added to his responsibilities, and it was clearly very difficult for Evel to accept that not only were his prime jumping days over, but that the only venues which he could now perform in were as small and amateurish as the ones he had started out in all those years before.

It is never easy for a celebrity to lose their fame – or wealth – and for a man as proud as Knievel to lose both was the worst thing he could have imagined. But a novelty act like his was always going to be a short-lived career, and, in truth, he did extremely well to stretch it out for as long as he did. Had he invested his millions wisely, he would still have been an extremely wealthy man who could have lived out his retirement on the golf course. Instead, he was constantly and desperately searching for a way, any way, in which to make more money. Still unable to dream up a suitable alternative to jumping, he resorted to squeezing his increasing girth back into the white jumpsuit which had always been his own version of Superman's costume; a costume which could transform him from an ordinary man in the street to a superhero. He was going to jump again.

Evel's last jumps have not been well documented, such was the
lack of interest in him after his jail sentence. He had been given a
second chance by his American public after disappointing at Snake
River, but, having blown that with the failed shark jump and his
arrogant attitude towards the penal system, he wasn't about to get
a third one. By all accounts (or rather, the few that exist), Evel took
to making small, easy jumps in small venues with few ticket sales, a
humiliating experience and one which did not earn him much
money. Having lost his Harley-Davidson contract, Evel reverted
to riding Triumphs again, but by now no one really cared. It was
1980, the beginning of a new decade, and people seemed eager to
put the Seventies behind them as quickly as they could. That meant
abandoning the icons of that decade, of which Evel Knievel was
undoubtedly one. The chest-beating, chauvinist macho male with
the medallion and anti-feminist outlook was no longer acceptable
and certainly no longer looked up to. Knievel had simply become
old-fashioned, and with his movie-star looks gone he was just
too old, broken in body as well as spirit. 'I was a gladiator and I
couldn't fight any more. My arms were broke, my legs were broke,
and my heart was broke. I still wanted to be in the arena; I wanted
to be a player and when that's taken away from you when you've
been so used to it, it's very hard.'

So ignored were his last jumps that his very last performance is
still argued over and Knievel himself, operating as he was through
a haze of alcohol at the time, struggles to remember the exact
details. He believes it was in Miami sometime during 1980 alongside Robbie, where the father-and-son team performed short
crisscross jumps together (Evel jumped in one direction as Robbie
jumped in the other), but other sources suggest it was in Pitts-
burgh. The very fact that the venue for his final jump is disputed
proves how far the once mighty Knievel had fallen. His career,

which had been one of the most publicised of the 1970s, ended not with one final spectacular performance or with a touching and emotional press conference, but with a whimper followed by total silence. It was a sad exit by anyone's standards, but Evel Knievel's motorcycle-jumping career was finally over.

He toured briefly with Robbie in 1981 to help promote his son's career but never again performed himself, and, with the touchy relationship between the two becoming more pronounced as Evel faced up to his son 'stealing' his fame, he got out of the motorcycle-jumping business once and for all after the '81 tour.

Robbie 'Kaptain' Knievel would go on to better all of his father's records, both in terms of total distance cleared and obstacles jumped, but there were two crucial differences between their careers. The first was that Robbie used a proper motocross bike which was much more suited to jumping and allowed him to easily out-distance his father's jumps (his 223-foot jump in Vegas in 1998 was almost 100 feet more than Evel ever managed), which were performed on heavy, unwieldy Harley-Davidsons, Triumphs and American Eagles. The other, even more important, difference was that Robbie was not the originator of the profession of motor-cycle jumping and was not blessed with the charisma of his father. People always remember firsts: the first man to run a four-minute mile; the first man on the moon; the first man to climb Everest. They are not nearly so interested in those who follow in the footsteps of originators – those who stand on the shoulders of giants. By the time Robbie was into his stride as a motorcycle jumper the novelty had passed and audiences were no longer interested in variations – however impressive – of the same theme. Had Robbie been as loud, brash and inventive as his father, he may have attracted more publicity, but as it was he not only replicated his father's jumps but he also used many of the same quotes which

Evel had been churning out since 1965, and even took to calling himself 'the last of the gladiators', just as Evel had. He wore an almost identical suit to Evel's, signed his autographs with 'Lucky Landings' (a variation on Evel's 'Happy Landings'), and even billed himself as 'Evel Knievel II' on occasion. He was, to all intents and purposes, a less entertaining clone of his more famous father and the public, by and large, were not interested. Robbie himself even admitted that 'My dad was flamboyant and I'm not like that. He created his own sport and you can't take that away from him. Back then, there was Elvis, Muhammad Ali and my dad.' Now there was only Robbie.

That is not entirely to take away from Robbie's achievements, however, which are considerable. He remains the only man to have conquered the fountains at Caesar's Palace (he cleared them with Evel in attendance in 1989) after youngster Gary Wells was almost killed in the attempt. Robbie also became the first and only motorcyclist to jump the Grand Canyon – a feat which his father was not even permitted to attempt – on a standard motorcycle, but although the jump was impressive it was over a tributary of the canyon and not over a three-quarter-mile-wide section as his father had attempted at the Snake River. Knievel junior does, however, plan to jump the Snake River Canyon in the future, though as yet it is unclear whether it will be on a standard motorcycle or in a steam-powered rocket. He has also jumped 30 limousines, 17 trucks (no-handed) and, rather embarrassingly, 10,180 dishes for a television commercial, all of which had reputedly been washed with just one ounce of Dawn dishwashing liquid!

Robbie's attempts to better all his father's jumps appear to be a desperate bid to win Evel's approval; a cry for attention since the two first went their own separate ways in the early 1980s. Robbie has made little attempt to carve out his own unique career-path and seems to be more than content trying to imitate and upstage his father. This desire to impress may have its roots in the fact that he desperately wanted Evel's blessing and help early in his career, only to be shunned. Evel tried to restrict his son to easy short jumps of no more than 10 vans, apparently on the grounds of safety, but Robbie began thinking his father had another, less caring motive. 'I started to think he might be jealous,' he admitted, 'and didn't want to pass the torch. I was his biggest fan. I just wanted his support.'

Robbie continues to jump and has performed other spectacular leaps including a building-to-building jump in Las Vegas, 13 storeys up without a safety net. While Evel never actually attempted such a stunt, he did lay the foundations by once toying with the idea of jumping between the doomed twin towers of the World Trade Center.

Robbie has also leaped from a ramp built on a railway line facing an oncoming train, taking off just a split second before the train smashed through the ramp in what was a most impressive stunt. But he continues to fail to capture the attention of the world at large in the way his father did. Part of this is undoubtedly because he approaches his jumps in a much more scientific manner than Evel ever did and, by doing so, eliminates much of the risk. In other words, there is much less chance of seeing Robbie being wiped out than there was with Evel. It's not that Robbie never got hurt – he has had his share of broken bones and concussions – but his body has not taken half as much abuse as Evel's.

Despite the fact that he never became anywhere near as big a star as his father, Evel became increasingly jealous of his son's achievements to the point where the two often went for years on end without talking. But the mutual animosity was not created exclusively by jumping rivalries; the pair had always endured a

stormy relationship and never more so than when a youthful
Robbie came home at 4 a.m. one morning when he was on
probation for breaking into a record store. Evel completely lost
his temper and lashed out at his son, knocking him to the floor.
'He wouldn't apologise,' Knievel senior said by way of explanation,
'so I knocked him down again. Then I kicked him in the face
and broke his nose. I broke his nose and it broke my heart [but]
I may break it again if he doesn't listen to me.' Evel took his son to
a plastic surgeon the following day and reputedly spent $100,000
having Robbie's nose fixed up. However, such incidents are
not easily forgotten and the relationship between father and son
remains inconsistent at best.

Evel has, however, finally found it within himself to declare
Robbie as the greatest motorcycle jumper in the world, and added
that 'the kid's got more guts and more balls than anybody in
the world'. But, still not willing to completely downplay his own
achievements, he added, 'Robbie has a tough thing to overcome
with me. It would be like Muhammad Ali's son wanting to be
champion of the world.'

If all Robbie wanted was recognition from his father it seems
he has achieved his aim. Recognition from the world at large is
another matter, and it seems certain that no matter how long
Robbie continues to jump and whatever else he achieves, he will
always be most famous for being the son of Evel Knievel.

After his abortive attempts to tour with Robbie, Evel finally
gave up the ghost and completely turned his back on motorcycle
jumping. Of his enforced retirement he said, 'I just dropped out of
sight and played golf and relaxed. I just completely withdrew from
the public eye. I tell ya, I came to a point in my life when I just
couldn't pull the gun outta the holster any more. Just couldn't do

it, couldn't pull the trigger. I mean, I'd been hurt 30-some times and every time I saw a bus or a truck comin' down the road I'd wince when I was driving a car. It's something I can't explain but, believe me, it gets to you.'

But his bitter disappointment at having to retire from jumping paled into insignificance in the face of his mounting financial difficulties. In 1980, the Miami Federal District Court found Evel liable for damages to his boat *Evel Eye 1*. Despite all his boasting to the contrary, Knievel didn't actually own the boat but rather leased it from the Transit Charter Company with the promise that he would eventually buy it outright. The bone of contention was that Evel had made $50,000 worth of unapproved alterations to the boat and now quite clearly was not in a financial position to buy it. Knievel rather pathetically argued that he had been taking painkillers at the time he leased the boat and his decision to do so had been clouded by their effects. He also admitted that he was in debt to the tune of $4 million, owing money to banks and credit-card companies, and the fact that he still owed $200,000 on his house in Butte.

Too proud to file for bankruptcy, Knievel had to face many of his assets being seized, including his luxury Butte home, forcing him to move his family into a much smaller and cheaper property in Crystal Street, Butte while he suffered the humiliation of watching a lawyer move into the house which had been built to his own specifications. As he said, 'Nobody likes to live like a king and realise that your throne may be jerked out from underneath you.' Knievel's throne may not have been completely jerked out from underneath him but it was being inexorably prised away.

But there was worse to come than the legal wrangling over the boat. The Internal Revenue Service now declared that Evel had failed to pay his taxes between 1972 and 1976, and that he owed

$1.7 million in back-payments, although Evel himself sometimes claimed this figure was as much as $21 million. Whatever the case, it was money that Evel simply didn't have and couldn't expect to earn now that his career was over and his name was of little interest to anyone. He had started the 1970s as one of the world's most famous stars and had entered the 1980s with nothing but hazy memories and a mountain of debt. It was the ultimate fall from grace and things got even worse in 1981 when the dreaded name of Sheldon Saltman re-entered Knievel's life.

With Evel's criminal sentence having been served, Saltman now attacked him through the civil courts and, on 22 December 1981, Los Angeles County Superior Court ordered Knievel to pay almost $13 million in damages to Saltman. Coupled with his tax bill, Evel was now in debt to the tune of at least $18 million without any obvious means of paying up. And so long as he continued failing to pay his taxes, so the penalties and interest increased. In a desperate bid to escape the attentions of the taxman, Evel quite literally ran away – or rather drove away – in a luxury tour bus and trailer (with a combined length of almost 100 feet) which was reckoned to be worth almost $500,000. It was to be his home for most of the 1980s but he remained defiant of the taxman and boasted, 'My Knievel toys made $300 million; I had the top-selling pinball machine; my Evel Knievel action figure outsold both GI Joe and Barbie combined. But yeah, most of the money has gone. The IRS claim I owe them $21 million. They can kiss my ass. And I told them if they send someone around to get it I won't be responsible for what happens to him. Money is for spending and enjoying and I sure did enjoy it.'

Linda opted to stay back at their small house in Butte to look after baby Alicia, even though she too was suffering from her husband's massive debts. She couldn't open a bank account herself or invest what little money she had left for fear the IRS would levy the cash, as they had vowed to do with any further earnings Evel was entitled to make from his Ideal Toy sales.

So, leaving Linda and Alicia behind, Evel packed up his bus and headed off aimlessly all over the United States, parking up as, when and where he saw fit. He soon settled into a circuitous annual route round the States, regularly taking in Atlanta, St Louis, Coeur d'Alene in Idaho, Deer Valley in Utah, San Francisco and Las Vegas. It was a lonely, miserable and depressing time for the man who had so recently been such a huge star. Drifting from town to town, he hustled for money in bars or on golf courses, he fished and he hunted, all with a bottle of Wild Turkey as his only constant companion. But at least he didn't have to worry about paying out $13 million to Saltman, as he later boasted. 'He hasn't received one single dime and he never will. He'll never get one single dime. I'd rather die.' Knievel figured that if he didn't have the money he couldn't pay it to Saltman, and no one knew where the hell he was anyway, so long as he just kept travelling around.

While Linda, in the depths of despair over her ruined existence, turned to the church and became a born-again Christian, Evel himself questioned the existence of any God who could have allowed him to fall from grace in such a way. He had fallen during many jumps and suffered horrendous injuries but this fall hurt a thousand times more than any before, and he simply couldn't come to terms with the new, inferior life which had been left to him and which he blamed the IRS and the US government for causing, due to the 80-per-cent tax bracket they placed him in. 'The US Government is run by a bunch of fuckin' thieves, liars and con men. To be a good politician in the US you've got to be a God-damned crook and a liar and a thief. That's what it amounts to. And the Internal Revenue Service is worse than the Gestapo.

They threaten people and lie and cheat. We need a business manager to run this country – a good one.' 'Abolish the IRS! Stamp out organised crime!'

Unlike Linda, Knievel never believed in religion in the standard acceptance of the word. 'I don't believe in hell. I don't believe in gods or Jesus Christ or sacred cows. I don't believe in that big fat-assed Buddha. Show me one piece of the tablets that Moses was supposed to have brought down from the mountain. Show me one piece of Noah's Ark. People need a crutch. They need to make up stories. I don't want to do that.'

Knievel harboured an extreme dislike for organised religion, especially when it came to those sects that specialised in raising 'funds' in the name of religion. In fact, there were few subjects which prompted Knievel into such a rant when given the chance to air his views. 'All these so-called Christian people, Catholic people and Jews and Seven Day Adventists and Mormons; all these people that profess they're men of God, all these silly-ass preachers . . . instead of takin' money from their people every Sunday they oughta give 'em all donor cards and let them become donors of their eyes and kidneys and hearts and livers. If you die, you can't take your liver to heaven with you, only your spirit goes. You've gotta leave your liver here to help somebody else live. Now, do you think you can do anything where God would bless you more than helping somebody live? So I challenge all of you so-called Christian people and all those believers in God. There's less than one per cent of them that are donors. Where's their heart at? Why should you give Jimmy Swaggart [a leading TV evangelist who resigned after a sex scandal] money? He'll just go spend it on a whore. Why should you give Jim Bakker [leader of a multi-million-dollar religious empire who was jailed for five years for fraud] money? He's just gonna spend it on some homo someplace.

Who knows what these preachers are doin' with our money? They're scam artists, and [it's] all tax-free. It's the biggest scam in the world, religion.'

As his drinking and depression got worse, Knievel realised he was finally slipping over the edge, out of control, and he had to do something about it. 'I think that I began to feel so bad from the alcohol hangovers, travelling alone like I did, partying like I did, that I really felt that I was beginning to lose touch with reality. I really started to feel bad and I knew that I was drinking too much alcohol and I had to do something with my life.'

He even checked himself into rehab in a bid to quit drinking, but, somewhat predictably, it didn't last. 'I stayed for two days then escaped. They filled me up on so much Valium and so much crap I couldn't even think for myself. I thought, "Hell, I'd be better off drunk," so I got the hell out of there.'

During this dark period Knievel spent a lot of time hanging out with mobsters in Chicago, who not only shared a passion for gambling but were willing to help out the former daredevil star financially at a time when Evel most needed help. He said of them, 'I had a lot of friends, especially in Chicago, who were really beloved pals at a tough drinking time, at a tough time when I really kind of lost control and didn't know which way to turn.' In a darker moment of reflection he even added, 'I came to a point in my life where I didn't want to continue.'

He dined and played golf with known mobsters like Tony 'Big Tuna' Accardo, Joey Lombardo and Jackie Cerone, but his association with the Chicago mob would eventually lead to trouble. In 1985, Knievel was subpoenaed before the Grand Jury to testify against a suspected mobster called Robbie Margolwitz whose legitimate profession was the jewellery business. Knievel wasn't fazed. 'The FBI had investigated my friendship with Lombardo,

Accardo and Cerone. My attorney, Fred Bezark, told the authorities flat out that they would have to grant me immunity or I would not even say "Good morning" to them. During the questioning, they asked me whether I knew that the FBI called Lombardo "the Stone killer". I replied, "Joey is a good man. If Joey Lombardo killed anybody, then they deserved killing."' According to Knievel, someone on the jury actually applauded this statement and Evel was swamped with autograph hunters during the lunch break before the case was thrown out of court.

But such excitement was rare, as Knievel spent most of his time just roaming America alone in his bus. The only other occasions when he appeared in public were whenever he could score a few bucks for appearing at the opening of a new car-showroom or at some golf tournament as a very second-rate celebrity, living off the fumes of his former glory and churning out the by now well-rehearsed anecdotes.

Desperate to see some sort of light at the end of his long, dark tunnel, Evel once again questioned the existence of a god, and asked Him to send a sign to prove He existed and hadn't completely abandoned the old daredevil he appeared to have spared so many times in the past. In a blistering tirade worthy of an evangelical preacher, he ranted, 'When I pray and when I question God I always say, "God, if you're really there, since I'm alone driving this motorhome down the road, I'm between Albuquerque and Phoenix, prove to me that you're here; send an angel down here in the middle of this road. Stop me right now, I'll let the angel in. Let this angel talk to me and tell me that you're real, that I better abide by the ten commandments, and that I better believe in God and do what's right. Once that angel has living proof that you are there ..." Sometimes I think, "Maybe he sent the baby [Alicia]. Maybe the baby's the angel." I thought to myself, "I've got a beautiful family,

I've got a beautiful wife and a little baby. There's more to life than just wasting yourself on alcohol."'

The thought inspired Evel to spend more time with Linda and Alicia, and, after two years of drifting aimlessly, he returned home to pick them up before returning to life on the road, this time with his family in tow. Knievel truly seemed to dote on his youngest daughter and treasured the time he spent with her on the road. 'The most precious times and special times with her are when I get to help her get into her little bath-tub, dry her off and hold her in my arms. Say her prayers with her before she goes to bed, kiss her goodnight and let her know that her daddy cares about her and that I love her. It's not that I love her more than I did my other children, I think I really just appreciate her so much because I'm older and I'm not out trying to conquer the world, and I know how fast my other kids grew up.'

In a rare television interview in 1986, Linda explained how Alicia had helped to reunite the family after such a trying time. 'It comes to a point where everybody needs to be needed, to be loved, and I felt my husband came to that point when he lost everything. He thought that he'd never run out of money and when he did it was a shock. It took him a couple of years to get over it. I thought that God loved him enough to give us this little girl. God placed a special love within her because right from the beginning she always loved her daddy. She's been very special to him and of course to me because she's so full of love. And he [Evel] can holler and yell at her and she'll just go over to him and give him a big hug and kiss and he'll just melt right back down.'

In 1986, the first post-famous documentary was made on Evel Knievel by Twin Tower Enterprises (*The Last of the Gladiators: Evel Knievel*), giving the retired stuntman his first chance to tell of his fall from fame and his financial ruin. It also gave him the opportunity to make a few dollars and to be paraded in front of an audience again. Evel allowed the film crew onboard his bus and reviewed his rise to fame and his fall from it. He also admitted he had been an alcoholic but claimed his 'angel' Alicia had cured him of it and that he was once again happy living with his family on the bus. Alicia herself, at just six years old, explained how she stopped her father from drinking. 'Every time he got a whisky I'd pour it on the floor. I said, "If you don't quit drinking I'm gonna pour every single bottle down on the floor." So he quit drinking and . . . so . . . I made him quit!'

Knievel told the cameras that he had beaten his addiction to alcohol, saying, 'The first couple of weeks were tough – just murder. But I got through it and all of a sudden it just became easier for me each and every day and I finally licked it.' It wasn't to last. Within months of the documentary being shown, Knievel was back on the bottle and the happy family atmosphere he had strived so hard to portray finally collapsed once and for all. Things were about to get even worse for Evel Knievel.

# 12
# Tainted Love

**'There is only one bastard in this family and that's me.'**

If golfing seemed a rather quaint pastime for a retired daredevil, the other big passion which had crept into Evel's life was even more surprising: he was dedicating much of his spare time (and he now had a lot of it) to painting. Although he had never mentioned it when he was at the peak of his fame as a daredevil jumper, Knievel now claimed that he had always been interested in art. However, only in the late Seventies and the Eighties did he have the time to pursue it more fully under the guidance of long-term friend and painter Jack Ferriter, who used to paint Knievel's trucks, planes, bikes and trailers. 'I was always creative and started painting when I was eight years old, but it wasn't until the Seventies that I truly understood the wonderful value of art. Jack Ferriter, an artist and genius who captures American history as well as any artist, including C.M. Russell, taught me the gentle stroke of a brush. You know, it's funny; one of the last things in the world people want to buy is art, especially from a guy with a reputation like I've got as a daredevil. Boy is it tough to overcome it and sell yourself as an artist.'

But even when it came to painting there were those who doubted Knievel's integrity, claiming it was just another scam in the Knievel book of cons. In his book, *Evel Incarnate: The Life and Legend of Evel Knievel*, author Steve Mandich suggests that Knievel was simply adding his signature to Ferriter's work and passing it off as his own as a means of making cash. Mandich claims to have the testimony of an artist (who remains unnamed) in Butte who was at school with Knievel and who says he was once approached by the daredevil and asked if he'd think about painting some pictures and allowing Evel to put his name to them. The pair could then sell them for handsome sums by exploiting Evel's name and then split the cash. The artist in question refused the alleged offer from Knievel but thinks it not beyond the realms of possibility that Knievel had managed to strike a deal with Jack Ferriter for the same purposes.

Knievel's paintings, mainly of American wildlife and Wild West scenes – with the odd foray into portraits of himself and even one of Mother Teresa in which he included his own blood – do bear a striking resemblance to Ferriter's, but that may be expected if Ferriter did indeed tutor him and Knievel followed his lead blindly without developing his own individual style. Interestingly, Evel has been filmed in a studio putting the finishing touches to a painting in the documentary *The Last of the Gladiators: Evel Knievel*, but since he is merely dabbing his brush here and there and the painting is practically complete it is impossible to say if he is genuinely finishing one of his own paintings or merely touching up one of Ferriter's. Naturally, both men vehemently deny any suggestion that the Knievel paintings are not genuine. In fact, Knievel was fond of boasting about the compliments his artwork received: 'The president of Brown & Bigelow, which is a big calendar company in Minneapolis and one of the biggest greeting-card companies in the world . . . he told me he's never seen anything in the world better than that watercolour I did of Mother Teresa, and he told me that I'd never do anything better; that it was the best that he'd ever seen in his life.'

Whatever the case, the paintings provided Knievel with at least some money, thanks to a tie-in with the Legend's (sic) Corporation of North Royalton, Ohio, who bought the rights to his lifetime's work in 1983. Knievel would spend several months in a studio in Cleveland before packing the paintings into his bus and touting them round the States, hoping to find individual or bulk buyers or anyone who was willing to display them. Once again, he started making some public appearances, this time to promote the paintings, but it was a far cry from the scenes of hysteria which used to surround him when he appeared in person in the mid-1970s.

Knievel's nomadic existence continued as one year drifted into another and he seemed destined to spend the rest of his days aimlessly following the American freeways, completely forgotten by the public. As he bitterly noted, 'Being a hero in America is the shortest-lived profession that anybody could hope to participate in – or hope not to participate in.' He bitterly added, 'You can be famous for a lot of things. You can be a Nobel-prize winner; you can be the fattest guy in the world; you can be the guy with the smallest penis. Whatever it is, enjoy it. It don't last forever.'

By the mid-1980s Linda had returned home to Butte, tired of Evel's drunken rages and bitterness at losing his fame and fortune. Of the wife who had stood by him for so many years, an ungrateful Knievel could only say of her return to Butte, 'She was bitching too much and I can't live with that. You know, I wasn't put on this earth to sit and listen to bitching all the time. I was put here to have

George Hamilton poses on the promotional poster for the 1971 film *Evel Knievel*. Evel later referred to him as 'a pussy'.

Knievel's first dramatic role was playing himself in the 1977 flick *Viva Knievel!* Becoming a member of the Screen Actor's Guild meant he could finally insure himself for the first time in his career.

ABOVE: Taking one last look at the task ahead at Wembley on 26 May 1975.
Note the new Union Jack-meets-stars-and-stripes-suit made especially for his UK audience.
BELOW: Warming up the sell-out crowd with a wheelie.

Movie star. Knievel was much more than just a motorcycle jumper – how many other stunt riders make it onto the covers of mainstream movie magazines?

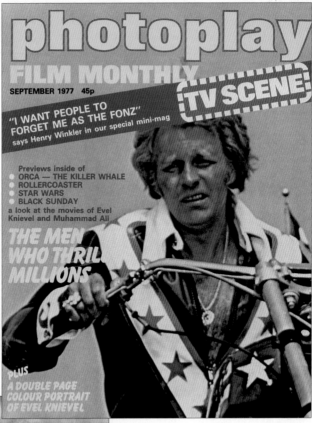

Evel and son Robbie have always endured a tempestuous relationship. Robbie still jumps but never achieved the legendary status of his father.

ABOVE: Evel's son Robbie becomes the first man to clear the fountains at Caesars Palace in 1989. Both his dad and stunt rider Gary Wells had been seriously hurt attempting the same jump.

BELOW: The Last of the Gladiators. Knievel returned to Caesars Palace in Las Vegas to b[e] wed at the location which had first made hi[m] famous more than 30 years before.

An incurable ladies man, Evel makes another nubile blonde's day during a recent public appearance – albeit in a more innocent fashion than in his heyday.

Pulling power, Even in his sixties, Evel is still a favourite with the ladies.

Into the jaws of death. A pre-jump publicity shot before Knievel's ill-fated leap over 13 Lemon sharks in Chicago, 1977.

fun. A woman is for loving and caring for; who said they have to bitch? I have got no time for all that.'

With his wife no longer there to restrict him, Knievel fell even deeper into the seedy life of a vagrant with no fixed abode and began to seek his sexual pleasures among the professional women of the streets. It was another measure of how far he had fallen: 10 years before he was hiring bodyguards to fight off the attentions of beautiful young women and now he was stalking the city streets hoping to pay for sexual favours. How often Knievel participated in such behaviour is known only by him, and this more sordid side of his life may never have come to light had he not approached an undercover policewoman in Kansas City named Cheri Williams, who was posing as a prostitute as part of an undercover operation to trap men like Knievel.

Evel was arrested on charges of soliciting and was once more fêted by the media, but again for all the wrong reasons. His arrest came just three months after the release of the *Gladiator* documentary in which he had gone to great lengths to prove himself a doting parent and loving husband. At a press conference held a week after his arrest, Evel typically put some spin on the situation and claimed he had known all along that the woman was an undercover cop and that all he had done was insult her. 'There's a little evil in all of us,' he said, 'but there might be a little more evil in your police department than there is in me.' Despite his initial claim that he did not try to solicit Cheri Williams, he did eventually plead guilty to a charge of disorderly conduct on 23 July 1986 and was fined $200. The damage to his reputation was somewhat more substantial.

Knievel's unhappy Eighties continued: he was drinking again, hustling on the golf course and gambling any winnings he picked up. When times grew particularly hard he wasn't too proud to accept handouts from old friends either. The late television presenter Flip Williams had been a good friend of Evel's in the 1970s and was one of several friends who were willing to help out a man who was down on his luck, as Evel explained: 'I was at Turnberry in North Miami playing golf. One night at the bar I was tapped on the shoulder and it was Flip's son. He handed me a cheque for $5,000 and said, "This is from my dad. He forgot to pay you on a golf bet while in Butte." Flip didn't owe me anything. He knew I was in financial trouble. I shall never forget him.'

Stumbling from one crisis to the next, Evel reappeared in the newspapers in 1989 amid another sex scandal. He had been playing golf with a friend named Clarence Paulsen before heading to the bar of the Ridpath Hotel in Spokane where the two were staying. At one point, Knievel announced he was going up to his room for a nap and left Paulsen alone at the bar. At around 9 p.m., Paulsen obtained a key to Knievel's room from reception, claiming that Evel had asked him to wake him at that time. When he opened the door he was more than a little shocked to find Knievel in bed with his (Paulsen's) ex-girlfriend. According to Evel, Paulsen attacked him and severely beat him, though Paulsen has always denied this.

At first, Evel tried to keep the matter secret, not wanting to appear in the press yet again for sordid doings. But when a local newspaper picked up on the story and made the matter public he decided to sue the Ridpath Hotel for invasion of privacy, on the grounds that a staff member had given Paulsen a key to his room. Knievel said it was this action which had caused him severe injuries and subsequent depression as well as public humiliation. He sought $130,000 in damages and was actually awarded $51,000, but not until 1995. But once again the case proved that public interest in Evel Knievel in the 1980s was so low that the only time he ever made the news was when he got into more trouble with the law; after all, no newspaper can ignore a 'former celebrity in trouble' story.

As the Eighties gave way to the Nineties, Knievel's tax bill had soared to $7.6 million, meaning that, added to the money he still owed Sheldon Saltman, he was in debt to the tune of $20 million. There still seemed to be no light at the end of the tunnel, no hope of ever making enough money to pay off his debts, no way of regaining the fame that he had so coveted and no way of reconciling with his wife, whose ever-stronger religious beliefs seemed to annoy Evel as much as his erratic and sordid behaviour annoyed Linda. Their marriage was effectively over by the mid-1980s although they never officially divorced until December of 1997.

Conservative and traditional as she was, Linda had desperately wanted to remain married and provide a solid upbringing for Alicia, and, to her credit, she endured more than most in pursuit of her goal. 'When you get married, you stay married and that's the way it is. I didn't want step-moms and step-dads around and I didn't want to be alone.' But everyone has their breaking point and Linda finally reached hers as far as any meaningful relationship with Evel was concerned. They still stayed in touch as they do to this day, but from the mid-1980s onwards Knievel had effectively been operating as a single man. There wasn't much he could be credited with when it came to being a husband but he at least owned up to the fact that the failure of his marriage was his fault alone. 'There is only one bastard in this family and that's me. There's never been a bad day with myself and my wife that was not my fault.'

Despite his mounting troubles, Knievel finally found something to smile about in 1991; something that made his life worth living again. At the ripe old age of 52, Evel fell in love. Her name was Krystal Kennedy and she was a 21-year-old senior on the Florida State University golfing team. Evel was already looking much older than his 52 years by the time the pair met at a charity golf match in Largo, Florida, but the age gap was not about to stop him turning on the charm he'd practised on countless girls over the years. After all, he *was* still Evel Knievel and he *had* been a major star, and it wouldn't be the first time that an impressionable young girl had fallen for a much older man under similar circumstances. Evel, as usual, put his own slant on the age issue, saying, 'She's a little young for me but what the hell – if she dies, she dies.' When the question of the age gap was put to him seriously he simply said, 'I don't see what all the fuss is about; I've had young women, I've had old women. So what?'

The only real problem for Evel was that Krystal told him on the day they met that she was due to be married in two weeks, but even that didn't put him off. Ignoring the fact that Kennedy had a fiancé, he confessed to being 'infatuated with her beauty, her smile and her personality' and added, 'I immediately knew pursuing Krystal was the right thing to do.'

For her part, Krystal certainly didn't seem to be completely suckered in by Knievel's boasts and storytelling. On the contrary, she appeared to enjoy his hoopla for what it was while being able to see right through him. 'I never met anybody in my life who had more colourful stories than he does. He weaves fact with fiction. There's a fine line there. He's good at that. That's the great thing with him – he can look you right in the eye and tell you a story and you don't know whether to believe him or not.'

Krystal believed enough of it to break off her engagement and join Knievel in his luxury bus on his apparently never-ending tour of the US. It seemed a partnership made in heaven: both loved to golf, both were good at it, and both loved to drink, party and gamble, pastimes they both excelled at too. It became even easier for Evel to hustle and win money on the golf course with Krystal in tow. He could bluff his opponents by feigning lack of mobility from his battered limbs while claiming that Krystal was just a little girl who hadn't played much. But both were more than capable of pulling out the right shots when they mattered, usually on the last hole when their opponents thought they had the win in the bag.

When they weren't staying in hotels and travelling around the country (which accounted for at least nine months of any given year), or back in Vegas – where Knievel had started hanging out again after ten years of being disillusioned with the city – the two stayed in Krystal's condo which overlooked the golf course in Clearwater, Florida.

Life seemed to have taken a turn for the better for Evel and he draped his young blonde on his arm like a prize trophy. Instead of feeling foolish for dating someone who was younger than three of his four children, Knievel was proud to be seen with Krystal and having a much younger partner obviously massaged his ego. He may not have been in a strong financial position but the pair were earning enough by hustling on the golf course to get by, and, since bets on a golf course were usually paid in cash, it meant the IRS couldn't seize any of their winnings.

While Knievel may have found happiness of a sort away from the limelight, something incredible was about to happen which he could never have foreseen; something that would completely change his life. It started slowly then gathered pace before positively snowballing into nothing short of a national craze. It was a revival; a revival that was instigated by a nostalgia for lost youth; a revival of everything and anything connected with the 1970s. Slowly but surely, the decade everyone had once tried to forget as being embarrassingly non-stylish was gradually becoming cool again, and the impact on Knievel, one of the true icons of the decade, would be massive. The light at the end of the tunnel that Evel had been waiting for was ignited slowly and dimly but would grow into an almost blinding brightness. Evel Knievel was about to make a comeback.

No revival of any period is an instant phenomenon and it is rarely caused by a singular event. So it was with the resurgence of 1970s culture in the 1990s. Certainly, the widespread availability of satellite television played its part by running endless replays of cheap-to-buy 1970s TV shows like *Starsky & Hutch* and *Kojak*. With compact discs having almost completely taken over from vinyl and music cassettes, music fans restocked their collections by buying old favourites on CD, leading to a massive increase in sales of 1970s music. Abba started selling again, the Grease soundtrack was a great memory for many, and Elvis's 1970s Las Vegas performances became more popular than they were first time around. Countless Seventies compilation CDs were released and swallowed up by a nostalgic music-buying public.

The grunge music of the early Nineties owed a lot to 1970s fashion too: long hair – which had been largely abandoned by mainstream culture in the Eighties – became 'cool' again, as did ripped and even flared denims. Guitar-based groups fought back against the electro-pop of the 1980s and even Hollywood cashed in on the gradual revival of Seventies culture. Quentin Tarantino's 1994 cult favourite *Pulp Fiction* completely revived the flagging career of Seventies icon John Travolta, while in 1997 *Boogie Nights* reintroduced macho Seventies star Burt Reynolds back to the big-time in a movie set in this revived decade.

The kids who had grown up in the Seventies were the

thirty-somethings who were now calling the shots as fashion designers, DJs, artists and television gurus. Naturally, they had been influenced by Seventies music, movies and fashion, and while they might have allowed some of their Seventies heroes to slip from their minds, they had never quite forgotten them altogether.

As stars like Travolta and Reynolds re-emerged, the public began to wonder what had become of their other Seventies heroes. More and more 'Where are they now?' features appeared in lifestyle magazines and more and more stars of the decade were re-discovered and fêted by the media once more, to be ridiculed or idolised in equal measure. Some fortunate-few celebrities had managed to retain their 'cool' with audiences over the decades (Tom Jones being one rather inexplicable example), while others were seen as a product of their time, and, as time moved on, they had lost the appeal they once held and were remembered only as jokes or has-beens.

Throughout the 1980s, Knievel had definitely fallen into the latter category. He was seen as a relic of the macho Seventies and was no longer regarded as cool. More effeminate make-up-wearing male actors and singers had stepped in to become the pin-ups of the Eighties, and the hairy-chested medallion-man image was most definitely out.

But the 1990s was another decade, and it was within this new nostalgic climate that Knievel made the greatest comeback of his life. After more than a decade spent in a drunken wilderness, he slowly found his name was beginning to mean something again and he started receiving offers to capitalise on it. Initially the offers were fairly low-key and quite often degrading. The Little Caesar's pizza company, for example, hit upon an idea for a television ad-campaign with the premise being that because their pizzas were so cheap and no expense was wasted on the consumer they could only afford third-rate celebrities to advertise them. Evel fitted the bill perfectly, and, dressed in his once-famous white suit, he performed a few easy manoeuvres on his motorcycle for two different adverts, both of which ended with a crashing noise off-screen, proving yet again that the collective public consciousness had remembered Knievel for his crashes more than his successes.

The adverts may have been degrading in a sense but Knievel was not yet in a position to be picky about job offers. The slots at least got him back on to television and also earned him some cash for his 'third-rate' celebrity status. Further, they alerted other companies to his presence, companies which were keen to cash in on Seventies nostalgia, and he soon found himself touting everything from breath mints to electric wheelchairs, and motel chains to gambling machines. But there were other offers which allowed Knievel to carry off a little more dignity, one of which was an invite to appear at the Grand Hotel in New York in 1994 for a screening of a video called *Evel Knievel's Greatest Hits*. Evel received a stunning reception from a mixed-age audience during a question-and-answer session and he was besieged with requests for autographs after the show from fans of all ages. His fame was on the ascent again.

What shocked those who remembered him from the Seventies more than anything else was Evel's appearance. He was old, had thinning grey hair and wore spectacles on a chain like their own grandfathers did. His hands were gnarled, scarred and swollen from arthritis, and his limp seemed even more pronounced with age. He even claimed he had mild Alzheimer's and needed to use Post-it notes everywhere to remind him what to do. The Evel Knievel with the movie-star looks had been replaced by a frail old man who looked much older than his 55 years. But the fact remained that he was incredibly lucky to be alive at all. As he said,

'I knew Elvis, I knew Frank Sinatra, I used to drink with Lee Marvin. Funny, if you had been asked back then to place your money on who would still be alive today, it wouldn't be the stunt-man you put your money on, would it? You wouldn't have put your money on me.'

Much of his shocking appearance was due to the abuse he had put himself through with alcohol in the late 1970s and throughout the darkest days of the Eighties, but recovering from the amount of injuries Evel had had also takes its toll on the body and often causes premature greying of the hair. Besides his physical injuries, Knievel had by now also contracted Type II (or late-onset) diabetes, a common but chronic condition. The cause of diabetes is still not known but can be contributed to hereditary factors in about 50 per cent of cases. Obesity is another often-cited cause, but while Knievel had certainly added weight over the years he could never have been described as obese. Diabetes can be well controlled if the patient follows a healthy diet, exercises well, does not smoke and does not overindulge in alcohol. While Knievel only smoked cigars occasionally, his battered body would not allow him to exercise to any great extent and his passion for alcohol had always been likely to lead to complications. For Evel, accustomed as he was to dealing with medical problems, diabetes was just another illness he had to deal with, and he was far more interested in retaining his status as a major star than he was in worrying about a pesky disease.

For a superstar to become a legend often necessitates a period away from the public eye; a time for the public to reassess their career and appreciate how talented and/or charismatic the individual was in the first place to achieve their fame. There is no finer example of this than the actor Sean Connery. For a period in the 1970s and early 1980s, Connery could not detach himself from the

James Bond tag and was consequently almost forgotten about as he made a string of below-par movies. It was only in the mid to late 1980s when he had gone through his own wilderness years that he reappeared and became bigger than ever with roles in films like *The Name of the Rose* and *The Untouchables*. With his powerful presence in these roles, the public suddenly remembered why they had so admired Connery in the first place and realised how much they had missed him while he was 'gone'. Once firmly back in the public eye, Connery found himself a bigger star than ever.

Knievel found himself in a similar situation: his public had grown tired of him in the Seventies and had temporarily forgotten about him, but now, with a slight jog of the memory, they were more than happy to accept him back again. The span of years that had passed since his earlier fame only served to exaggerate his legend.

But Evel still proved he had an uncanny knack of falling foul of the law, and in 1994, just as it looked like he was getting his life back on track, he found himself in trouble again. This time it was for allegedly beating Krystal. The pair were staying at the Comfort Inn motel in Sunnyvale, California on the night of 9 October when a night porter overheard a violent argument coming from Knievel's room and called the police. Upon arrival, the police found Knievel had left but Krystal was still in the room and had bruises on her face and neck. While the police were questioning Krystal, Evel called from a nearby topless bar, the Brass Rail, and two police cars were immediately sent to apprehend him. He was arrested quietly and without fuss and was taken to the Santa Clara County Jail. His beloved 1984 Aston Martin Lagonda Sedan was also impounded there as a matter of routine – a routine which would lead to even more trouble for Knievel.

Upon searching the car, again as a matter of routine, police found a veritable arsenal of guns and knives in the boot, including a .44 calibre handgun with laser sights and two clips of ammunition, a loaded .38 calibre revolver, a stun gun and an array of knives. Knievel had long had a fascination for guns and it's a fascination that continues to this day. He still sleeps with a Smith & Wesson .357 under his pillow at night and carries a Magnum .357 in his golf bag, in case there are any arguments over high stakes owed. He also keeps a Dirty Harry-style Magnum .44 in his car at all times. When asked why he feels the need to arm himself practically everywhere he goes, Knievel replied, 'Do you know how many murders and car-jacks we have in this country? I don't go on any trip without a Goddamned shotgun and a pistol with me. If I killed somebody, I'd rather have 12 people judge me on a jury than have six people carry me in a coffin to my grave. That's the way it is.'

To this day Evel harbours a rather unhealthy fantasy of killing someone and makes no attempt to disguise the fact. 'I've done everything in the world I've ever wanted to do except kill somebody. There are a couple of guys I know who need shooting. They represent the rectum of humanity.'

Unfortunately for Knievel, the Santa Clara police didn't quite see things the same way, and matters were only made worse by the fact that Knievel was an ex-con and as such was not permitted to carry firearms. He had already been fined $120 back in August for having a loaded handgun on the passenger seat of his car while driving in Helena, Montana, and it now looked increasingly likely that Evel's semi-comeback was going to be remarkably short-lived and he would be sent back to county jail. As matters transpired, Krystal played down the assault, blamed herself for starting it and refused to press charges. Evel did, in time, confess to beating Krystal. When asked what lessons he had learned looking back upon his life, he responded, 'Loving someone doesn't mean that you can love her for six days [of the week] and then beat the crap out of her on the seventh.'

Even so, Krystal stood by her man when he appeared before Santa Clara County Superior Court in September 1995 to face weapons charges. He was sentenced to 200 hours of community service, which entailed lecturing to kids on the importance of wearing crash helmets, something which, in fairness, he had been doing for some time and which he did appear to be passionate about. 'I always said I'd pay $1,000 to anyone who ever saw me making a jump or doing a wheelie without a helmet in public. There was a time when I took some heat from the motorcycle groups opposing mandatory helmet laws. I will always campaign for those laws. Senator Floyd credits my testimony before the California Transportation Department for the eventual passage [passing] of California's helmet law.' Knievel was, however, quite happy to ride round the streets of Butte some years later without a helmet for television cameras, while filming the documentary *Evel Knievel's Great Ride*.

Evel continued endorsing products, even at the expense of his credibility, because he desperately needed money and he desperately wanted to become mainstream famous again. In 1995 he was the perfect choice to endorse a pain-relieving product called 'The Stimulator' – a heat-generating device intended to warm muscles and soothe pain. While there was no medical evidence to suggest the product worked, Knievel tried his best to convince television audiences that he swore and lived by it. He also promoted a spin-off product called 'Evel Knievel's Pain-relieving Gel', but in the same year Knievel discovered he had something much worse than arthritis to worry about: he had contracted hepatitis C, a potentially fatal disease which he believes he contracted during one of his many blood transfusions.

His condition was discovered during tests for another condition that he had brought about himself with alcohol abuse. Evel had passed out several times with massive haemorrhages in his neck, which resulted in excessive blood loss, and he was repeatedly rushed to Morton Plant Hospital in Clearwater, Florida. After one particularly serious incident he said, 'I thought I was going to bleed to death. The veins in my throat literally exploded.' He confessed, 'The drinking got me – I had a bleeding oesophagus [part of the alimentary canal which links the pharynx to the stomach] from drinking too much – I had to quit. I almost died from drinking.'

While treating Evel for a bleeding oesophagus, a Dr Barsilo ran several blood tests and discovered his celebrity patient had contracted hepatitis C, the most deadly of the hepatitis viruses. The disease was ravaging Knievel's liver, which was already severely damaged from drinking. Dr Barsilo gave Evel five years to live.

Hepatitis C (as opposed to the A and B strains) was only discovered in 1989 but affects an estimated 170 million people worldwide, with 3.9 million sufferers in the United States alone. Like the AIDS virus it can be contracted through sexual contact or needle sharing among intravenous drug users, but in Knievel's case it was determined that he was infected with the virus during a blood transfusion operation. His liver failure, while being partly due to his hepatitis, was also brought on by years of alcohol abuse for which he only had himself to blame.

It seemed terribly ironic that a man who had stared death in the face on so many occasions, and had come so close to dying but always fought back, was now facing his toughest challenge of all from a debilitating, silent killer, which no amount of bravery or determination would overcome. The only thing that could save Knievel now was a new liver. In the short term, Evel was treated with Ribavirin tablets (to boost his immune system) which he took three times a week, but the looming possibility that his liver would eventually fail him, and thereby kill him, must have played on his mind considerably.

As it was for now, the show had to go on. Evel was determined to continue his gradual rise back into the public eye, and if he now had to treat diabetes *and* hepatitis C along with his usual aches and pains, so what? His career as the king of the stuntmen meant he was no stranger to pain and the possibility of death. He even foolishly showed no regard for his doctor's orders concerning alcohol, even though he had already stated that he had quit drinking. 'They told me to quit drinking . . . I am a stubborn man. I have been a big-shot all my life. I thought I knew it all so I continued to drink. I have punished my liver, I can tell you, and that just helps hepatitis C even more.'

Knievel did eventually stop drinking but was still suffering much of the time, drained of energy and hobbling around like a man 30 years his senior. But he was revelling in the new recognition he was now being showered with as the originator and founding father of a whole new lifestyle, one which was gathering momentum throughout the States and would eventually spread worldwide – Extreme sports.

While Evel had been primarily associated with motorcycles, he had once strapped himself into a steam-powered rocket and had also planned to freefall from an aeroplane at 30,000 feet to land on some hay bales, stunts which make him more than just a motorcycle jumper. He had no shortage of imitators over the years – whom he more often than not despised as they threatened to steal the limelight away from him. The Extreme-sports fanatics, however, are much closer in spirit to Evel than any of his imitators were. They invented their own ways to live life on the edge, and with it they invented a whole new lifestyle, fashion industry and music form. Whether it was extreme surfing, base jumping, snowboarding or freestyle motocross, a whole host of youngsters ushered in an enviable new lifestyle, all wearing designer brands like Oakley, Fox, On Fire and RipCurl gear and opting to drop out of humdrum society in order to chase thrills. They wore cool shades, baggy pants, beanie hats, combat trousers, covered themselves in tattoos and body piercings and listened to Nu-Metal music. They rebelled against the nanny state and thrived on taking risks and inventing new challenges, just as Evel had done a generation before. For them, copying Evel's suit and replicating – or even trying to better – Evel's stunts would have seemed utterly pointless. It had been done before, so where was the risk or triumph in that? They possessed far too much originality to become mere clones; then they would be little better than the thousands of overweight Elvis Presley impersonators who merely dyed their hair black, donned a pair of aviator sunglasses and squeezed into a white-tasselled jumpsuit.

Many of these kids were too young to even remember Knievel, but the older members of the Extreme community began hailing Knievel as the godfather and originator of everything they did and believed in, and the message soon spread to the younger participants thanks to the back-catalogue of Knievel videos. From being a relic of a forgotten decade and little more than a washed-up joke, Evel Knievel was finally finding the respect he had always craved, and it was coming from a youth that he respected – a youth which embodied the very lifestyle and attitude he had single-handedly created.

# 13
# The Return of the King

## 'He gave me a gift of life through his liver so that I could go on living.'

Golf does not have the reputation of being a particularly dangerous sport but Evel Knievel seemed to have a knack for getting hurt wherever he went or whatever he did, even in the most relaxed of environments. In December of 1997 he finally underwent the surgeon's knife in Tampa General Hospital to have a complete hip replacement after falling over during a round of golf and once more smashing his fragile hip. It was, as one would expect, found to be in a terrible state of repair when surgeons opened Knievel up to begin the operation. 'The doctors said they had never seen a worse hip in their lives,' he commented.

It may not have been the most glamorous way to injure himself (wiping out at Caesar's Palace carries heaps more credibility), but the operation to insert a titanium hip was successful and meant that, for the first time in 30 years, Knievel's legs were both the same length and he no longer had a limp – or the need for his famous cane. Prior to surgery, Evel had been suffering badly with his hip and was told by doctors to use a Zimmer frame to take his weight off it. Pride, however, prevented Knievel from doing so – at least in public – and he insisted on using only his cane, even though it was woefully inadequate for the job.

The injuries didn't stop there either. Some months later Evel slipped while getting out of a Jacuzzi and broke a rib to add to his quite outstanding list of injuries. But all these problems paled into insignificance as Knievel's hepatitis C approached a critical point much earlier than had been expected. In April of 1998 doctors gave him between three and six months to live. 'Three years ago,' Knievel said, 'the doctor diagnosed five years, but now it's just crept up on me so fast.'

The virus was sapping Evel's strength and forcing him to remain in bed for up to a week at a time. He was also losing weight fast and was down to 165 lbs from his usual 180 lbs. If he didn't undergo a liver transplant within the next three-to-six months, Evel Knievel was going to die. But finding a suitable donor is never easy, and being rich and famous (which he was now slowly becoming again) didn't make it any easier, as he explained: 'Some people think that if you're rich you'll just get a transplant. It doesn't work that way. The person who needs it the most and is a donor match will get the transplant. It doesn't matter if you're Mickey Mantle, Evel Knievel, Walter Payton or Joe Smith. And what if the body rejects the first one you're given? You can't just say, "Hey doc, I'm rich, here's another $467,000. Go find me a new one." Believe me, they're just not available.'

If Knievel was to be lucky enough to find a matching donor in time, there was still, as he said, no guarantee that his body would accept it. Even if it did, he estimated that a new liver would only buy him about seven years. To further add to his worries there was every chance that his hepatitis would immediately attack the new liver all over again.

Part of Knievel's appeal in his glory days was that he simplified things, even death itself. He faced a ramp, gunned his bike up it, and tried to bridge the gap. He either landed successfully, got hurt or got killed. Gruesome but simple. And if he did get killed, chances are it would have been so quick that he wouldn't even have known about it. Now he was in a very different situation, little better than a prisoner waiting on death row hoping his appeal will grant him life. But to his eternal credit, Knievel faced this new form of death in exactly the same way he had faced it in a different guise. He talked openly about his illness and remained philosophical.

'It is a bitch,' he admitted, 'but I am not scared of it – nothing much scares me – but I just don't want to die. Hepatitis C is worse than AIDS. There is no cure. If I do get a liver the disease will start attacking the new one as soon as it is put in. It is a damn rattlesnake this thing.'

Knievel was issued a pager to carry at all times, which would alert him if and when a suitable liver was found. He was one of 10,000 patients in the US holding on for the news that might save their lives and was acutely aware that a quarter of those patients die before their pagers ever go off. The sickest patients are pushed to the top of the list, and at one point Knievel was nearing the top after twice coming extremely close to death. On both occasions his body's near-superhuman ability to fight off pain and injury, coupled with the steely determination that had allowed him to become Evel Knievel in the first place, allowed him to recover sufficiently well to embark upon what looked like being his last-ever road trip. Evel's doctors advised him to visit his family and friends while he still could, as it might be his last chance.

By this time, Evel had not only his own four children to think about but eight grandchildren too. Sadly, he could not see his beloved grandmother Emma who had raised him as a child; she had passed away the previous year aged 103.

Evel set out on a heart-breaking trip to Montana to visit as many friends and relations as possible, knowing full well he might never see them again. He might not have been an ideal father to his own children but as he grew older he doted on his grand-children, five of whom were Tracey's children, two Robbie's and one Alicia's. It was a trying time for all involved with so many uncertainties hanging over Evel, but he retained his optimistic outlook, despite hearing of his youngest grandson (Tracey's son) Jesse's ambitions. 'He's just seven and [he] came up to me and said, "Granddad, you know it's going to be up to me and my brother Josiah to keep the family name going." He was wearing his bicycle helmet and sitting on an Evel Knievel bike. I just rolled my eyes and said "Jesus."'

Upon returning from his 'last trip', Evel continued making personal appearances when he felt well enough and he also gave interviews and played golf, even though his arthritis meant he had to run his wrists under a hot shower for twenty minutes before he could even think about holding a golf club. 'I have bad arthritis,' Evel admitted, 'and it hurts me to get up in the morning. I have to be very careful in the mornings because of the injuries I have; I'm a slow starter.' When the pain was too great he even took to rubbing horse liniment into his body to try and ease the pain in his muscles and joints.

Helped along by widespread and remorseful reports of his deteriorating health (the public often forgets how much they admire celebrities until these celebrities are dead or in danger of dying), the Evel revival continued to gather momentum. The Playing Mantis toy company announced that the famous Knievel toys would be re-released in time for Christmas and his new official website was selling a whole new range of Knievel-labelled merchandise, from which Evel naturally got a cut. Replica leather jackets, Evel Knievel cigars and aftershave, commemorative coins, T-shirts, caps, posters and signed photographs were all available at a price. If Evel Knievel merchandising had been a phenomenon in its own right back in the 1970s, it was well on its way to being so again.

Evel relished the fact that he was now finally able to make money without having to risk life and limb to do so; it was a scenario he had dreamed of since his career started going downhill back in 1976. Of the multitude of businesses offering him appearance money he said, 'They don't ask me to jump; I just turn up, smile, pose for the cameras and they give me the money. It is quite a career. In the old days, the promoters wanted more and more from me. They wanted me to jump or spill my blood and break my bones. Every time they wanted me to jump farther and farther and farther. Hell, they thought my bike had wings.'

The endorsement deals kept flooding in. In 1998 Evel linked up with world BMX champion Matt Hoffman to produce an Evel Knievel BMX bike. Hoffman had long idolised Knievel and was one of the many Extreme-sports fans to view him as the grand-daddy of the movement. HoffmanBikes was recognised as being at the forefront in producing stunt bikes and the Knievel signature-series model was, naturally, designed primarily for long jumps rather than more intricate stunts. Hoffman himself often jumped over lines of cars on his BMX by being towed at speed behind a car then letting go of the rope as he reached the ramp. The bikes sold for $800 and Knievel seemed delighted, not only with his cut in the franchise (by 1998 he was making around $300,000 a year) but in being recognised by current world champions like Hoffman. At the time, Hoffman was a nine-time world champion and Evel described him as 'One of the finest young men I have ever met – a true competitor.' Hoffman himself penned a poem in honour of Evel, which ended with the lines 'On behalf of the past and future generation, thanks for the inspiration.' It summed up Evel's contribution to the Extreme movement perfectly.

But the product endorsement didn't stop with BMX bikes; for the first time ever, motorcycle riders could now buy a genuine Evel Knievel signature-series motorcycle. The California Motorcycle Company (CMC) announced in 1998 that it would be building a limited-edition run of 1,000 bikes, each painted up in the familiar red, white and blue starry logos Knievel made so famous, and different models would be made in honour of Evel's most famous jumps: Caesar's Palace, the Snake River and Wembley. They were certainly not intended as stunt bikes, however, but rather as Harley-Davidson-style cruisers. The 1440cc S&S engines pumped out a relatively puny 75 brake horsepower, but the bikes were not designed for performance but rather for show, as the gold-coloured trimmings and acres of chrome testified. The bikes went on sale for $25,000 and in November of 1998 CMC merged with Indian Motorcycles and seven other companies in a $30 million deal to form the Indian Motorcycle Company Incorporated. Unfortunately, failure to produce targeted numbers of bikes resulted in the company finally closing its doors in 2003.

Knievel must have been extremely frustrated throughout 1998. His name had never been hotter since his heyday and he was boldly predicting that he would make more money in the next 10 years than he ever made in the Seventies. But his new-found success was continually tainted by his illness and the nagging, depressing thought that he might not be around to enjoy the rewards of his comeback. His condition meant he often couldn't even enjoy the present. 'This disease is a bitch,' he admitted. 'Some days I just can't get out of bed. It saps your energy. Some days are good, some are bad.'

Yet still the recognition kept rolling in. Knievel was awarded the prestigious *Motor Cycle News* Dave Taylor Lifetime Achievement Award in September 1998. Taylor had been a stunt rider of some repute himself and had campaigned endlessly on safety issues before sadly dying from cancer. *MCN*, established in 1956, is the biggest-selling motorcycle weekly in the world and had chronicled Knievel's career from the moment he became famous. It was also significant that Knievel was being recognised by an enthusiasts' motorcycle title rather than as a mainstream celebrity, a fact that was not lost on Evel and one he was particularly proud of.

Knievel was too frail to fly to the UK for the awards ceremony but spoke to the audience via a pre-recorded video tape. Speaking of the cancer that killed Taylor and the liver disease that was well on its way to killing him, Knievel said, 'I know how painful cancer can be. I'm sick myself, not from cancer but from liver disease. I have hepatitis C and it's . . . everything that ails us is tough for a human being to get along with. God put you here on earth to do the best and be the best and live the best that you can, and when he's ready he's gonna take you and I don't think that a human being can ask for anything better than that.'

Fully expecting that Knievel was on his last legs, there were few in the audience – made up of the cream of the British motorcycle industry – with dry eyes. Knievel came across as being humble and in full acceptance of his condition. His speech was as far removed from his usual bravado and gung-ho rhetoric as it was possible to be, and the fact was not lost on his audience, many of whom had grown up marvelling at the crazy stuntman from across the Atlantic. Some of them had even been present at Wembley way back in 1975.

The UK was caught up in a Seventies revival just as much as the US, and in November of 1998 BBC2 honoured Evel with a special Evel Knievel Night – a whole night of programmes dedicated to the Seventies icon. A new documentary, *A Touch of Evel*, was aired along with the 1977 movie *Viva Knievel!*, an episode of *The Simpsons* which featured a Knievel-type character called Captain Lance Murdock, and some short documentaries on other famous stuntmen and women including Britain's own answer to Knievel, Eddie Kidd, who sadly suffered brain damage in a jump in 1996 and is now confined to a wheelchair. Having a whole evening's programmes dedicated to one man on a channel as respected as the BBC was a true measure of how much Knievel still meant in the UK, almost a quarter of a century after his only performance here.

He continued to be celebrated in the US too, as the world-famous Smithsonian Museum in Washington opened a permanent Evel Knievel museum in December. In what is one of the largest exhibits in the museum dedicated to just one person, Evel donated many of his personal belongings including the Harley-Davidson XR-750 that he used to make his longest successful jump at Kings Island in 1975 and one of his famous white jumpsuits.

But, as always, Evel Knievel and trouble were never very far apart, and in December Evel attracted further bad press when he was reported to the police for making threatening phone calls to a Cleveland-based motorcycle collector. Knievel had apparently not learned his lesson after being jailed for breaking Sheldon Saltman's arms back in 1977 and was now threatening the same punishment to a man whose name was not revealed. A business associate of Knievel's called Carl Forbes told the press that the man in question had been 'manufacturing jump bikes and using Knievel's name to advertise them'. Cleveland police-chief Kurt Laderer said, 'Since this happened over the phone, we have no way of truly knowing what happened. All we can do is put the man's residence under house watch.'

Given Knievel's state of health it is unlikely he could have broken anyone's arms; he was now gaunt and frail, a shadow of his former overweight self in the 1980s, and his skin tone was a sickly yellow. He had also become increasingly depressed by the prospect that he might die relatively young – if he didn't get a liver transplant in the first few weeks of 1999 he was a dead man and he knew it. Knievel had by now fallen so ill that he was taken into Tampa General Hospital to be cared for round the clock as he waited and prayed for news of a suitable donor.

Finally, on 27 January, Evel was told his body was shutting down and he was given just 48 hours to live. He decided he would prefer to spend his last hours at home with Krystal and die peacefully there rather than in hospital. After a lifetime of defying death, Knievel was finally forced to accept that he was going to lose, and for the first time in his life he practically gave up the fight. He had been repeatedly warned by doctors that this battle would be the biggest and most serious thing he would face in his life and it now looked like the defiant Knievel was finally beaten. At least he had put up one hell of a fight.

Clearwater, Florida, where Krystal and Evel had their condo, is linked to the city of Tampa by a 12-mile-long land bridge. Krystal helped Evel from the hospital into his car to drive across it on what he knew was his last journey, his last sight of the outside world and the Florida sunshine. He was going home to die. In the end it wasn't to be a 'glorious death' as George Hamilton had predicted in his 1971 movie; it was to be a slow, painful degeneration, sinking into nothingness, that was finally to fell Evel Knievel. The obituaries were sure to note the irony in a few days' time, if they didn't already have them written up.

Then, when everything appeared to be lost, it happened. It wasn't Evel's pager that went off, it was his mobile phone. 'As she [Krystal] was driving across the bridge I got that call on the phone from a nurse named Debby, and she said, "Evel, where are you at?" and I said, "I'm on the bridge back to Clearwater." She said, "There's been a car wreck in Miami. There's been a young man killed who has your exact blood-type. We think his liver's perfect and he is a donor. He was 23 or 24. Can you turn around? Your transplant surgeon is on his way to Miami on a Learjet. He's gonna get the liver, put it in a solution and come right back."'

Knievel wasn't out of the woods by any means but his journey home to die had suddenly turned into a race for life. He now at least had a chance, and when Evel Knievel had a fighting chance he usually came out the winner. Krystal floored the accelerator and screeched the car over to the other side of the bridge, ignoring a 'Do Not Cross' sign. Within minutes the pair were back at Tampa General and Knievel was readied for the life-saving operation he'd been waiting on for so long. He had been on the waiting list for a whole year, and now Knievel had a chance to defy death one more time he wasn't about to waste it. 'They wanted to open me up right away,' he later explained. 'I said, "Well, if you open me up and you take my liver out and throw it in the garbage and this [new liver] doesn't work, I'm a dead man." The surgeon said, "Well, you're the daredevil, what do you want to do?" I said, "Take it out."'

Dr Hector Ramos (MD) of the LifeLink Transplantation Institute went to work on what was Knievel's sixteenth major operation. Krystal paced the hospital corridors praying her frail but determined partner could stand up to the surgeon's knife just one more time; praying that he wasn't too weakened by the disease to take the anaesthetic, that he would have enough strength to pull round and come through. Most importantly, she prayed that Evel's body would accept the new liver. If it didn't, it was too late to find another. The operation simply had to work.

It did.

Evel awoke some hours later to the news that the operation had been a complete success and that his body was accepting the liver of the unfortunate donor, who had lost his life to give Evel Knievel a new one. The sadness was not lost on Evel when talking about the youngster. 'He gave me a gift of life through his liver so that I could go on living. He gave me life and I don't even know him. And I do love him . . . In the near future I hope to know his family. Not many of us ever have the chance at another go in life.'

Showing his legendary ability to recover from injury and illness, Evel walked out of hospital just five days after his transplant, despite saying that '. . . when they take your liver out of ya and put another one in, it's like replacing a football in your stomach'. He would need to take a weekly injection of Interferon and three Ribavirin tablets (both medicines help boost the body's immune system) every week for the rest of his life, but at least he had a life to live again after coming closer to death than even he had managed before. Some weeks later it was discovered that Knievel's hepatitis C was attacking the new liver, but since the liver itself was functioning perfectly there was a good chance the organ would last for many years.

The operation transformed Knievel's appearance: he regained weight and a much healthier pallor and found he had more energy than he'd enjoyed for years. It was time to get back to business with a new vigour and taste for life. Knievel fans the world over breathed a sigh of relief as the old gladiator once again showed them that they should never give up hope and never give up trying. Death had tried a new, stealthier, underhand tactic on him, and had been defeated again. He really was beginning to appear superhuman.

On 2 April 1999, in his first major post-operation public appearance, Evel returned to Caesar's Palace, the venue that had made him famous 32 years before, to launch the CMC Evel Knievel signature-series motorcycle. The massive billboard outside the complex bore the legend 'Evel Rides Again' and Knievel posed for pictures with the bike as well as riding it round the fountains, up the steps and into the casino itself, all without a helmet. This time Caesar's was more forgiving – he didn't crash.

Having apparently forgiven Las Vegas for all its sins against him, Knievel again returned to Caesar's on 19 November, but this time with an altogether different purpose: he had decided to marry Krystal. The couple had been together for nine years but ill health had prevented Evel from marrying over the last year and prior to that he'd seemed in no great rush to re-tie the knot. So now, with a relatively clean bill of health, he had decided to tie the knot for the second time in his life. The ceremony itself was pure Las Vegas kitsch, with scores of beautiful people dressed as Romans and gladiators, and Cleopatra flanking Knievel and his 30-year-old bride. Now 61, Knievel proudly rode his CMC bike to the ceremony and was pictured, unusually, wearing a suit in front of a decorative arch that featured several jumping motorcycles spanning its length. 'I feel like I got a chance at a new life,' Knievel told the press, 'so Krystal and I decided to start a new life right here where it all began.' Evel's son Kelly acted as best man (even though he was nine years older than his new stepmother) and, as the ceremony was open to the public, several hundred people watched on.

With a new liver, a new wife, and his name providing a licence to print cash again, life looked good for Evel once more. The dark, drink-saturated days of the Eighties were well and truly behind him. Once more, Hollywood came knocking with the intention of making a much more realistic and grittier film of Knievel's life story than the sugary George Hamilton vehicle had been. Producer Marco Brambilla had sold the idea to Universal Studios and had chosen Betty Thomas to direct. Thomas had already directed the movie *Private Parts*, based on the life of shock American DJ Howard Stern, as well as directing the *Brady Bunch* movie. Heart-throb Mathew McConaughey was selected to play Knievel after *True Romance* star Christian Slater had been briefly considered. It was inspired casting as *U-571* and *Reign of Fire* star McConaughey bears an uncanny resemblance to the younger Knievel and looks even more like Evel's son Kelly. In fact, the two look so alike that Knievel told McConaughey they could be twins.

Brambilla had been working on the project since 1996 and a budget of $60 million was being bandied about, but wheels can turn slowly in Hollywood and, as the new millennium rolled around, talk of the movie died away and it seemed it would never actually be made.

Knievel's rejuvenated ability to make money was not making him as rich as it should have done, thanks to his ongoing dispute with the IRS, and he was naturally cagey when discussing his earnings. 'I have an agreement with a big investment firm that I've signed everything to,' he explained. 'I just live on a salary plus expenses. But as far as expenses go, I can have anything I want – from a Learjet to a horse.' Significantly, he had neither, but his name was usually enough to ensure he'd be given items of cash value free of charge, simply because people wanted to be able to say they had some kind of link with the man who had by now become a bona fide living legend. 'I can call up and order a $4,000 super charger and there's no charge. I order a motorcycle and I get it four days later – no charge. There's lots of companies and shops that do everything for me.'

Whenever possible, Evel wanted cash upfront for any personal appearances and had even been known to demand cash for giving interviews – an unorthodox method of self-publicity. What the taxman didn't know about, he couldn't take, which is why gambling continued to be a safe way of making (or losing) money for Knievel.

Evel was still spending several months of the year in the Maxim Hotel and Casino in Las Vegas, mostly in the complex's Cloud Nine bar, his favourite watering hole outside Butte, which also acted as his 'office' when it came to betting on various sporting events. With a new liver in place, Knievel decided he could afford to have the odd drink again, even though Krystal regularly watered down his beer when he wasn't looking. But he had at least given up on the Wild Turkey that had been his undoing in the 1980s, claiming he had taken his last shot back in 1989 because he had 'just had enough of it'.

When he wasn't in Vegas or making public appearances, Evel's day-to-day life in Clearwater was remarkably normal. He'd stop by the pharmacy and pick up his family-size prescription of drugs for his diabetes, hepatitis C and chronic arthritis (he now has to take 37 pills every day as well as his injections). He'd play a round of golf, visit his tailor to have his carefully faded jeans let out to accommodate his weight gain, and would drop into McDonald's like everyone else for a burger. But the difference between Knievel and most other celebrities was that he never made any attempt to be conspicuous. Evel loved being recognised, and since word had got round that he lived in Clearwater during the winter it wasn't hard for fans to spot him in his Evel Knievel-liveried Cherokee Jeep. A whole new generation of kids who admired the Extreme-

244 ★ Life of Evel

sports lifestyle and had learned of the godfather of the movement honked their horns and yelled at him as he drove round Tampa and Clearwater, and Knievel loved every minute of it. 'I can't even go in a grocery store without people wanting an autograph or wanting to kiss or hug me,' he explained without any hint of complaint. 'But it goes with the territory. I earned it so I might as well enjoy it.'

He continued riding his CMC motorcycle, especially when he visited Montana in the summer months when Clearwater became too hot and humid for him. When he was there, he assisted in the organisation of a whole new Knievel spin-off which would prove to be one of the biggest compliments of his career: his hometown was planning to stage an annual event called Evel Knievel Week, which would hopefully attract people from all over the US and further afield to celebrate the town's most famous son. Few living people have been granted such an honour.

Evel had already had a river named after him in Arkansas, and in 1998 had received a fax from the Governor of Alabama declaring that 4 July, Independence Day, was to be declared Evel Knievel Day in that state. They were both great honours, which were followed up by *Icon* magazine naming Evel as their 'Icon of the Year' for 1998. But an annual event held in his own honour was something else altogether, and it gave fans the world over the chance to travel to Butte and ride with their hero; a hero who really was back from the dead.

# 14
# A Life Less Ordinary

*'Dying is a part of living and none of us is going
to get out of here alive.'*

While his professional life could hardly have been improved upon,
Evel Knievel's private life was an unmitigated disaster by 2001.

He had been suffering from mood swings that often resulted in
violence, and according to Krystal she was usually at the receiving
end of it. Knievel blamed the medication he had been taking since
his liver transplant, but matters were not helped when he began
to suspect that Krystal was being unfaithful to him.

By July, the couple's 10-year relationship had reached the point
of no return and they were divorced less than two years after their
fairy-tale wedding in Las Vegas. But this was one girl that Knievel
couldn't let go of and he swallowed his Butte pride in a bid to win
Krystal back. Thrown out of the condo in Clearwater, Knievel went
back to living in his bus, and for a while he parked up in Roosevelt
Boulevard in Clearwater so he could be near Krystal, a position
that Krystal found increasingly uncomfortable. 'He initially would
leave flowers and cards at the door and on my car but once he
understood we were not going to reconcile – I made it very clear

I wished for him to leave me alone – he turned very angry.'

The fact that Knievel even attempted a reconciliation with Krystal was at odds with his long-held attitude towards women. Just a few years before he had, with typical bravado, commented, 'Women are like buses: good to ride on for 15 minutes but they forget that if you get off there will be another one along in 15 minutes – and another one, and another one.'

Krystal became so concerned for her safety that she eventually took Evel to court in February 2002 seeking an injunction against him. At Pinellas County Courtroom on 20 February, Krystal accused Knievel of hitting her and making constant threatening phone calls, prompting Judge Amy Williams to order a permanent injunction against Knievel, who was listed in the court papers as a 'retired daredevil'. Knievel was ordered to stay away from his ex-wife and forbidden from attempting to make any contact with her.

Bizarrely, Knievel filed for his own injunction, claiming that Krystal always 'packed a gun' and had made various threats towards him, one of which was threatening to shoot him in a tug-of-war over her jewellery collection. Judge Williams also granted this injunction and ordered Krystal to stay away from Evel for a period of four years. It was a messy and undignified end to a relationship that, on the surface at least, had appeared close to perfect.

As usual there were hordes of autograph seekers outside the courtroom hoping to meet Evel, who was dressed in his regular flashy style wearing tinted spectacles, glitzy jewellery and blue alligator-skin cowboy boots. Putting on a brave face, he told reporters he was glad to be rid of Krystal, saying, 'There's just some things a man can't live with.' He then admitted he had asked Krystal to forgive him but added that he was not prepared to put up with her infidelities and snarled, 'She's lucky I didn't hit her. I never want to see her again.' To another reporter, however, he let his guard slip and bemoaned, 'Any way you look at it, it's a sad situation. I came here with a broken heart.'

It was a very revealing statement on Knievel's behalf; he had never before admitted weaknesses and certainly not where women were concerned, but his recent behaviour in showering Krystal with flowers and messages had proved just how much he wanted her back in his life. As it was, Evel had been forced back into a sad, lonely existence on the road. At 63 years old, he was on his own again and full of bitterness. 'I went through a pretty tough marriage with a girl who wasn't what I thought she would be. I was tied to a tree by a rattlesnake for 11 years. She wanted me to stop being Evel Knievel. I am who I am. I'm not going to change. I'll settle down the day they put me in a six-foot pine box.'

Given the mess he had repeatedly made of his private life, it was somewhat ironic that Knievel was now to be found dishing out advice on all kinds of personal matters via his 'Ask Evel' website. He had been offered a spot as a monthly advice columnist on *www.tripod.com* back in 1998 and had accepted the post whole-heartedly, even though he couldn't seem to offer himself much advice on managing his own affairs. 'I'm looking forward to sharing my perspective with Tripod members,' he said. 'I've pretty much done it all. You can ask me for advice on just about any-thing.' Anything except, perhaps, relationships.

But Knievel had other things to worry about than his ruinous love life; the taxman was still chasing him and by August 2001 was claiming that Knievel still owed almost $6 million. The Depart-ment of Revenue filed two charges against Evel totalling $395,000 and claimed that court records in Butte showed he owed $800,000 in back-taxes to the State of Montana and $5.3 million in federal taxes. Knievel naturally disputed this and he and his attorney,

Wade Dahood, claimed they had reached a settlement under which Evel was obliged to pay only a fraction of that amount – just $15,000 in total. Knievel produced a letter from the IRS addressed to Robert C. Knievel which stated 'You have completed the payment requirements of your Offer in Compromise. This settles any previous owed Federal income taxes, according to the terms of the agreement between you and the Government.' The IRS refused to discuss the matter publicly but Dan Hoffman, an administrator for the Montana Department of Revenue, did go on the record to confirm that Knievel was finally catching up with the back-payments he owed the State of Montana. Hoffman said claims for $395,000 of the back-taxes had 'made it through the proper channels for collection'. Wade Dahood remained tight-lipped about the affair, but it seemed that after so many years of living on the run from the IRS, Knievel was finally catching up with his debts.

He spoke openly about his tax problems at the annual Butte Press Club meeting where he was a special guest for the 2001 session. In an unusually sombre mood, Knievel used the event not only to help promote Butte but to clear his name of past misdemeanours. He read out letters from various US government officials relating to the Sheldon Saltman incident, his arrest for soliciting in Kansas City, and, mostly, his tax debts, which he now promised to settle by the end of the year. Knievel also vowed to help promote Butte in any way he could in a bid to attract more visitors back to the once great town. 'We have no choice,' he told the assembled journalists and officials, 'this town is dying.'

Evel backed a proposal to erect 200–300 signs promoting Butte all over the state of Montana and even promised to put up some of the money for the project himself, as well as promoting the town as much as possible during his many television show appearances and radio and press interviews. He even made a travel documentary for the Travel Channel called *Evel Knievel's Great Ride* in which he took viewers on a tour of his beloved hometown in a bid to entice them to visit.

While it may have been a minor revelation to hear Knievel sounding humble and dipping his toe into council matters, there was much more of a revelation to come when he stunned the world by announcing the unthinkable: he was going to jump again. Those who were familiar with Knievel's sense of hyperbole sniggered at the very thought of such a suggestion, but there were others who believed – after all, there had been thousands who thought his promise to try and jump the Snake River Canyon would come to nothing and he had proved them wrong that time. Who was to say he wouldn't do so again?

And it wasn't going to be a short exhibition-style jump either; Knievel vowed he was going to jump further than he had ever jumped in his life – more than 200 feet – prompting fellow motor-cycle jumper Johnny Airtime to remark: 'The only way Knievel could leap 200 feet would be to take 200 amputated human feet, put them side by side and jump over them.'

Knievel made the startling announcement on 1 June while attending the launch of an Evel Knievel tribute car at the Galpin Ford dealership in the San Fernando Valley, Southern California. The Ford car was dubbed the Evel Knievel F-150 Gladiator and came in a choice of two Knievel-inspired paintjobs – the famous white with blue and red, or the dark blue Wembley colour-scheme.

Of his proposed jump he said, 'At that time [spring 2003] if I'm still strong enough and feel like I do [now], I'm going to make my last jump. When I get ready to go, I hope you're all there. Stay on the take-off side and when I take-off blow like hell – you'll get me clean over.' The initial statement did sound very tongue in cheek;

however, Knievel continued to boast about his comeback jump throughout the year, although the details changed every time he was interviewed. 'I don't know what I'm going to jump over yet. I have a lot of companies who want me to jump their trucks and cars so . . . we'll see. I may jump over 200 beautiful naked women, laying face down. I jump ramp-to-ramp and rump-to-rump. If I miss, the landings will be so smooth and soft. No problem.'

Knievel hadn't even worked out how far he was going to jump or what bike he was going to use, both factors pointing to this being nothing more than a publicity stunt. 'I'll jump over 200 feet . . . I may jump 300, who knows? I'm looking into the bike now. There's a lot of motorcycles out there as good as a Harley-Davidson. I'm gonna test them and when I come up with one you can be assured it'll be the fastest, safest, best motorcycle in the world. I'm not decided yet. Maybe a Triumph, Triumph from England. I love Triumph.'

Knievel showed how completely out of touch he was with modern motorcycling by adding, 'Triumphs are the best handling motorcycles in the world. I jumped the T120 Bonneville; [it] runs at 115mph, a great motorcycle.' Evel did in fact jump the T120 but that was way back in 1967 and before the advent of the modern Japanese Superbike, many of which will now top 180mph straight out of the crate. And the handling of motorcycles since the late 1960s has improved in quantum leaps. If Knievel had been serious about making one last jump, the only realistic option open to him was to use a motocross bike as all other jumpers – including his son Robbie – rode.

Still, the boasting continued: he was going to jump over those 200 naked women; he was going to leap three tractors and trailers end-to-end, with 20 Ford trucks added for good measure; he was going to jump 220 feet because that figure represented his current age on top of the furthest distance he had jumped before (64 feet for the age he was to be in 2003 and 156 for the furthest jump which he, incorrectly, claimed to have made).

In theory, Knievel could easily make such a distance using a motocross bike, which would be light enough, powerful enough and have enough suspension travel to absorb the landing; but was there any real possibility of a man who had to warm his wrists under a shower for 20 minutes just to play a round of golf being able to hang on to a bike as it landed at 100mph from a 200-foot jump? It seemed unlikely.

Even the planned location of the jump varied from day to day. One day it was to be held on the Nevada/California border while his next announcement was that he'd been meeting with the Italian government to gain permission to jump the Colosseum in Rome. Other potential sites were named as the Sturgis Rally in South Dakota (which attracts 750,000 bike fans each year), Yankee Stadium and even Butte itself. There was a lot of room for cynicism despite Evel's protestations that his coming out of retirement would be good for the American public. 'By jumping again at my age and after all I've been through, the way ups and the way downs, both physically, financially and spiritually, through all the greatest triumphs and the lowest turmoil of my personal life, I feel like maybe I can inspire the people of America to get up again, no matter what they've been through.'

Evel insisted all the major television networks had approached him about televising the event and he figured he could make $12 million from the jump, his optimism obviously un-dampened by the financial disappointment of the Snake River broadcast rights. 'If I make this last jump, I'm gonna come at it so fast that if you blink you're gonna miss it. I'm gonna take off and I'm gonna be so high and go so far you'll wonder where the hell I went . . . If I have an ounce of life in me I'm gonna do it. I will outdraw every event there ever was in this last jump. You watch me.'

In many ways it was rather sad to listen to Knievel's talk of a comeback; to bear witness to the old gladiator who was simply not able to lay down his sword and enjoy his freedom. After all, Knievel had earned his 'rudius' – the wooden sword presented to gladiators who had proved themselves brave enough and won their freedom. He had taken the pain and made his name a legend; he had nothing to prove to anyone. But even though he was back in the limelight as a revered icon of the 1970s, Evel desperately wanted to recapture his former glory. He wanted to be the Evel Knievel of old one last time; to fly through the air with his famous helmet and jumpsuit on and his cape billowing in the wind. Only then could he, at least in his own mind, be in his mid-thirties again, a man commanding the attention of a nation, being watched by millions of fans old and new. There was even some speculation that Knievel's wish to jump again was the result of a darker motive; that he would have preferred to go out in a blaze of glory with one spectacular crash rather than just falling prey to a slow illness and dying in a hospital bed. He even hinted at this himself on occasion, saying, 'Things have been so damn tough around here I wouldn't mind taking a vacation for the rest of my life. Anyone who's afraid of dying is an idiot.'

But in brighter moments Knievel was happy to pick up the flag for pensioners and hoped he could inspire them like he had inspired the youth of the 1970s. 'Just because you're 65 years old does not mean that you have to quit life and retire. If you've worked in the job and you're going to retire, well, that's fine, but take something else up. I'm not telling everybody to get on a motorcycle and jump over a huge distance like I do, but, you know, for exercise some old people think that they got to get up and walk around the couch two or three times and scratch their ass then sit down and just quit life. In other words, they don't do anything – they become couch potatoes. I don't believe in that. I want to live and live and live until the day I die. That's just the way I am.'

Whether people believed him or not, Knievel had said he would make his last jump in the spring of 2003 but as the date came and went, with no jump, older fans were reminded of the continual postponement of the Snake River attempt. In the meantime, Evel had his upcoming Evel Knievel Week to think about. The event ran from 29 July to 3 August and served two purposes: one was to honour Knievel and the other was to attract much-needed tourist money to Butte. Knievel had always been proud of his hometown and offered his services free of charge for the festival in order to give something back to Butte. 'I've given a couple of weeks of my time here,' he said. 'I'm very happy about it but I have cancelled a couple of events that could have meant quite a bit of income for me but that doesn't matter. Giving back to the community and to the friends that I grew up with is what's important to me.'

Butte hadn't really done much to promote the Knievel phenomenon in past years and hadn't even erected a statue, opened a museum or celebrated his fame in any significant way. There had been some talk of naming a street after Evel and there were many supporters in favour of the idea, especially County Commissioner Mike Sheehy who proposed the notion. But complaints from businesses who would have to change their stationery and addresses at their own cost scuppered the proposal, at least temporarily.

Butte did, however, arrange for a museum of Knievel memorabilia to be opened in time for Evel Knievel Week as part of its $60,000 investment in the event. Evel himself attended to open the exhibit, which officially kicked off the week's activities. The exhibit was housed in Butte's Piccadilly Museum of Transportation

Memorabilia and Advertising Art, and included the crumpled X-2 Sky Cycle, Evel's Wheelie Bike, the early mock-up Harley-Davidson 'jet bike', the XR-750 he crashed when jumping the shark tank, a life-size statue of Evel and a collection of toys and other memorabilia.

It was estimated that between eight and ten thousand people descended upon Butte for Knievel Week, most of whom were on their way to the famous Sturgis Rally – which was due to be held the following week – and were looking for a warm-up party. There was certainly plenty to entertain, as visitors could watch live bands, see stuntman Spanky Spangler set himself alight and leap from the ninth floor of the Finlen hotel onto an airbag, attend custom bike and car shows and generally party in the streets until their hearts (and livers) were content.

True Knievel fans also had plenty of opportunities to meet their hero in the flesh as Evel led a 100-bike ride-out round the 'Knievel Loop', a newly signposted route through Butte that took in many sights connected with Knievel's life. Die-hard fans could even part with $50 to attend a dinner hosted in Evel's honour with the man himself in attendance.

While Evel Knievel Week might have been a thrill for his more ardent fans, the event was not a financial success and was reduced to just three days in 2003 and renamed Evel Knievel Daze (sic) in a bid to make it more cost-effective. But the real surprise of the 2003 event was the woman who accompanied Evel throughout the activities – Krystal Kennedy. Evel's persistence in following her and bombarding her with flowers, cards and telephone calls had obviously paid off and the two erstwhile lovers were reunited despite the tempestuous nature of their relationship. Knievel was full of praise once more for his ex-wife and explained all that she had had to put up with over the years. 'I was an alcoholic. I had hepatitis C and didn't know it. She went through my alcoholism; she went through a condition I had called a bleeding oesophagus; she went through a hip transplant, all the time nursing me back to life and back to health . . . I had a temperament problem, a bad one . . . I was on drugs like Zoloft [an antidepressant] – it was like dropping a pill in the Pacific Ocean. After the divorce I finally fought back and got on medication that would help me, help the damage I did. She then returned to me – she came back. And together we're trying to make every day a good day. Hopefully we'll get married again some day.'

Krystal had indeed been Knievel's guardian angel in the years that she had been with him and had saved his life on more than one occasion, as she explained without presuming to take credit for the fact. She had rushed him to hospital at least 15 times since meeting him, 'And I don't mean for stupid stuff but in life-threatening situations. He's been bleeding internally well over half those times.'

Yet again in his roller-coaster ride through life, things seemed to be going Evel's way, and work began on the Evel Knievel Xperience Café in Primm, Nevada, a casino/resort development town on the Nevada/California border. It was a project Evel had long dreamed of as he had kept all his bikes (14 of them according to his own estimate), trucks, trailers and assorted memorabilia and had always wanted to display them all in one place, either in a themed restaurant or bar. This at least seemed like a realistic project, and one which could have been easily achieved until Evel started talking of virtual-reality theme rides being incorporated so visitors could experience crashing into the Snake River Canyon and flying through the air on a Harley-Davidson – all without the pain he himself had endured in the same attempts. 'I have a ride that you can get on and you can jump 30 cars yourself, on the ride. Then you experience a crash which you may not be able to get up from. You can jump in my rocket car, jump the Snake River Canyon, hit the wall, go down in the river, and when you hit at 130mph the water splashes right in your face.'

The Evel Knievel Experience was set up as a three-way venture between Talisman Companies, Kirk Kerkorian (owner of the MGM Grand among other casinos and resorts) and Net Net Inc., a Nevada corporation owned by Evel's son Kelly who had turned his mind to business after turning his back on stunt-performing in the 1970s. Kelly had also been making a name for himself on the golf courses of Nevada. Having won the Las Vegas City Amateur Championship in 1998, he progressed to the Southern Nevada Golf Association Championship where he took consistent top-ten placings. He might not have followed his father into professional motorcycle jumping but Kelly Knievel certainly shared Evel's passion for golf.

Knievel senior expected to make either $1.35 million a year from the Xperience or, alternatively, would opt for one third of the profits. As well as the virtual-reality rides, he also envisioned various games based on his career being included in the Xperience as well as a sports bar and a restaurant serving up traditional truck-stop food. An existing roller coaster which spans the freeway in Primm was also due to be renamed the 'Evel Knievel Great American Daredevil Roller Coaster' in a link-up with the Café.

Knievel had planned for his resort to open in 2003 but, just like his planned comeback jump, it never happened. In fact, he had begun telling reporters that his jump would take place at the opening of the Café, which is a half-hour drive from Las Vegas. However, when one year after the initial date for both events had passed, nothing had materialised.

What did materialise was another sudden surge of interest in

Evel, both from Hollywood and a more unlikely source – a small Los Angeles-based theatre company. In the spring of 2003 it was announced that Evel had signed over the rights to the Zoo District theatre company to make a rock opera based on his life. Musical director and composer Jef Bek approached Evel with a seven-song demo he'd been working on for two years and won the approval of his childhood hero to produce 'Evel Knievel: The Rock Opera'. 'He was a living superhero,' said Bek. 'He knows I get him and he knows I understand what's really significant about his legacy.'

Bek (not to be confused with rock singer/guitarist Jeff Beck) was inspired by Knievel as a child and was determined to become a motorcycle stunt-rider himself before crashing his bicycle into a tree stump and realising he might not be made of the same stuff as Knievel. Knievel himself thought the project – which would include songs influenced by Seventies giants Led Zeppelin and Pink Floyd – was 'a wonderful compliment' and even suggested he might make a cameo appearance during the show's opening nights, whenever they might be.

But it was the attention from Hollywood which really promised to make Evel an 'A list' celebrity once again. The much-hyped movie *Pure Evel* had sunk without a trace back in 1998, and most assumed the project had been shelved indefinitely. But in 2004 it was announced that *Pure Evel* had been given the green light by Universal Studios and would be directed by Joseph McGinty Nichol (better known as McG), who had recently enjoyed big box-office success with *Charlie's Angels* and *Charlie's Angels: Full Throttle*, both based, appropriately enough, on the 1970s hit television series. The script was to be written by another major Hollywood player, Andrew Walker, whose previous credits included *Se7en* starring Brad Pitt, *Sleepy Hollow* with Johnny Depp, and *8MM* starring Nicolas Cage.

The movie, tentatively scheduled for a 2005 release, was to be centred around the Snake River Canyon jump when Evel's fame was at its peak, and, in contrast to the George Hamilton biopic, it promised to be a warts-'n'-all portrayal of the darker side of Knievel. McG had long been fascinated by the Knievel legend and confessed that Knievel had been one of the characters he fantasised about in his 'Walter Mitty childhood'. 'Here the fact really is stranger than fiction,' he said. 'This is a guy who was a bank robber, who carried Wild Turkey in a cane. This is a guy who painted his name on his Learjet and then bought a second one to fly alongside so he could look at it from the air. The picture is about a man and that which made him great will also be his un-doing. I want to tell darker stories. This will be a dramatic piece.' McG planned to produce the movie under his Wonderland Sound and Vision company and would be aided by Stephanie Savage as executive producer. It was once again rumoured that Mathew McConaughey would play Knievel, but nothing was confirmed in the press release as far as actors were concerned.

Knievel hit the headlines again in early 2004 when it was announced that the industry standard for mobile gaming – the Superscape Group – was to launch a state-of-the-art Evel Knievel game for mobile phones using highly realistic images of the stunt-man and his bikes. Superscape's chief executive Kevin Roberts said that 'Given the worldwide interest in this personality and his spectacular exploits, I believe that the Evel-ution game will prove a great hit for gamers worldwide.'

Hard on the heels of the announcement that *Pure Evel* was set to enter production came the news that American cable-television giants TNT were to start shooting a made-for-television movie about Evel's life in April 2004. It was to be produced by Mel Gibson's Icon Productions, the company responsible for the five-Oscar-winning movie *Braveheart* among others. While Gibson would act as executive producer, actor George Eads from hit television show *CSI* (*Crime Scene Investigation*) would play Knievel in the film, which would follow Evel's whole life-story rather than just part of it. The script was written by Jason Horwitch, whose past movies had included the 1998 Harvey Keitel/Bridget Fonda vehicle, *Finding Graceland*. TNT's senior vice president Michael Wright also appeared to be a personal fan of the subject of his new movie: 'Evel Knievel is that rare larger-than-life character from which good film biographies are made. I grew up – like a lot of other kids in the Seventies – thinking Evel Knievel was the coolest guy on the planet. Now, after going through the development process with this project, I see him as a fascinating and complex character, a guy with an admirable streak of self-confidence, determination and pure grit.'

Nothing cements and increases a person's fame as much as a major Hollywood movie, and while Knievel is already a hero to millions around the world, *Pure Evel* and *Evel Knievel* look set to make him a hero to a whole new generation who were not even born at the peak of his fame. *Pure Evel* may not cover his whole life-story, but no two-hour movie – including, presumably, *Evel Knievel* – could ever hope to cram in every aspect of such an incredible life; a life which was perfectly symbolised by the jumps that made Evel famous in the first place. His willingness to have a go and to get back up and try again if he failed applied to his private life just as it did to his jumps. The willingness to accept and deal with the pain and injuries he was sure to suffer along the way; the highs and the lows; the good times and the bad; the falls from grace as well as the perfect landings. The fame and the fortune, the glitz and the glamour, his fall from glory and the alcohol-soaked wilderness years followed by his remarkable comeback; not to mention the illnesses he fought and is still fighting, and his fiery romances, have all combined to make Evel Knievel's life anything but an ordinary one, and certainly a far-from-perfect one. But these are the things that made him Evel Knievel and the man himself is quick to point out that he wouldn't have had things any other way. He played the cards he was dealt, switched them when necessary and always kept an ace up his sleeve. He lived a life that few of us would have the courage to follow and he has enjoyed every minute of it. 'I've had a good life. I've lived a better life than any king or prince you've ever had in England. There is no president, no athlete – nobody – that has ever lived a better life than I.'

On another occasion Knievel reflected, 'Some people can only dream of such a life. I lived it. I was watching television the other day – a biography on the History Channel of Aristotle Onassis. They talked about his wealth, his riches, and I wasn't impressed. I had bigger boats than he did, bigger yachts; I had more Rolls-Royces, more Ferraris. I had more racehorses than he did. I screwed more women than he did – and they were better looking too.'

When Knievel started performing, his jumps genuinely amazed spectators in an age when such feats were anything but commonplace. That era has now been superseded by one in which we are desensitised to outrageous stunts as people continue to push the limits of what is possible. Knievel's simple ramp-to-ramp jumps have been replaced by freestyle riders performing acrobatics in mid-air, hanging off their bike in contorted positions as they soar over much greater distances than Evel ever did. Apart from all the Extreme athletes, we are also constantly subjected to madcap stunts through programmes like *Jackass* where the participants appear more than happy to perform any number of life-threatening capers in order to raise a laugh or a wince from the audience. The *Jackass* crew, like the Extreme sportsmen, are the direct descendants of Knievel in that they are prepared to shed skin and break bones in order to thrill themselves and their audiences and break away from the confines of 'normal' everyday society. While Evel's jumps may look tame by today's standards, his crashes certainly don't, and his reputation as the originator of a whole new lifestyle remains intact, and is, if anything, growing.

There have been few regrets in Knievel's extraordinary life: with the exception of a 'couple of women' that he would have liked to have slept with and a couple of people he would have liked to have killed, he only wishes he could have gone a little faster on a few jumps and made the landings stick. He also regrets not having access to today's modern high-tech safety equipment such as back protectors and body armour, equipment which could have saved him a great deal of pain and injury. 'I tell ya, I don't know what was the matter with me. I thought I was a superman. [My suits] had a little bit of padding in the knees, a little in the shoulders and a little in the elbows. When I hit that pavement at 70 or 80mph those suits just ripped. If I had to do it all over again I'd a [sic] had shoulder pads on like a quarterback wears; I'd a [sic] had hip pads on, therefore I wouldn't have broken my left hip five times; I'd wear a better pair of gloves so my hands weren't so scarred up and burnt. What the hell, I guess I thought I was Elvis Presley, but I'll tell ya something; all Elvis did was stand on a stage and play a guitar. He never fell off on that pavement at no 80mph.'

When Knievel does finally succumb to the multitude of aches and pains, breaks, diseases and viruses he fights each day, he insists he isn't afraid of dying and never has been. For many it is a miracle that he has made it this far. And in true Knievel style he even has his own version of heaven already planned out, just the way he wants it. 'I want to go to my own kind of heaven. It's got a canyon I can jump across safely; it's got a golf course I can par every day, buses I can jump easily. It's got draft beer that doesn't make you fat. It's got a lot of beautiful girls running around and none of them will be the jealous type; and my kids stay small all of their lives and don't talk back to me. There's no state tax, no federal tax and no politicians. Now that's my kind of heaven.'

Even as a young man, Knievel had figured out that the way he would like to die was to be in bed with a good-looking woman at 100 years old. And if he doesn't make it to 100, he's got that one covered too. After cheating death so many times Knievel is still very much aware that dying is the only sure thing in this world and the one thing that unites all of humanity. As he says, 'If I die then I'd just be getting somewhere quicker than you're going and I'll wait for ya – that's all. I'll sit there and have a cool beer and wait for ya.'

However long he manages to beat Father Time, Knievel can be assured of one thing: nothing and no one, not even death itself, can ever erase his legend. For as long as human beings take risks and for as long as they continue to pick themselves up after failure and refuse to be beaten, the spirit of Evel Knievel will survive.

# Major Career Statistics

## 1965

Date: Unknown
Venue: Moses Lake, Washington
Distance/obstacle: 40 feet over a box of rattlesnakes and two
    mountain lions.
Bike: 350cc Honda Twin
Details: Made the jump but clipped box on landing.
Injuries: Sprained ankle

## 1966

Date: 23 January
Venue: National Date Festival Grounds, Indio, California
Distance/obstacle: 45 feet over two pick-up trucks parked end to
    end.
Bike: 750cc Norton
Details: The jump was successful and was the climax to a show by
    his newly formed troupe 'Evel Knievel and his Motorcycle
    Daredevils'.
Injuries: None

Date: 10 February
Venue: Barstow, California
Distance/obstacle: n/a*
Bike: 750cc Norton
Details: Wind prohibited motorcycle jump so Evel attempted a
    star jump over speeding motorcycle but was struck in the groin.
Injuries: Several broken ribs

Date: 1 June
Venue: State Line Gardens, Post Falls, Idaho
Distance/obstacle: n/a
Bike: 750cc Norton
Details: n/a
Injuries: n/a

Date: 19 June
Venue: Missoula Auto Track, Missoula, Montana
Distance/obstacle: 13 cars
Bike: 750cc Norton
Details: Cleared 12 cars before landing short and crashing out.
Injuries: Knocked unconscious and suffered broken left arm and
    several ribs.

Date: 21 August
Venue: Great Falls Speedway, Great Falls, Montana
Distance/obstacle: n/a
Bike: 750cc Norton
Details: Still injured from his Missoula jump, Evel merely made an
    appearance while his 'Motorcycle Daredevils' performed. This
    was the last performance from the troupe before Evel went solo.
Injuries: None

Date: 30 October
Venue: Naranche Memorial Drag Strip, Butte, Montana
Distance/obstacle: 14 cars
Bike: 750cc Norton
Details: Successful
Injuries: None

# 1967

Date: 9 March
Venue: Ascot Park Speedway, Gardena, California
Distance/obstacle: 15 cars
Bike: 650cc Triumph Bonneville T120
Details: Successful
Injuries: None

Date: June
Venue: Ascot Park Speedway, Gardena, California
Distance/obstacle: 16 cars
Bike: 650cc Triumph Bonneville T120
Details: Successful
Injuries: None

Date: 28 July
Venue: Graham Speedway, Tacoma, Washington
Distance/obstacle: 16 cars
Bike: 650cc Triumph Bonneville T120
Details: Cleared the cars but fell off on landing.
Injuries: Light concussion

Date: 18 August
Venue: Graham Speedway, Tacoma, Washington
Distance/obstacle: 16 cars
Bike: 650cc Triumph Bonneville T120
Details: Successful
Injuries: None

Date: 24 September
Venue: Evergreen Speedway, Monroe, Washington
Distance/obstacle: 16 Chevrolets
Bike: 650cc Triumph Bonneville T120
Details: Cleared the jump but landed hard.
Injuries: Compression fracture to lower spine.

Date: 23–26 November
Venue: San Francisco Civic Center, San Francisco
Distance/obstacle: 100 feet over three motorcycles, a Triumph
    Banner, a Volkswagen bus and a van.
Bike: 650cc Triumph Bonneville T120
Details: Three successful jumps over a three-day period.
Injuries: None

Date: December
Venue: Long Beach Sports Arena, Long Beach, California
    (indoor)**
Distance/obstacle: 10 cars
Bike: 650cc Triumph Bonneville T120
Details: Successful
Injuries: None

Date: 31 December
Venue: Caesar's Palace, Las Vegas, Nevada
Distance/obstacle: 141 feet over the fountains outside Caesar's
    Palace hotel/casino.
Bike: 650cc Triumph Bonneville T120
Details: Cleared the fountains but crashed heavily on landing.
Injuries: Multiple broken ribs, broken left hip, crushed pelvis, 29-
    day coma and hospitalised for 37 days.

# 1968

Date: 25 May
Venue: Beeline Dragway, Scottsdale, Arizona
Distance/obstacle: 13 cars
Bike: 650cc Triumph Bonneville T120
Details: Crashed on landing.
Injuries: Broken leg and fractured foot.

Date: 3 August
Venue: Meridian Speedway, Meridian, Idaho
Distance/obstacle: 13 cars
Bike: 650cc Triumph Bonneville T120
Details: Successful
Injuries: None

Date: 26 August
Venue: Spokane Interstate Fairgrounds Speedway, Spokane,
    Washington
Distance/obstacle: 13 cars
Bike: 650cc Triumph Bonneville T120
Details: Successful
Injuries: None

Date: 7 September
Venue: Missoula Auto Track, Missoula, Montana
Distance/obstacle: 13 cars
Bike: 650cc Triumph Bonneville T120
Details: Successful
Injuries: None

Date: 13 & 15 September
Venue: Utah State Fair, Salt Lake City, Utah
Distance/obstacle: n/a
Bike: 650cc Triumph Bonneville T120
Details: n/a
Injuries: n/a

Date: 13 October
Venue: Tahoe-Carson Speedway, Carson City, Nevada
Distance/obstacle: 10 cars
Bike: 650cc Triumph Bonneville T120
Details: Crashed on the tenth car.
Injuries: Broke right shoulder and re-broke left hip. Contracted
    staph infection while in hospital.

# 1969

Date: 24–27 April
Venue: Los Angeles Memorial Sports Arena, Los Angeles,
    California.
Distance/obstacle: 80 feet over eight cars.
Bike: 750cc American Eagle (manufactured by Laverda)
Details: Successful
Injuries: None

# 1970

Date: 23 January
Venue: Cow Palace, San Francisco (indoor)
Distance/obstacle: 11 cars
Bike: 750cc American Eagle (manufactured by Laverda)
Details: New indoor record
Injuries: None

Date: 5 April
Venue: Seattle International Raceway, Kent, Washington
Distance/obstacle: 13 cars/18 cars
Bike: 750cc American Eagle (manufactured by Laverda)
Details: Blew out rear tyre during practice jump over 13 cars then
    cleared 120 feet over 18 cars, a new personal best.
Injuries: None

Date: 10 May
Venue: Yakima Speedway, Yakima, Washington
Distance/obstacle: 100 feet over 13 Pepsi-Cola delivery trucks.
Bike: 750cc American Eagle (manufactured by Laverda)
Details: Landed on safety ramp covering thirteenth truck and fell
    off bike.
Injuries: Broken collarbone

Date: 19 June
Venue: Pacific Coliseum, Vancouver (indoor)
Distance/obstacle: 12 cars
Bike: 750cc American Eagle (manufactured by Laverda)
Details: Successfully set new indoor personal best.
Injuries: None

Date: 4 July
Venue: Seattle International Raceway, Kent, Washington
Distance/obstacle: 19 cars
Bike: 750cc American Eagle (manufactured by Laverda)
Details: Set new outdoor personal best but slid off after landing on
    wet grass.
Injuries: Several cracked ribs and fractured vertebrae.

Date: 16 August
Venue: Pocono International Raceway, Long Pond, Pennsylvania
Distance/obstacle: n/a
Bike: 750cc American Eagle (manufactured by Laverda)
Details: Crashed on landing.
Injuries: Cracked vertebrae, broken shoulder and broken right
    hand.

Date: 12 December
Venue: Lions Drag Strip, Los Angeles, California
Distance/obstacle: 13 cars
Bike: 750cc Harley-Davidson XR-750
Details: Successful
Injuries: None

# 1971

Date: 2 January
Venue: Houston Astrodome, Houston, Texas (indoor)
Distance/obstacle: 13 vehicles
Bike: 750cc Harley-Davidson XR-750
Details: Twice cleared indoor record of 13 vehicles.
Injuries: None

Date: 27–28 February
Venue: Ontario Motor Speedway, Ontario, California
Distance/obstacle: 129 feet over 19 cars.
Bike: 750cc Harley-Davidson XR-750
Details: Successfully set new personal best.
Injuries: Fractured right hand during preliminary jump.

Date: 26–28 March
Venue: Chicago International Amphitheater, Chicago, Illinois
Distance/obstacle: n/a
Bike: 750cc Harley-Davidson XR-750
Details: n/a
Injuries: n/a

Date: 8–11 July
Venue: Madison Square Garden, New York (indoor)
Distance/obstacle: Nine cars and one van
Bike: 750cc Harley-Davidson XR-750
Details: Made four clear jumps over four nights.
Injuries: None

Date: 15–17 July
Venue: Lancaster Speedway, Buffalo, New York
Distance/obstacle: 13 vehicles
Bike: 750cc Harley-Davidson XR-750
Details: Successful
Injuries: None

Date: 29–30 July
Venue: Pocono Downs horse track, Wilkes-Barre, Pennsylvania
Distance/obstacle: 12 Stegmaier Beer trucks
Bike: 750cc Harley-Davidson XR-750
Details: Successful
Injuries: None

Date: 27–28 August
Venue: Philadelphia Spectrum, Philadelphia, Pennsylvania
Distance/obstacle: 10 Chevrolets
Bike: 750cc Harley-Davidson XR-750
Details: Successful
Injuries: None

Date: 16–18 September
Venue: Great Barrington Fair, Great Barrington, Massachusetts
Distance/obstacle: 16 cars/10 cars
Bike: 750cc Harley-Davidson XR-750
Details: Cleared 16 cars on first night but lost control after
    landing. Second night cancelled due to rain, cleared ten cars on
    third night.
Injuries: None

Date: 25–26 September
Venue: Kansas State Fair, Hutchinson, Kansas
Distance/obstacle: 10 Kenworth trucks
Bike: 750cc Harley-Davidson XR-750
Details: Successful
Injuries: None

Date: 21 October
Venue: Oregon Memorial Coliseum, Portland, Oregon (indoor)
Distance/obstacle: 12 cars and 2 vans
Bike: 750cc Harley-Davidson XR-750
Details: Set new indoor record but suffered heavy landing.
Injuries: Broken left hand

# 1972

Date: 23 January
Venue: Tucson Dragway, Tuscon, Arizona
Distance/obstacle: 12 cars and 3 vans
Bike: 750cc Harley-Davidson XR-750
Details: Successful despite rough landing.
Injuries: None

Date: 11–13 February
Venue: Chicago International Amphitheater, Chicago, Illinois
Distance/obstacle: n/a
Bike: 750cc Harley-Davidson XR-750
Details: Successful
Injuries: None

Date: 2–3 March
Venue: Cow Palace, San Francisco, California
Distance/obstacle: 12 cars/15 cars
Bike: 750cc Harley-Davidson XR-750
Details: Successfully cleared 12 cars on first night but crashed
    heavily while landing on second night.
Injuries: Broken ankle, heavily bruised hand and ribs.

Date: 24–26 March
Venue: State Fairgrounds Coliseum, Detroit, Michigan
Distance/obstacle: 13 cars
Bike: 750cc Harley-Davidson XR-750
Details: Successfully cleared 13 cars but crashed into a wall after
  landing.
Injuries: Broken collarbone

Date: 8–9 April
Venue: Emerson Ranch, Plymouth, California
Distance/obstacle: 100 live rattlesnakes and 2 vans
Bike: 750cc Harley-Davidson XR-750
Details: Successful
Injuries: None

Date: 11 June
Venue: Lakewood Speedway, Atlanta, Georgia
Distance/obstacle: 13 Cadillacs
Bike: 750cc Harley-Davidson XR-750
Details: Overshot practice jump over 4 trucks and crashed, ruling
  out scheduled Cadillac jump.
Injuries: Hurt both hands and suffered compression fracture in
  back.

Date: 17–18 June
Venue: Oklahoma State Fairgrounds, Oklahoma City, Oklahoma
Distance/obstacle: 3 cars on day one, then 5 cars and 2 vans
  thereafter.
Bike: 750cc Harley-Davidson XR-750
Details: Successful
Injuries: Still wearing a back brace for compressed vertebra.

Date: 24–25 June
Venue: St Louis International Raceway, East St Louis, Illinois
Distance/obstacle: 10 cars
Bike: 750cc Harley-Davidson XR-750
Details: Successful
Injuries: None (still wearing back brace)

Date: 16 July
Venue: Minnesota Dragway, Coon Rapids, Minnesota
Distance/obstacle: n/a
Bike: 750cc Harley-Davidson XR-750
Details: n/a
Injuries: n/a

Date: 30 July
Venue: Continental Divide Raceways, Castle Rock, Colorado
Distance/obstacle: 7 trucks and 4 cars
Bike: 750cc Harley-Davidson XR-750
Details: Successful
Injuries: None

Date: 1–2 September
Venue: Evergreen Speedway, Monroe, Washington
Distance/obstacle: 22 cars
Bike: 750cc Harley-Davidson XR-750
Details: Cleared 21 cars but came down on safety ramp above
   twenty-second car. Remains the highest number of cars he ever
   jumped.
Injuries: None

# 1973

Date: 5–7 January
Venue: Las Vegas Convention Center, Las Vegas, Nevada
Distance/obstacle: Several jumps leading up to 13 vans.
Bike: 750cc Harley-Davidson XR-750
Details: Successful
Injuries: None

Date: 19–21 January
Venue: Dallas Convention Center, Dallas, Texas
Distance/obstacle: n/a
Bike: 750cc Harley-Davidson XR-750
Details: n/a
Injuries: n/a

Date: 18 February
Venue: Los Angeles Memorial Coliseum
Distance/obstacle: 50 cars (piled)
Bike: 750cc Harley-Davidson XR-750
Details: Successfully cleared the cars which were piled two-to-
    three high making the numbers deceptive and, in distance
    terms, equivalent to jumps he had completed before.
Injuries: None

Date: 23–25 February
Venue: Cleveland Convention Center, Cleveland, Ohio
Distance/obstacle: n/a
Bike: 750cc Harley-Davidson XR-750
Details: Successful
Injuries: None

Date: 2–4 March
Venue: Nassau Coliseum, Uniondale, New York
Distance/obstacle: n/a
Bike: 750cc Harley-Davidson XR-750
Details: Successful
Injuries: None

Date: 16–18 March
Venue: Lakewood Fairgrounds Exhibit Hall, Atlanta, Georgia
Distance/obstacle: n/a
Bike: 750cc Harley-Davidson XR-750
Details: Successful
Injuries: None

Date: 23–25 March
Venue: Chicago International Amphitheater, Chicago, Illinois
Distance/obstacle: n/a
Bike: 750cc Harley-Davidson XR-750
Details: Successful
Injuries: None

Date: 30 March & 1 April
Venue: State Fairgrounds Coliseum, Detroit, Michigan
Distance/obstacle: n/a
Bike: 750cc Harley-Davidson XR-750
Details: Successful
Injuries: None

Date: 13–15 April
Venue: St Paul Civic Center, St Paul, Minnesota
Distance/obstacle: n/a
Bike: 750cc Harley-Davidson XR-750
Details: Successful
Injuries: None

Date: 27–29 April
Venue: Cincinnati Gardens, Cincinnati, Ohio
Distance/obstacle: n/a
Bike: 750cc Harley-Davidson XR-750
Details: Successful
Injuries: None

Date: 22–24 June
Venue: Great Lakes Dragway, Union Grove, Wisconsin
Distance/obstacle: n/a
Bike: 750cc Harley-Davidson XR-750
Details: Successful
Injuries: None

Date: 29 July
Venue: Lincoln Downs Race Track, Providence, Rhode Island
Distance/obstacle: n/a
Bike: 750cc Harley-Davidson XR-750
Details: Successful
Injuries: None

Date: 6–7 October
Venue: Wisconsin International Raceway, Kaukauna, Wisconsin
Distance/obstacle: 10 cars/3 trucks
Bike: 750cc Harley-Davidson XR-750
Details: Successfully cleared all obstacles in first performance but crashed during repeat show.
Injuries: Fractured bone in left hand, bruised back and kidneys.

Date: 20 October
Venue: JFK Stadium, Philadelphia, Pennsylvania
Distance/obstacle: 13 vehicles
Bike: 750cc Harley-Davidson XR-750
Details: Successful
Injuries: None

## 1974

Date: 17 February
Venue: Green Valley Raceway, North Richland Hills, Texas
Distance/obstacle: 11 Mack trucks
Bike: 750cc Harley-Davidson XR-750
Details: Successful
Injuries: None

Date: 29 March
Venue: Oregon Memorial Coliseum, Portland, Oregon (indoor)
Distance/obstacle: 16 vehicles (9 cars and 7 vans)
Bike: 750cc Harley-Davidson XR-750
Details: Successfully equalled own indoor record.
Injuries: None

Date: 13 April
Venue: Fremont Raceway, Fremont, California
Distance/obstacle: Ten Mack trucks
Bike: 750cc Harley-Davidson XR-750
Details: Successful
Injuries: None

Date: 20 April
Venue: Orange County International Raceway, Irvine, California
Distance/obstacle: Ten Mack trucks
Bike: 750cc Harley-Davidson XR-750
Details: Successful
Injuries: None

Date: 28 April
Venue: Kansas City International Raceway, Kansas, Missouri
Distance/obstacle: Ten Mack trucks
Bike: 750cc Harley-Davidson XR-750
Details: Successful
Injuries: None

Date: 5 May
Venue: Tulsa International Speedway, Tulsa, Oklahoma
Distance/obstacle: Ten Mack trucks
Bike: 750cc Harley-Davidson XR-750
Details: Successful
Injuries: None

Date: 25–27 May
Venue: Dragway 42, West Salem, Ohio
Distance/obstacle: Ten Mack trucks
Bike: 750cc Harley-Davidson XR-750
Details: Successful
Injuries: None

Date: 20 August
Venue: Toronto Exhibition Stadium, Toronto, Ontario
Distance/obstacle: 105 feet over 13 Mack trucks
Bike: 750cc Harley-Davidson XR-750
Details: Successful
Injuries: None

Date: 8 September
Venue: Snake River Canyon, Twin Falls, Idaho
Distance/obstacle: Three-quarter-mile-wide canyon
Bike: X-2 Sky Cycle
Details: Parachute blew out on launch leaving Knievel to drift
   down into nearside canyon wall.
Injuries: Minor facial scrapes and cuts.

# 1975

Date: 26 May
Venue: Wembley Stadium, London, England
Distance/obstacle: 120 feet over 13 single-decker buses
Bike: 750cc Harley-Davidson XR-750
Details: Landed badly on thirteenth bus and suffered heavy crash.
Injuries: Fractured pelvis, broken hand, concussion

Date: 25 October
Venue: Kings Island Family Entertainment Center, Kings Mills,
Ohio
Distance/obstacle: 133 feet over 14 single-decker Greyhound
buses
Bike: 750cc Harley-Davidson XR-750
Details: Furthest distance ever jumped without crash or injury.
Injuries: None

# 1976

Date: 11 October
Venue: Fitton Field, Worcester, Massachusetts
Distance/obstacle: 4 vans/7 vans/10 vans (75 feet)
Bike: 750cc Harley-Davidson XR-750
Details: Successfully made two leaps over 4 vans, three leaps over
7 vans and one leap over 10 vans.
Injuries: None

Date: 29–30 October
Venue: Kingdome, Seattle, Washington
Distance/obstacle: 7 Greyhound buses
Bike: 750cc Harley-Davidson XR-750
Details: Successful
Injuries: None

# 1977

Date: 31 January
Venue: Chicago International Amphitheater, Chicago, Illinois
Distance/obstacle: 90 feet over a tank containing 13 live lemon
   sharks
Bike: 750cc Harley-Davidson XR-750
Details: Crashed in practice jump and injured television
   cameraman.
Injuries: Fractured collarbone and right arm and suffered heavy
   bruising.

# 1979

Date: February
Venue: Australia
Distance/obstacle: n/a
Bike: 750cc Triumph T140 Bonneville
Details: Performed wheelies and hosted touring stunt-show 'Evel
   Knievel Thrill Spectacular'. Did not perform any jumps.
Injuries: None

# 1980

Date: March
Venue: Puerto Rico
Distance/obstacle: n/a
Bike: 750cc Triumph T140 Bonneville
Details: Performed wheelies and hosted the touring show which
   focused on son Robbie's jumping. Did not attempt any jumps.
Injuries: None

AUTHOR'S NOTE:

The distances recorded are those claimed by Knievel and/or those quoted in contemporary reports. Many are questionable and in some cases no reliable claims can be made.

** Indoor indicates the jump/s were performed at an indoor venue and were therefore usually of shorter distances.

* n/a denotes an absence of details in the available press material.

# References

## CHAPTER 1

p. 13, 'Everything that my grandparents got': *The Last of the Gladiators: Evel Knievel*, Twin Tower Enterprises, 1986.

p. 13, 'There were 500 prostitutes': *A Touch of Evel*, BBC/The Learning Channel, 1998.

p. 13, 'In ten years in these whorehouses': *Evel Knievel's Great Ride*, Tri-Crown Productions, 2003.

p. 15, 'I had never seen anything like it': *Evel Ways: A Daring Approach to Life*, GraF/X, 1999.

p. 18, 'He was an individualist': *The Last of the Gladiators: Evel Knievel*, Twin Tower Enterprises, 1986.

p. 19, 'I could hardly wait to get out': *A Touch of Evel*, BBC/The Learning Channel, 1998.

p. 24, 'One time the police caught me and another boy': *Penthouse*, 1974.

p. 25, 'He went around on the south side': *The Last of the Gladiators: Evel Knievel*, Twin Tower Enterprises, 1986.

p. 26, 'When he was a doorknocker': *The Last of the Gladiators: Evel Knievel*, Twin Tower Enterprises, 1986.

CHAPTER 2

p. 34, 'It got to be kinda fun': *The Last of the Gladiators: Evel Knievel*, Twin Tower Enterprises, 1986.

p. 35, 'I learned to do wheelies': *Motor Cycle News* (1 July 1998).

p. 35, 'I was goin' up and down mine hills': *Evel Knievel's Great Ride*, Tri-Crown Productions, 2003.

p. 43, 'This guy started running around': *Penthouse*, 1974.

CHAPTER 3

p. 55, 'The Triumph was a much better': *Motor Cycle News* (1 July 1998).

p. 55, '. . . a piece of crap': *Top Gear* (March 1999).

p. 56, 'He told me, "Step off 40 steps"': *Icon* (April 1998).

p. 58, 'The more I studied on it': *Sports Illustrated* (2 September 1974).

p. 59, 'I'm going to try and jump': *Evel Knievel*, Grosset & Dunlap, 1974.

p. 64, 'The one thing I remember': *Sports Illustrated* (7 October 1996).

CHAPTER 4

p. 69, 'I was hurt real bad': *POPsmear* (September/October 1998).

p. 70, 'The film that was shot': *The Last of the Gladiators: Evel Knievel*, Twin Tower Enterprises, 1986.

p. 73, 'America was down on its ass': *Cycle World* (March 1998).

p. 79, 'All my jumping risks were calculated': *Evel Ways: A Daring Approach to Life*, GraF/X, 1999.

p. 80, 'Football players fall down on Astroturf': *The Last of the Gladiators: Evel Knievel*, Twin Tower Enterprises, 1986.

p. 81, 'Just before the Caesar's Palace jump': *Evel Ways: A Daring Approach to Life*, GraF/X, 1999.

p. 85, 'These guys are dogs': *A Touch of Evel*, BBC/The Learning Channel, 1998.

p. 87, 'Evel was a double-edged sword': *Cycle World* (March 1998).

p. 87, 'I saw this little bastard': *A Touch of Evel*, BBC/The Learning Channel, 1998.

p. 88, 'He made a derogatory remark': *www.liveworld.com* (22 May 2000).

## CHAPTER 5

p. 94, 'My bikes are Harley XR-750s': *Evel Ways: A Daring Approach to Life*, GraF/X, 1999.

p. 99, 'I'd never have another one': *Top Gear* (March 1999).

p. 100, 'I don't need a licence to fly an airplane': *Penthouse*, 1974.

p. 100, 'No, he just sits': *Rolling Stone* (7 November 1974).

p. 100, 'I knocked a wingtip tank off': *Penthouse*, 1974.

p. 101, 'I saw him on TV one time': *Evel Knievel's Great Ride*, Tri-Crown Productions, 2003.

p. 105, 'He was certainly the most courageous': *A Touch of Evel*, BBC/The Learning Channel, 1998.

p. 107, 'The motorcycle crowd back in those days': *Icon* (April 1998).

## CHAPTER 6

p. 009, 'Women wanted me for my fame': *FHM*, October 1998.

p. 110, 'I think if a guy's married': *Penthouse*, 1974.

p. 110, 'I was very promiscuous': *Penthouse*, 1974.

p. 111, 'I treat women the way I always did': *Playboy* (May 1978).

p. 111, 'Women's lib groups are a pain in the ass': *FHM* (October 1998).

p. 112, 'You know, women are the root': *the-vu.com* (September 1998).

p. 112, 'It got to be a real problem': *the-vu.com* (September 1998).

p. 112, 'Use the mathematics': *Icon* (April 1998).

p. 112, 'I used to be bitter and resentful': *The Last of the Gladiators: Evel Knievel*, Twin Tower Enterprises, 1986.

CHAPTER 7

p. 131, 'Well, those two didn't really fail': *Rolling Stone* (7 November 1974).

p. 131, 'You know what? I'm gonna try and spend a million dollars': *Penthouse*, 1974.

p. 136, 'I tried to talk him into': *Rolling Stone* (7 November 1974).

p. 136, 'After I'd worked with him a while': *Rolling Stone* (7 November 1974).

p. 137, 'You sonofabitch': *Rolling Stone* (7 November 1974).

p. 139, 'The night before the canyon jump': *The Last of the Gladiators: Evel Knievel*, Twin Tower Enterprises, 1986.

CHAPTER 8

p. 148, 'I hope that no one ever sees': *The Last of the Gladiators: Evel Knievel*, Twin Tower Enterprises, 1986.

p. 151, 'We were certain he was dead': *Evel Ways: A Daring Approach to Life*, GraF/X, 1999.

p. 151, 'I was so used to him surviving every jump': *Evel Ways: A Daring Approach to Life*, GraF/X, 1999.

p. 152, 'That idiot fired my parachute team': *Icon* (April 1998).

p. 153, 'If I had made it across that canyon': *The Last of the Gladiators: Evel Knievel*, Twin Tower Enterprises, 1986.

CHAPTER 9

p. 157, 'won $5 from Cosgriff on the afternoon': *Sports Illustrated* (2 September 1974).

**p.** 157, 'I like to gamble': *the-vu.com,* September 1998.

p. 158, 'I'd never been to England': *Classic Bike* (February 1999).

p. 160, 'The English crowd and people were great': *Classic Bike* (February 1999).

p. 161, 'They were about to put on a show': *A Touch of Evel,* BBC/The Learning Channel, 1998.

p. 161, 'The first time he looked over': *A Touch of Evel,* BBC/The Learning Channel, 1998.

p. 164, 'I just didn't have enough speed': *Classic Bike* (February 1999).

p. 165, 'Doctors in the UK': *BBC Top Gear* (March 1999).

p. 166, 'It was always scary from the very beginning': *The Last of the Gladiators: Evel Knievel,* Twin Tower Enterprises, 1986.

p. 168, 'I was prettier and just as great': *Evel Ways: A Daring Approach to Life,* GraF/X, 1999.

CHAPTER 10

p. 170, 'Eight inches may not sound like much': *The Journal Herald* (27 October 1975).

p. 171, 'I've never been in a better frame of mind': *Dayton Daily News,* 1975.

p. 175, 'The descending ramp was built': *The Journal Herald* (27 October 1975).

p. 175, 'People said I wasn't scared': *the-vu.com* (September 1998).

p. 176, 'Evel Knievel was the star of the movie': *A Touch of Evel,* BBC/The Learning Channel, 1998.

CHAPTER 11

p. 185, 'He said I was a drug-taker': *FHM* (October 1998).

p. 191, 'Aw, what the hell, you know?': *POPsmear* (September/October 1998).

p. 192, 'They caught me playing golf': *POPsmear* (September/October 1998).

p. 192, 'It was degrading': *FHM* (October 1998).

p. 192, 'I was in there cos I chose to be in there': *POPsmear*, (September/October 1998).

p. 193, 'Guess who they put in with me?': *Icon* (April 1998).

p. 194, 'If somebody tells lies about you': *A Touch of Evel*, BBC/The Learning Channel, 1998.

p. 201, 'My dad was flamboyant': *Maxim* (October 1998).

p. 202, 'I started to think he might be jealous': *Maxim* (October 1998).

p. 205, 'My Knievel toys made $300 million': *the-vu.com*, (September 1998).

p. 206, 'The US Government is run': *FHM* (October 1998).

p. 207, 'All these so-called Christian people': *POPsmear*, (September/October 1998).

p. 208, 'I think that I began to feel so bad': *The Last of the Gladiators: Evel Knievel*, Twin Tower Enterprises, 1986.

p. 208, 'I stayed for two days then escaped': *Minnesota Motorcycle Monthly* (June 2001).

p. 208, 'The FBI had investigated': *Evel Ways: A Daring Approach to Life*, GraF/X, 1999.

p. 209, 'When I pray and when I question God': *The Last of the Gladiators: Evel Knievel*, Twin Tower Enterprises, 1986.

p. 210, 'The most precious times': *The Last of the Gladiators: Evel Knievel*, Twin Tower Enterprises, 1986.

p. 210, 'It comes to a point where everybody needs to be needed': *The Last of the Gladiators: Evel Knievel,* Twin Tower Enterprises, 1986.

## CHAPTER 12

p. 212, 'I was always creative': *Evel Ways: A Daring Approach to Life,* GraF/X, 1999.

p. 214, 'The president of Brown & Bigelow': *POPsmear,* (September/October 1998).

p. 214, 'You can be famous for a lot of things': *Esquire* (July 1999).

**p.** 214, 'She was bitching too much': *the-vu.com* (September 1998).

p. 216, 'I was at Turnberry in North Miami': *Evel Ways: A Daring Approach to Life,* GraF/X, 1999.

p. 217, 'When you get married, you stay married': *St Petersburg Times,* (21 June 1998).

p. 218, 'I never met anybody': *Icon* (April 1998).

p. 223, 'I knew Elvis, I knew Frank Sinatra': *the-vu.com* (September 1998).

p. 225, 'Loving someone doesn't mean': *Esquire* (July 1999).

p. 226, 'I always said I'd pay $1,000': *Evel Ways: A Daring Approach to Life,* GraF/X, 1999.

p. 228, 'They told me to quit drinking': *the-vu.com* (September 1998).

## CHAPTER 13

p. 231, 'Some people think that if you're rich': *Evel Ways: A Daring Approach to Life,* GraF/X, 1999.

p. 232, 'It is a bitch': *the-vu.com* (September 1998).

p. 233, 'He's just seven': *the-vu.com* (September 1998).

p. 234, 'They don't ask me to jump': *the-vu.com* (September 1998).

p. 239, 'As she [Krystal] was driving': *Hollywood Five-O* (spring 2003).

p. 240, 'He gave me a gift': *Evel Ways: A Daring Approach to Life*, GraF/X, 1999.

p. 240, '. . . when they take your liver out': *Minnesota Motorcycle Monthly*, (June 2001).

p. 242, 'I have an agreement with a big investment firm': *Motor Cycle News* (1 July 1998).

p. 244, 'I can't even go in a grocery store': *Motor Cycle News* (1 July 1998).

CHAPTER 14

p. 245, 'He initially would leave flowers': *St Petersburg Times* (21 February 2002).

p. 246, 'Women are like buses': *the-vu.com* (September 1998).

p. 250, 'I don't know what I'm going to jump': *www.knievel korner.co.uk*

p. 250, 'I'll jump over 200 feet': *www.knievelkorner.co.uk*

p. 251, 'By jumping again at my age': *New York Press*, Volume 15, Issue 34.

p. 251, 'If I make this last jump': *Evel Knievel's Great Ride*, Tri-Crown Productions, 2003.

p. 253, 'I've given a couple of weeks of my time here': *Evel Knievel's Great Ride*, Tri-Crown Productions, 2003.

p. 254, 'I was an alcoholic': *Hollywood Five-O* (spring 2003).

p. 255, 'I have a ride that you can get on': *www.knievelkorner.co.uk*

p. 258, 'Given the worldwide interest': *The Mail on Sunday* (25 January 2004).

p. 260, 'Some people can only dream': *the-vu.com* (September 1998).

p. 261, 'I tell ya, I don't know what': *Minnesota Motorcycle Monthly* (June 2001).

# Select Bibliography

Albers, Buckby, 'Evel's Act Ends Abruptly', *The Journal Herald* (27 October 1975).

Atyeo, Don, *Blood & Guts: Violence in Sports* (Paddington Press, 1979), pp. 323–327, 350–353.

Bachman, Scott, Sam Cassel, Tracy Cassel and Kevin Nelson (eds), *Evel Ways: A Daring Approach to Life* (GraF/X, 1999).

Barker, Stuart, 'Captain America', *Two Wheels Only* (June 2001), pp. 118–123.

Barker, Stuart, 'God's Own Stuntman', *FHM* (October 1998), pp. 122–128.

Barker, Stuart, 'Evel Knievel: I Did It Fly Way', *Motor Cycle News* (1 July 1998).

Brown, Roland, *On 2 Wheels: An Encyclopedia of Motorcycles and Motorcycling* (Southwater, 2001), pp. 154–155.

Caldwell, Alicia, 'Knievel Ordered to Leave Ex Alone', *St Petersburg Times* (21 February 2002).

Collins, Ace, *Evel Knievel: An American Hero* (St Martin's Press, 1999).

Coombs, Davey, 'The Sum of all Evel', *Cycle World* (March 1998), pp. 66–70.

Erickson, P. J., 'Evel Knievel Knocks on Wood after Coming up Short on Jump', *Tucson Daily Citizen*.

Eszterhas, Joe, 'King of the Goons', *Rolling Stone* (7 November 1974), pp. 40–58, 68–73.

Ewing, Russ, 'Penthouse Interview: Evel Knievel', *Penthouse*, 1974.

Fleury, Richard, 'Hitching a Ride with Evel Knievel', *BBC Top Gear* (March 1999).

Gilbert, Don, *'Evel Knievel: The World According to the American Daredevil'*, POPsmear (September/October 1998), pp. 42–52.

Hawthorne, Mark, 'Viva Knievel', *Bike* (September 1997), pp. 108–114.

Hoffer, Richard, 'Where Evel Lurks', *Sports Illustrated* (7 October 1996), pp. 78–84.

Jones, Robert F., 'Make It or Break It', *Sports Illustrated* (Time Inc., Sept 1974), pp. 52–62.

Kerwin, Robert, 'Women's Lib and Me', *Playboy* (May 1978), pp. 100–104, 110, 228–230.

Leach, Andrew, 'Knievel makes the Leap into Mobiles', *The Mail on Sunday* (25 January 2004).

Leslie, David, *New York Press*, Volume 15, Issue 34.

Lowitt, Bruce, 'Evel Irony', *St Petersburg Times* (21 June 1998).

Mandich, Steve, *Evel Incarnate: The Life and Legend of Evel Knievel* (Sidgwick & Jackson, 2000).

Marx, Tony, *Minnesota Motorcycle Monthly* (June 2001).

Pomerantz, Gary M., 'The Icon Profile: Evel Knievel', *Icon* (April 1998), pp. 100–109, 157–158.

Sager, Mike, 'What I've Learned: Evel Knievel', *Esquire* (July 1999), pp. 98–99.

Saltman, Sheldon, *Evel Knievel on Tour* (Dell Publishing, 1977).

Scalzo, Joe, *Evel Knievel* (Grosset & Dunlap Inc., 1974).

Scalzo, Joe, *Evel Knievel and Other Daredevils* (Grosset & Dunlap Inc., 1974).

Shapiro, Harvey, 'Evel Has No Fear of 14-Bus Jump', *Dayton Daily News* (1975).

Smith, Kevin, 'Evel Knievel', *www.the-vu.com* (September 1998).

Spiegel, Marshall, *The Cycle Jumpers* (Scholastic Book Services, 1973).

Watson, Peter and Stuart Barker, 'Knievel's Wembley Wipeout', *Classic Bike* (February 1999), pp. 18–22.


NEWSPAPERS

*Cycle News East, Daily News, Dayton Daily News,*
*LA Herald-Examiner, National Tattler, Rocky Mountain News,*
*St Petersburg Times, Sunday Chronicle-Herald, Sunday News,*
*The Globe and Mail, The Hutchinson News, The Journal Herald,*
*The Mail on Sunday, The Mercury, Tucson Daily Citizen,*
*Chicago Herald-Tribune, The Montana Standard.*


WEBSITES

*www.antiquelynx.com, www.borntoride.com, www.billingsnews.com,*
*www.butteinfo.org, www.cbsnews.com, www.csifiles.com,*
*www.divorcemag.com, www.evel1.com, www.evelknievel.com,*
*www.evelknievel.us, www.filmforce.ign.com, www.focusonhepc.com,*
*www.foxnews.com, www.gamblingmagazine.com,*
*www.hollywoodfiveo.com, www.liveworld.com,*
*www.knievelkorner.co.uk, www.mainstreetbutte.org,*
*www.montanaforum.com, www.piccadillymuseum.com,*
*www.pinball.org, www.reviewjournal.com, www.sunnews.com,*
*www.the-vu.com, www.tvzap2it.com, www.twincities.com*

# Index